The Popes and the Jews
in the Middle Ages

QUEST BOOKS

This series—searching for truth on matters that are of concern to both Christians and Jews, and thereby fostering their brotherhood—is sponsored by the Institute of Judaeo-Christian Studies, Seton Hall University.

The Popes
and the Jews
in the Middle Ages

By Edward A. Synan

Preface by John M. Oesterreicher

The Macmillan Company, New York
Collier-Macmillan Limited, London

1965

Nihil obstat
James A. Reynolds, Ph.D.
Censor Deputatus

Imprimatur
✠Francis Cardinal Spellman
Archbishop of New York

May 11, 1965

The nihil obstat and imprimatur are official declarations that a book or pamphlet is free of doctrinal or moral error. No implication is contained therein that those who have granted the nihil obstat and imprimatur agree with the contents, opinions or statements expressed.

First Printing

The Macmillan Company, New York. Collier-Macmillan Canada Ltd., Toronto, Ontario. Library of Congress catalog card number: 65-20172. Designed by Michael Marchner. Printed in the United States of America.

CONTENTS

Preface   vii

I   Indictment and Intentions   1

II   Christian Roman Law   17

III Age of the Fathers   31

IV   Interim   51

V   The Crusades   66

VI   The Pontificate of Innocent III   83

VII Thirteenth-century Popes   103

VIII The Last Two Hundred Years   125

IX   Reflections   148

     Notes   165

     Appendices   215

In memory of the esteem
in which my father
held his Jewish friends

PREFACE

This is the second volume in the series of Quest Books. Sponsored by the Institute of Judaeo-Christian Studies, Seton Hall University, and inspired by the vision of Pope John, it is dedicated to a reordering of the relationship between Christians and Jews.

My one objection to *The Popes and the Jews in the Middle Ages* is the author's modesty. "By no means a work of erudition," he writes, "this collection of texts does not pretend . . . to break new ground." The reader will not have to turn many pages before discovering that he is in the presence of urbanity, learning, and culture. Formerly a student, now a colleague of Etienne Gilson at the Pontifical Institute of Mediaeval Studies in Toronto, Father Synan gives us far more than a collection of texts, even more than a fresh translation of them.

True, Father Synan has not unearthed documents hitherto unknown to scholars. Instead, he unfolds in this book records not easily accessible so that, now, all who have an intelligent concern for the past and future relationship between Church and Synagogue can learn about—and from—them. This is no mean achievement. In opening wide the archives, he introduces and explains the interaction of Pope and Jews in the Middle Ages, but his comments never intrude. They never interfere with his theme; its servant throughout, he helps the reader make his own assessment.

An outstanding characteristic of this book is the author's view of the past. The common attitude to it is either one of complete approval or one of utter disapproval. To those who live, as it were, by discontent, the past appears as the sum of all that is good; to those who think that their own

vii

age nears paradise, "past" is a synonym for evil. Need I say that Father Synan belongs to neither category? He is not what Horace called *laudator temporis acti*, hymner of an age gone by (*Ars Poetica*, 173), nor is he its contemner. To praise or to denounce former times is an inexacting business, worthy of sophomoric minds. In particular, to arraign the long-distant past is rarely a sign of deep morality, more often one of pretentious moralism. The truly moral stance is that of the prophet who, at great risk, castigates the sins of the present. "You are the man!" (2 Kg 12 : 7)—words like those of the defenseless Nathan before the mighty David are the true witness of the Spirit.

Father Synan reads the words and deeds of medieval popes in their historic context. He does not demand that they conform in every way to our own insights. Indeed, he knows they cannot. Everyman, the Christian being no exception, is a child of his age. This he cannot help. He fails only when he lets himself become its slave. It would be wrong to think that men can do nothing, save what their era allows them, but it would be no less an error to assume that man's possibilities are at all times limitless, that at every moment he can fulfill the ideal of his humanity to the utmost.

Giants though they were, the Greek philosophers mistook the excellence of man for the excellence of the man born free. In his first book of *Politics*, Aristotle discusses at length the nature of slaves: to him, they are on the same plane and of the same worth as chattels, no more than useful tools, as Father Synan himself notes. Fruitful and far-reaching thinker though he was, Aristotle failed in so fundamental a question as the dignity of the human person to leap over the frontiers of his society and age. Only a person with no regard for the fetters of time will thus turn up his nose at the Philosopher.

The situation of medieval man was similar. Though there is not the slightest warrant for it in Holy Scripture, he held that Jews were condemned to lasting servitude for not having accepted Jesus as the Christ. I find this tenet outrageous. Still, I can well understand how a society unified on the one hand and rigidly structured on the other (one need only think of its system of guilds), how a society of kings and vassals, lords and serfs, knights and servants, masters and apprentices, led, almost impelled, its members to assume that heaven, and not they, had decreed the bondage of Jews. Medieval man put "chains" on the Jews because his own mind was "chained"— not by faith, but by an imperfect understanding of it. Only a deluded modern who thinks he bears no shackles, simply because he cannot see them, will despise the medieval Christian.

I have spoken of fetters, chains, and shackles: the scandal of history—not to be confused with history's scandals. But the limits time imposes on us offend only him who does not realize that these limitations are the necessary concomitants of the wonder of time, as shadows are of light. It is in time that we grow. Time is needed for man to grasp and, even more, to realize his potentiality. Time, too, is needed for the Christian to fathom his calling, his role in the world, and his bond to those who do not share his beliefs. Time had to elapse before Christians could more fully understand their bond with the Jewish people.

Thanks to the Lord of history who guides but never forces it, our generation is favored to observe—indeed, to participate in—a spiritual and moral ascent few other generations have known. New horizons have opened. Without betraying the uniqueness of the gospel, rather in obedience to the breadth, and length, and height, and depth of Christ's love (Eph. 3 : 18–19), we have come to understand better than ever the ties that bind Christians to non-Christians, especially to the Jews. Yet, this ascent is by no means completed, this understanding by no means assured. They will not reach their appointed goal without prayer and work, without study and vigilance.

The Middle Ages considered the Jews of all times caught in a web of guilt. It could do so because philosophy as well as theology had not sufficiently progressed to distinguish with precision between collective guilt and communal responsibility, between the guilt of the guilty and the burden it imposes on the guiltless. Man knows so little. Without pain, he knows even less; he remains dumb before certain issues. A cruel awakening seems to have been needed for him to understand the tremendous difference between the misdeed of one or of a few, and the way it involves or affects others, indeed a whole nation, at times even the community of nations. Our age has had an experience painful enough to teach it the proper distinctions. It has thus no excuse. The simplistic notion of collective guilt, whether applied to the Jews or to any other body, must go!

To sum up, Father Synan's book makes a definite contribution to the renewal of the Church. Its empathy with the events of the past, its humility before the movements of history, its compassion for men of former days, will, paradoxical though this sounds, equip us better for the task ahead. As Cicero has it, history told by an "orator" bears witness to ages past, sheds light upon their reality, enlivens our memory, and guides our existence; it is *testis temporum, lux veritatis, vita memoriae, magistra vitae* (*De Oratore*, II, 36). Father Synan's book admirably fulfills this purpose.

JOHN M. OESTERREICHER
Institute of Judaeo-Christian Studies
Seton Hall University

I

INDICTMENT AND INTENTIONS

Critics find many complaints to register against medieval popes, and on no subject are these more pointed than on their relationship with the Jews. Europe dominated by the papacy, it can be argued, knew neither equality nor justice; medieval legislation was as savage in its intentions as in its penalties, and the brunt of these fell upon the helpless Jewish population. The medieval Jew went in fear of mob violence, a threat often tolerated and, at times, incited by the authorities responsible for public order. Badge and ghetto sealed with humiliation a systematic drive to degrade the whole Jewish community. Obscurantist zeal led Christians to burn cartloads of precious Torah scrolls and of manuscript copies of the Talmud, that monument of learning and religious jurisprudence so dear to Jewish sensibilities. The Church was not ashamed to make use of disingenuous devices to allure converts; she was ready to reward the apostate from the faith of Israel,[1] to threaten the steadfast, to force the attendance of simple Jewish believers at conversionist sermons.[2] Crusades, in theory organized to recover the Palestinian shrines, to combat Christian heresy, or to expel Islamic invaders from Christian states, meant incidental suffering for the Jews. Marauding bands of armed men terrorized the Jewish quarters of cities on the crusading routes, emotional sermons on the passion of Jesus could not fail to excite the indiscriminate wrath of the Christian populace against the whole people held guilty of the crucifixion; bankers were deprived of their interest on loans they had made in good faith. Persecution, if intermittent, proceeded on principle. The harsh regime that marked the whole medieval period in Christian Spain,

1

one historian has complained,[3] counted as more "Catholic" than that of popes who spoke out inconsistently for methods milder than those dictated by the doctrine that remained official.

For all this the popes have been held chiefly responsible. The papacy had shown no reluctance in assuming the right to govern Europe, and, if effective control was not always within the power of the Holy See, in theory at least, responsibility rested with Rome. At the same time, it is held, the ineffective character of papal efforts to protect the Jews must render unreal and pretentious, indeed, no more than verbal, expressions of concern by the popes for Jewish suffering.

In Jewish eyes, too, the limited benevolence shown their medieval forebears by the popes of those days is vitiated by the motives on which it was based. Did not every pope believe that in the end of time the Jews would be converted to the Church? Did not their defense of the Jews' right to life on the fringe of society bear witness to a hope that the ultimate conversion might begin the sooner, and the apostates be the more numerous, rather than to any disinterested goodwill toward the victims of injustice? Let the popes claim that a sharing in the Christian faith is the fulfillment of Torah and of the prophets, read "according to the spirit," and a pledge of eternal beatitude; for the convinced Jew, baptism remains apostasy, while friendship proffered with a view to apostasy is seduction. Christian overtures to the Jews in our own day have met with comparable resistance. Nor would it be reasonable to expect Jews to take any great pleasure in the role assigned them by Christian spokesmen as witnesses—in their dispersion and miseries—to the error, or worse, of their fathers in rejecting Jesus of Nazareth as Messiah. No doubt medieval Jews preferred to escape massacre, even on such grounds as these, but they cannot have failed to resent so tendentious a theory of protection.

A Catholic is understandably uneasy in the presence of these accusations. Can medieval Christians—those in the highest place, most of all—have flouted so grossly the charity and the justice that their leaders propose to modern Christians? What has changed within the Church to make a benign ecumenicity normal, even modish, now? Is the record of medieval Jewry one of unrelieved conflict with the Church?

Were papal policies with respect to the Jews—whether those of repression or those of protection—capriciously formulated, reducible to the personal bias of each pope? Or did they proceed from intelligible convictions consistently applied to a developing situation? Is the ultimate intention of those policies coherent?

Questions such as these will not remain merely historical ones for the Catholic of our day. Unless he is blind, he will have noted that in their attitude toward the Jews not all Christians reach the standard set by Pope John XXIII. In his country club and neighborhood, in some rectories, kinship according to the flesh with the Nazarene all Christians call their Lord does not count necessarily as a patent of nobility. The reflective Catholic inevitably asks: What has the medieval experience to teach us on the justice and the wisdom of ecclesiastical appeals to police power, on the coordination of the temporal and eternal goals of a Christian state, on that ultimate ethical value, the upright conscience? Although in some dimensions she transcends time, the Church he esteems is the Church in history, as burdened by her knaves and fools as she is glorious in her saints. It is the Church who has taught him the truths that give him pause when he reflects upon the record of churchmen. No Platonic archetype—ideal, unmixed, immobile—the real Church is in this world of men, leavening with the divine, if the believer is right, our tragicomic doings.

Perspective

Precisely because we come to history with an interest in a particular theme and period, an ineluctable distortion warps our seeing. The least mischievous consequence of this is that our own interest becomes a principle of selection and our last standard of judgment. Periods, personalities, events, all receive attention thanks to our concern rather than to any intrinsic importance they might have. Physicists report that the very conditions that render subatomic observation possible change, and thus falsify, the phenomena to be observed; something comparable renders the work of every historian suspect. To bring his materials into focus he must impose upon them an order alien to them, suppress what in fact coexisted with what he chooses to retain, tend to exaggerate that on which his interest bears. The work of men dead for centuries is evaluated from points of view unknown—indeed, unknowable—to them; casual decisions, incautious phrases, their unreflective acceptance of propositions no contemporary would dream of contesting, now count as the norms that enable a later generation to pass judgment on the dead. Questions posed by the presence of Jews in medieval Christendom, our present concern, can hardly have appeared to a single pope of the period as among the most pressing he was called upon to face; only a tiny fraction of the immense documentation left by the medieval papacy refers to matters that affected the Jews.

Still, who could find it in his heart to blame the Jew of our time, still agonizing over the catastrophes of 1933–1945, who asks what the record can tell of the popes who preceded John XXIII? Would any earlier pope have been disposed to greet Jewish visitors, as did Pope John, with the words of the patriarch who dispensed grain in a time of famine: "I am Joseph, your brother" (Gen. 45 : 4)? Above all, what were the words and the deeds of popes in the days when the papacy was endowed with the ambiguous advantages of terrestrial power, when the pope, the first of all bishops, was also the first of all princes?

We cannot hope to transcend our human limitation when we call the writings of men now dead into council, but to remember and to question, to attempt interpretation, are human aspirations that only cowardice would urge the living to forgo.

The "Middle" Ages

Convenient to the point that it is all but indispensable, the term "Middle Ages" nevertheless remains a stone of stumbling. More than a century of scholarly reevaluation has not sufficed to purge the expression of its emotional overtones. According to one extreme interpretation, the phrase evokes a "good" period, a golden age of chivalry and faith and artistic accomplishment—knightly honor and idyllic Franciscan anecdotes, glass membranes glowing between stone cathedral ribs. Those centuries were blemished, their defenders will concede, by scandals and failures, but these are easily excused as vagaries inseparable from human weaknesses—invitations, therefore, to an apologetic that must convince all but the wilfully blind.

Other observers—and these seem the more numerous—still equate the Middle Ages with the Dark Ages, count it a time of barbaric cruelty and abysmal ignorance, of oppression and of slavish submission.

These contradictory estimates—neither of which is without a certain foundation and neither of which is adequate—are fragmentary reflections, we must assume, of the complex and ambivalent realities that the term "Middle 'Ages" denotes.

Nor do the discrepancies that attend the interpretation of those centuries fall exclusively within the order of value judgments; not every observer sees the same ages as "Middle," and our theme demands a decision on which centuries ought to be chosen. The Latin rhetorician or grammarian sets limits that need not coincide with those that please the historian of philosophy and theology; specialists in medieval Islam do not share the perspectives of Latin Christendom. Between what limits and on what basis can any block of centuries be established as "Middle"? Besides, no matter to what centuries the rubric be assigned, those years were modern times for those who lived through them. Who but Augustine, always original, has ever been so little the prisoner of time as to be able to see his own days from a metahistorical standpoint and to conceive of himself as a man living through what he called "this middle season," *in hoc interim saeculo*?[4] Less a historian beguiled by the temporal than a theologian aspiring to eternity, the Bishop of Hippo had his own ideas as to where the limits of "this middle season" fall. Those boundaries he set at the first Advent of Jesus, come to redeem us, and at the Second Coming, the Lord's Parousia as Judge of all the earth. Without contesting the theological value of Augustine's vision, historians will be excused if they confine themselves to a less apocalyptic plane. Last, a delimitation of the Middle Ages is not rendered any simpler by the application of the term to the Jewish experience.

The Middle Ages of the Jews

In fixing the limits of the Middle Ages, Jewish historians are accustomed, and not without reason, to adopt the partition of European history into ancient, medieval, and modern periods, but not one of these is an altogether satisfactory division of specifically Jewish history. It has even been suggested that if the Jews are to be described as having passed through a "medieval" period of their own—conceived as a time of darkness between a light ascribed to Greece and Rome, and that other light that reconciles us to our own times—then the beginning of the Jewish Middle Ages must be calculated from the Christianization of the Roman Empire and the consequent loss of the privileged position Jews had enjoyed under pagan imperial law.[5] For were not the Jews, within a few generations, victims of emperors newly baptized and, worse yet, victims of imperial popes, who were only too ready to emulate that policy of religious repression by law from which the Christian community had so lately suffered?

No doubt many a reservation must be registered against this reading of Judaeo-Roman relations; not every pagan Roman was a friend to Israel. Pre-Christian Rome produced Pompey to invade Palestine, to violate the Holy of Holies, to subject the sacred nation to the Senate and the Roman People. The emperors Caligula and Claudius figure in the history of legally sanctioned anti-Semitism. The suppression of Jewish revolts by Titus, Vespasian, and Hadrian needs no commentary, and there are ambiguities in the legal exemptions of Jews under pagan Roman Law. Furthermore, Jewish historians, who are by no means blind to the shortcomings of the popes, record repeated papal efforts to protect the Jews.[6]

So also, to end the Middle Ages with the fifteenth-century Renaissance, as the custom is, finds small justification from the standpoint of Jewish history. If the "Middle Ages" are to be both Jewish and dark, they can end no earlier than with the Enlightenment—more precisely, at least for most of Europe, with the definitive emancipation of the Jews under Napoleon. In the Rome of the popes, the end was longer delayed, for there the civil disabilities of the Jews—far more rigorously conceived after Reform and Counter-Reform than during the earlier centuries—perdured until the dissolution of the Papal States and the consequent loss of temporal power that had made repression possible. Thus, the "Middle Ages" of the Jews were at their most "medieval" (if the term be taken to mean their darkest phase) during precisely that

period when the rest of Europe was emerging from the
religious upheavals of the sixteenth century into what we
confidently call "modern" times.

The Papal Middle Ages

So early does the enigma of Israel confront us with an
irreducible discrepancy: popes and Jews lived through the
same years, yet their respective "Middle Ages" are not
identical. Posed bluntly, this would constitute an insoluble
puzzle, but the destinies of Synagogue and Church are
mysteries rather than puzzles. Persons and faith and love and
sin are not wholly subject to conceptual, still less to mathe-
matical, expression; a time of grace or a season of rebellion
cannot always be calibrated according to the calendar. Because our theme is the papal response to the presence of
Jews in Christendom, it has seemed legitimate to take the
notion of "Middle Ages" from the side of the popes. The
historical initiatives that popes exercised with respect to the
Jews from the fifth to the fifteenth century are sufficiently
different in quality and scale from those of the centuries that
preceded and followed that millennium to qualify the period
as "medieval."

Medieval Faith

"Ages of Faith" is a characterization of the Middle Ages
that labors under many a disability, but it does serve to
emphasize one undeniable and persistent quality of the time.
Despite every failure, those centuries were marked by the
profound commitment of Christian, Jew, and Moslem to their
respective faiths. Unyielding theoretical consistency, considerably tempered in practice, led men to the sharp definition
of the boundaries that set off faith from faith. Not everyone
would go so far as did the more zealous of the Moslems, but
their striking oriental formula conveys the atmosphere of total
dedication to a creed, and the correlative total alienation
from every other community begotten by medieval faith. On
one side, there was Islam, the "territory of surrender," where
men delivered themselves, surrendered to Allah as revealed
by his prophet; on the other side lay the land of the "infidel"
—the "territory of warfare."

Belief and Disbelief: Fides and Perfidia

What precise points of belief divided, and divide, Christian from Jew? At the root of all our dissent is the figure of Jesus the Nazarene, rejected by the Sanhedrin of his day but accepted by Christians as the authentic Messiah, as the Anointed of YHWH, sent to save his People and to be the Light of the Gentiles. For Christians, confident that this in no way wounds their commitment to the unqualified monotheism that remains the glory of Jewish faith, Jesus is the only begotten Son of God; with the Father He is the principle of the Holy Spirit, who invisibly gives form to the royal and priestly people that is the Church, the new *qehal* YHWH. To the Jew, this Trinity seems incompatible with the divine Unity in a fashion as obvious as it is outrageous; trinitarian doctrine, he maintains—redolent of pagan polytheism in its multiplication of divine Persons—descends to pagan philosophy, that pseudo-wisdom, for its theological exposition in terms of nature and person. It goes without saying that from this fundamental dissent there flow contradictions without number. Mary, the Virgin of Nazareth, is either, as the Catholic holds, the miraculously fruitful mother of a Person who is the eternal Word of God, or, as the Jew must insist, she is the mother, in the fashion usual with our race, of one who may have had some claim to esteem as a preacher of righteousness but who cannot have been the Messiah, and still less the "son" in any literal sense of the God of Abraham and Isaac and Jacob. Torah is, or is not, still in force; messianic prophecies have been, or have not been, fulfilled; the observant Jew awaits with sure hope the Anointed of his rescuing God, or he has failed to recognize the passing of the Lord. These options are consequent upon the answer men make to the question Jesus himself formulated: "What think you of Messiah? Whose son is he?" (Matt. 22 : 42).

The Church was born into a world through which the Jews had been sown broadcast, and it was to the synagogue of each city that Paul of Tarsus first resorted with the news of salvation he felt called upon to preach. Even for the Apostle of the Gentiles, first the Jews, then the Gentiles (Rom. 2 : 9) remained the order of precedence, and this despite the consistent rejection of his preaching by those in

whose hands lay the destinies of what was to become normative Judaism. To a world turned Christian, the diaspora of the
Jews, their miseries and helplessness, invited the judgment
that Jewish incredulity had earned these evidences of divine
wrath. The notion of corporate responsibility, learned as it
had been from the Jews, rendered all Jewish disasters easily
intelligible: the whole nation, Christians thought, labored
under the guilt assumed by High Priest and Sanhedrin on the
night of Jesus' trial.

But the scattered Jews interpreted their calamities in
another fashion. Taught by the prophets to scrutinize their
own failings, they could add to shortcomings of their own
that had called down the successive scourges of Egyptian
and Assyrian, Philistine and Persian, and Greek and Roman,
yet another cause for those disasters: Christian cruelty and
religious caprice. Long since familiar in a thousand forms,
oppression—now by Christians—was new only in that the
Church laid claim to a superior understanding of the Hebrew
Law, prophets, and writings, and in the name of that understanding rejected, not without contempt, the intricacies of
rabbinical tradition, abandoned the sacred ceremonies of the
Law, scorned Torah's safeguards against idolatry. As Jewish
disbelief in Jesus' divinity outraged Christian sensibilities, so
Christian "liberty" in the presence of Torah exposed Jewish
nerves to the intolerable pain of blasphemy.

Hard Sayings

Jewish-Christian controversy in the Middle Ages is
marked by language that is offensive in the extreme. Common
to both communities, this usage was in part an expression,
and thus far an effect, of theological dissent on issues where
personal commitment made martyrdom the norm not only
in theory but also in practice. Still, this mutual vituperation
must have functioned in part as a cause of ever-deepening
group hostility. One reason that an emotive vocabulary was
common to both Jews and Christians is that both echoed the
passionate language of Scripture. That prophet and psalmist
used harsh language against sinner or infidel is as evident as
the fact that they used Hebrew or Greek. Is it possible to
honor their total devotion, their heroic fidelity in bearing
witness against a world as corrupt as it was powerful, yet

wish they had spoken with detachment and serenity? Medieval Jews and Christians found in their Bibles the teaching that faith demands unreserved dedication of the believer to his God, that life itself is not as dear as fidelity to the Lord of faith, that any distortion of authentic faith is the ultimate disaster. Language that might seem to erupt from hatred here springs from love. No one loved the Jews more than did their prophets, and that love is the tinder that set their words afire. If the Christian claims to be free from the constraint of the Mosaic Law and Christian faith in Jesus seemed blasphemous to the Jews, the resistance of Jews to that same faith seemed blasphemous to Christians; their language did nothing to ease the tension. Hebrew Scriptures proclaim a theme and counter-theme; the *qehal* YHWH, the assembly of the Lord, is gratuitously chosen, established, protected, loved; to fail in fidelity, to rebel, to prefer heathenish consolations, all this calls down the Lord's wrath, as measureless as the love of which it is the obverse.

We shall scarcely find a theologian of any community who has been more profoundly aware of the values cherished by other believers than was the Jewish master of the interior life, Bahya Ibn Pakuda. But his readiness to adopt the insights of Moslem and Christian did not prevent his use of more than one hard saying on the Christian doctrine of the Trinity, so hard that medieval Hebrew translators thought it better to leave them in the obscurity of the author's Arabic text. "Numerous causes," he wrote, "can corrupt the confession of the unity of God professed by a heart without guile. Among these we count associating anything whatever with God, belief in two Principles, or in a Trinity."[7] But not all Jews confined their pejorative vocabulary to abstract theology. The medieval Hebrew accounts we shall have occasion to cite with respect to the persecution Jews suffered at the hands of Crusaders, for example, refer to Christ as "the gibbeted one," "the son of the excommunicated," "the gibbeted bastard," and to a Christian church as a "house of filth," "a horror," "a house of alien slaves," and so on. So stereotyped had such terminology become that its very generality tended to diminish its malice, and the chroniclers went so far as to put abusively anti-Christian terms on the lips of Christians, thus posing an editorial problem to their modern translator not only on the plane of courtesy but even of intelligibility.[8]

In this connection we may remark that the term "Marrano," used by the "old" Christians of Spain to designate converts from Judaism, was so offensive to Jews of that day that it was forbidden by civil law.[9] Modern readers will not take kindly to the figure nearly always employed by popes with respect to converts from Judaism who relapsed into their former persuasion; they are regularly described as returning "like a dog to his vomit." But the popes borrowed the phrase from their first predecessor, Peter himself (2 Pet. 2 : 22); he, in his turn, had found it in no less respectable a source than the Book of Proverbs (26 : 11).

Language of this stripe was not confined to Judaeo-Christian polemics. Christian saints spoke out with a vigor that offends our more circumspect habit. Not only against heretic and infidel, but against other Christians too, the saints sharpened their tongues; we have but to read Saint Bernard on the tragic Abelard:

We now have in France a novel theologian in exchange for the old school-master who, when he was young, did his trifling in the art of dialectic, but who now does his raving on Sacred Scripture. . . . He has no care for what he says, goes rushing into the mysteries of faith, irreverently invades and shreds the hidden treasures of piety, for he thinks neither piously nor with faith. . . . His theology is more accurately a "fool-ology"![10]

We shall see the same Saint Bernard defending Jews while they were excoriated by Peter the Venerable, Abbot of Cluny, but this is not the only question on which they disagreed; both sons of Saint Benedict, they exchanged acidulous pleasantries on how the rule of monks ought to be lived:

With faltering steps you go astray in devious and unknown paths, contriving your own laws for yourselves in any way you like—and then pronounce them sacrosanct, throw out the precepts of the Fathers in favor of your own traditions; at once teachers and pupils in the same affair—a grotesque sight![11]

More than once echoes of this omnipresent energy of expression will enliven the account of medieval popes and

Jews. If we are wise, we shall listen with medieval ears to words pronounced by medieval lips. To register the dismay that would rightly greet language of this sort today can only distort our understanding of its significance for those who used and endured it then.

Hierarchy and Privilege

Human affairs beget, and are in turn conditioned by, a collective reality that can hardly be reduced to the sum of the individuals who constitute a society. Suspect though such conceptions must be, it is safe to say that for the total medieval period social structure was hierarchic, both in the political sense that equality was neither a fact nor an ideal and in the etymological sense that the gradations of society rejoiced in sacral warrants. True enough, no competent medieval theologian failed to distinguish with precision between the eternal and the temporal goals of man; nor did the Church ever falter in her effort to give the distinction effect by freeing her own clergy from the world of temporal concerns. The Church and her "men"—for she did not hesitate to make her own the lexicon of feudalism—had their own law, their many-faceted "privilege," a system of special courts. From the beginning of the medieval period until its end, there were territories in which the popes ruled without an effective secular rival. Everywhere, however, the terrestrial polity was considered to function within the Church, and her moral preeminence was universally accepted in principle, however much contested in practice. The notion of privilege did not connote a necessarily tyrannical favoritism; it was no more than a normal provision for a restricted group, a particular law contrived by legislators conscious of the special characteristics that then distinguished one collectivity from another. No medieval town or kingdom was monolithic. A typical medieval state included irreducibly diverse groups, and each one might have its own law and custom. The will of Alphonsus I, King of Aragon and Navarre, drawn up in 1131, illustrates the complex structure of a medieval realm as well as the king's consciousness of his obligation to rule within the provisions of law and custom; in it the king transmitted:

The dominion which I hold, in all the lands of my Kingdom, and the principate and right which I hold with respect to all the men of my land, clerics as well as laymen, bishops, abbots, canons, monks, noblemen, knights, townsmen, rustics, merchants, men and women, the small and the great, the rich and the poor, Jews too, and Saracens, with such law and custom of the sort that my father and my brothers and I have held up until now, and ought to hold.[12]

Not only through law and custom did the heterogeneous character of medieval society reveal itself, but through symbols too. Dress, place of residence, the carrying of arms, all were adjusted to what were conceived to be evident communal facts. The clergy wore a distinctive garb, carried no arms; free from the jurisdiction of the king's judges, clerks were answerable to the bishop's court, and to the canons of pope and council. A tightly woven web of decretals and dispensations, of laws and constitutions," consecrated the separation of clerics from the Christian layman, who was indeed *vir catholicus,* a "Catholic man," but not in the fashion of the cleric, who was, in the feudal sense, the Church's "man."

Disparate though their conditions were, Jew and cleric were at once alike and unlike in the paradoxical way of opposite extremes within the same class. We need not be medieval alchemists to agree that since hot and cold both qualify temperatures they are in an opposition more acute than the non-identity observable between hot and white. In the Middle Ages, both Jew and cleric belonged to restricted groups which law and custom conspired to identify by external signs. The Jew, in fact and by choice, lived outside the organic structure of Christendom, and the law that bound the Christian precisely as a Christian—the sanction of excommunication, for instance, by which the lawless baptized man might be brought to terms—could exert only an indirect pressure on the unbaptized Jew. True enough, the ingenuity of canon lawyers devised a way to make excommunication effective against Jews over whom the Church could claim no direct jurisdiction; the Jew could be isolated quite as effectively as an excommunicated Christian by forbidding the mass of the population, under pain of excommunication, to have any dealings with him. Thus the Knights of the Hospital, finding themselves in straits more onerous than those of simple excommunicates when local authorities thus isolated them, complained that they had been "judged with the judgment of the Jews"!

Nor was the exceptional status of the Jews in every sense a pejorative one. Providential guardians of documents that ground the Christian as well as the Jewish faith, kinsmen to the founder of the Church, destined, so Saint Paul assured his readers, to enter the Church in the world's last days of terror and majesty (Rom. 11 : 1-17), the Jews could as little be assimilated to Moslems or to heretics as to Christians, and still less to the pagans. Jews, in short, were a special case for Christian legislators; the laws could neither ignore the fact nor fail to provide for its consequences. Necessarily outside the interlocking relationships of feudalized Christendom, the Jews might be assigned for the reciprocal service and protection that constituted medieval political life to some feudal authority, a status not without the ambiguities inseparable from feudal arrangements and their terminology. Under the Emperor Frederick Barbarossa, for instance, the Jews counted as serfs of the imperial administration, *servi camerae*; in the next century, the eldest son of a Count of Soissons could enter into a convention with the King of France on "their" Jews. The King of France, the Count agreed, "cannot, from this day forward, detain my Jews . . . and I cannot detain the Jews of the Lord King."[13]

Method

It is not only because total recall is impossible that no one who speaks of the past can shirk responsibility for selection. Still more perilous than the selection, what has been selected must be organized and given form, for undigested material is hardly intelligible. Thus two doors gape for the apologist or the propagandist. A reader may fear he has been victimized by sleight of hand, suspect that under the manipulated shell there is no more than a bean, perhaps nothing at all. The brutality of the pruning that reduces a thousand years, the popes of ten centuries, myriads of Jews, within limits so narrow demands an explicit statement of the rationale that has inspired it. Like a map at night, a principle of organization is useful only to the point it can be rendered visible.

This essay will proceed in two phases. In the first, documents have been adduced to recount with what acts and
with what attitudes the popes of the period selected met
the necessities and challenge of Israel. Most of these texts
are legal ones, official letters and constitutions, but sometimes
a remark in a sermon, a comment on a theme or a verse
from the Bible, can supplement our understanding of those
long-dead popes. All texts are freshly translated, and a serious
effort has been made to give the Latin original of every term
or phrase, however casual, the translation of which might
appear tendentious. That total fidelity in translation is an
impossible ideal cannot well be denied; there is an inevitable
loss, if not of meaning, at least of atmosphere when the words
of one idiom are substituted for those of another. Hence the
reader will find at his disposal the evidence necessary to
evaluate each crucial expression. Texts from the Bible are
translated from the Latin found by medieval popes in their
"Vulgate" version; where the number of a Psalm in that
version differs from the number assigned in translations from
the Masoretic Text, the second number is given in paren-
theses. Proper names that end in Hebrew with the letter *he*
are transcribed with a final "h" rather than with the "s" that
reflects the Septuagint Version's transcription of such names
into Greek.

This first phase has been ordered around pontificates
generally conceded to have had special significance in Jewish-
papal relations, and it opens with some considerations on
Roman Law as a necessary prelude to a reading of the texts
of Pope Gelasius I and Pope Gregory I, both of whom belong
in the age of the Fathers. For many reasons, the pontificate
of Pope Innocent III has been taken as the central instance
of the medieval confrontation of popes and Jews. With his
reign, all the major principles have been formulated and
reduced to practice; new institutions and unprecedented
events justify our attention to the pontificates that follow his,
but the main lines had been drawn by the time this most
powerful of popes died. No pope will serve better than
Alexander VI to close the file of medieval pontiffs. A Span-
iard, familiar with the acute form Jewish-Christian animosity
had reached in his native country, Alexander is the very
figure of the renaissance pope, as yet unchastened by intima-
tions of Reform. No man to anticipate the self-searchings of

the Counter-Reform, a monarch ready to intervene between Spain and Portugal and so, perhaps, to block an all but universal war, this last pope on our list can show forth the strength and weakness of the tradition bequeathed him by his medieval predecessors as they confronted the kinsmen of Jesus, who still declined to be His disciples.

Lest we remain on the plane of straight narrative, in a second phase some reflections are ventured on the significance of what the documents have to tell us. As Augustine was fond of remarking, the remembered past survives and bears fruit in our present understanding. We live in a world in which nearly everything ceaselessly gutters back into nothingness, but Jews and popes have survived all erosion; our faith and our hope assure us that this will always be so. If a collection of texts can nourish the memory of our medieval fathers, Jews and Christians alike, it would be unforgivable should we neglect to weigh their doings and sayings with love, and with what wisdom we can muster.

These pages are intended neither as an apologetic in the interest of the popes nor as a questionable venture in philo-Semitism; the faith of Israel and the faith of the Church, the grandeur and the miseries of Jews and Christians, move on a plane above that of factions contending for dialectical victories. By no means a work of erudition, this collection of texts does not pretend to be exhaustive or to break new ground, and still less to provide a philosophy of even a small fragment of history. The goal is more modest: it is to supply evidence adequate for a well-grounded estimate; to maintain scientific integrity, but to avoid a tiresome, perhaps pedantic, deluge of repetitious materials; to reverence the divine image in all men that our biblical faith, Jewish and Christian, makes visible to us. Thus, it is hoped, the perennial response made by medieval popes to the fact that Jews lived in the world of Christians without sharing the faith that formed it may become intelligible. Only where evidence is examined with precision and respect can the legitimate interests, whether of Jews or of Christians, be served.

II

CHRISTIAN ROMAN LAW

The first popes who are known to have intervened in the affairs of the Jews ruled the Church during the "age of the Fathers." Here, as in so much else, the Church follows in Jewish footsteps when she names great men of the past her "Fathers," recognizing that their influence on succeeding generations resembles that of fathers on their sons. Despite their creativity in Christian history, the Fathers of the Church were themselves the offspring of religious and cultural antecedents. For all their undeniable originality, they were no Melchizedeks, themselves bereft of parents; they depended upon the materials that lay to their hands as they fashioned Church traditions. To understand them, therefore, is to see their work as that of men formed by late classical antiquity. Inheritors of a tradition, pagan and humanistic in its origins, but already in their day penetrated to a degree by Christianity, the Fathers of the Church were important agents in advancing that penetration.

It is a truism that the Church Fathers, in order to deepen their understanding of faith, exploited what the pagan schools of philosophy had taught them, but their learning was by no means restricted to Greek speculation. For those among them whose rank made the magistracy accessible, it was normal that education include some training in Roman Law. That imposing legal construction, gradually "Christianized" from the time of the Emperor Constantine, was composed of a mass of statutes and expert opinions, first collected in orderly fashion under the authority of Theodosius II,[1] and promulgated to take effect from January 1, 439, both in the East and in the West. A second collection, that of Justinian the

17

Great, extant in the supplemented edition of 534, superseded that of Theodosius for the East.[2] Here it should be noted that the "codes" of Theodosius and Justinian are not organic and deductive systems in the style of the Napoleonic Code. The term *codex*, "book," is to be taken literally: It is a book into which the most significant decrees of past emperors were copied and by their inclusion given current validity, but their collection is not in every sense a "codification." Further, not only certain texts, but also the legal tradition of government in accord with decrees of past executives, continually modified and augmented by the "new laws," *leges novellae*, of the reigning sovereign, was inherited by the popes. Thus, what is in Gregory the Great no more than an aphorism to explain his decision on one case involving Jews, by the twelfth century had become the famous "Constitution concerning the Jews," called, from its opening words, *Sicut Judaeis non*, and its growth was not to cease with the twelfth century. In the formulation of papal policy on the Jews, the popes to whom all later ones would look for precedents were significantly influenced by the law of the Christian empire. Chief among these was Gregory the Great, and there can be no impropriety in conceding that, in spirit as in chronology, Pope Gelasius I belongs at the side of the Church Fathers. To read those Fathers with perception requires some acquaintance with what they had been taught to accept as civil law.

The Spirit of the Law

If popes, priests, devout laymen, and bishops, have all had their share in the development of Christian speculation from pagan philosophical materials, the Christianization of Roman Law has been the work of emperors and their jurisconsults, not one of whom has qualified as a Father of the Church. This has doubtless had its consequences, not least among them the fact that when responsibility for public order devolved upon the popes of the early Middle Ages, they found in the existing law statutes to define the rights and disabilities that Christian emperors, heavy-handed champions of their new faith, had been pleased to assign the Jews. It is well known that pagan Rome had been singularly favorable toward the Jews. Despite the brutality of Pompey's conquest of Judaea and of the Jewish Wars Rome waged in

66–73 and 132–135, a tradition of Roman favor toward the Jews, which dated from the days of the Maccabees (1 Mac. 8 : 17–32), could still be traced in the legislation that Christian emperors undertook to emend.

Those new Christian laws, the work of Constantine and his successors, gave Christianity unqualified preeminence as the established religion of the Empire. The titles of the Theodosian Code, 8 and 9 of Book 16, that legislate on the Jews, the *Novellae* of Theodosius himself, and the Code of Justinian, 1, 9, are characterized by a theme and countertheme: Christianity is recognized by the law as the sole authentic worship of God; Judaism retains real, if diminished, privileges, guaranteed by statute, and in stark contrast to the law's all but unmitigated severity with respect to paganism.[3] Those privileges accorded to Judaism certainly derive from the long tradition of Jewish favor with Roman legislators, but this must have been reinforced by the incontrovertible prestige of the Jews: There is no moment, from the beginning to the end, when Christian legislation on the Jews is silent on their providential role, especially as guardians of Scripture and as destined for final salvation. That Jews are the people first chosen by God and never abandoned, an Elect whose failure, for all its tragedy in Christian eyes, is less a fall than a "stumbling" (Rom. 9 : 1–11, 32), remains Catholic teaching. In general, the Christian Roman law tended to render permanent the existing religious settlement by securing the position of Christianity as the faith of the majority against all rivals, and by inhibiting the expansion, if not the existence, of dissenting minorities. The Jews could expect that the rights and privileges conceded them in the decrees of past emperors would be vindicated in the imperial courts, but with respect to synagogue buildings, conversions, mixed marriages, slaveholding, and certain honorific careers their freedom was sharply curtailed. True enough, the emperors who formulated and enforced those statutes were under the influence of bishops,[4] the Bishop of Rome not excluded, but not even Saint Ambrose found an emperor his puppet when the legal rights of Jews seemed excessive to a bishop. The difficulty with which Ambrose prevailed over emperor and Jews shows how unreal it would be to minimize the distance that separates an emperor from a pope.[5] In any case, the popes who found themselves responsible for enforcing public law found the law already in being, and it was a law contrived by emperors.

Popes who had been trained in Roman law were equipped with a number of legal concepts that bore on the general problem of religious pluralism. Pagan Rome had nourished a multifaceted official religious worship, as no section of the population knew better than did the recusant Christians and their bishops. It was characteristic of Roman life that the law defined the right of that official worship, conceived as an indispensable element in the security of the commonwealth, to an organic role in civic affairs. Hence, to describe this aspect of the pagan empire in terms of a union of "church" and "state" would only falsify a reality that was in no sense a union because its elements were in no way separate; they were, in fact, hardly distinct. The emperor counted among his titles that of *pontifex maximus,* "supreme pontiff," and Christian popes would not disdain to adopt it; but the same man was *imperator,* "commander" of the legions, a function scarcely to be sought in the vicars of a Lord who had made it clear that his kingdom is not of this world.

Pagan Rome had admitted cults other than her own in coordination with the official religion; these were recognized at law and thus were "licit." Under the pagan emperors, Judaism was such a licit religion, whereas Christianity was not. This Roman juridical conception of a tolerated religion—outside the official worship of the Pantheon, to be sure, yet licit for all that—is still visible in a decree of the Christian co-Emperors, Theodosius, Arcadius, and Honorius. "It is clear enough that the sect of the Jews is prohibited by no law," this decree asserted, in assigning severe punishment, proportioned to the "excess" of those "who, under the name of the Christian religion, presume to do what is unlawful—strive to destroy and to plunder synagogues."[6]

The remark has often been made that Rome could rule the world because she knew what concessions to local traditions and structures were compatible with her essential hegemony, and the privileges of the Jews under pagan law are an instance of this perspicacity. The popes, in their turn, would not scruple to concede the rights of the Jews under the law as reformulated by the Christian emperors.

From pagan Rome too—and it is a heritage the Christian

emperors had done almost nothing to mitigate[7]—the popes received a tradition of legal brutality revolting to our conscience. The worst elements of this tradition are the use of judicial torture and the device of execution by fire. Witness to Verdun and Dachau, to Dresden and Hiroshima and Rotterdam, to the nauseating ingenuity of lynching mobs, impatient of due process, our century knows only too well the lengths to which ideologies can drive us. Still, the men of our day are rightly dismayed by the stake and the rack, those relics of pagan fury—above all because they were employed in the name of faith and justice, directly or indirectly, by the institutional Church herself. The medieval "question," inherited from Roman law, and the horrifying penalties of the "secular arm," put at the disposal of Church courts, are there to remind us how slowly and how imperfectly Christian men extricate themselves from their pagan antecedents. As we try to put this grim problematic into context, and thus to understand it, we must make it a point of honor not to accredit as a defense what can be no more than an explanation. There is much that explains medieval cruelty; like all cruelty, it remains indefensible.

Patriarchs, Self-rule, and Exemptions

Jews living in the Empire had the right to every protection Roman law provided, both in suits that involved their own religious interests and those that pertained to the "forum," where their civil rights depended upon specific imperial statutes. But the same law acknowledged that they had the option of consenting to accept Jewish referees, even in civil suits, and the decisions reached by such referees were automatically given legal status equivalent to that of judgments by the "ordinary" justices of the imperial courts.[8]

No aspect of Roman civic life was open to more serious criticism than was the collection of taxes, a function normally farmed out to speculators, who were notoriously venal. A decree of 429 shows Jewish officials, appointed by their own community, charged with the collection of the traditional Jewish tax which, in former times, had been the responsibility of their patriarchs.[9] Constantine himself had consecrated the privileged status of Jewish officials, "patriarchs," and "elders"; they were immune from personal and civil duties, *munera,*

even though they might possess the dignity of the decurion-
ate, and so too were Jewish "priests," "synagogue chiefs,"
and "synagogue fathers" granted legal immunity by the Emperor who had freed the Christian Church.[10] The personal
dignity of the "illustrious patriarchs" was protected by a
decree of 396, and to make "contumelious mention of them
in public" was an actionable offense.[11] The co-Emperors
Arcadius and Honorius, who had signed this decree, explained in another promulgated the next year that in maintaining the privileges of the Jews they were conscious of
following the example of their ancestors, *veteres imitemur,*
and that it was their intention to give Jewish religious dignitaries a status comparable to that of Christian clerics; to
that end, the Emperors exempted such officials from curial
responsibilities and charged them to rule their lives according
to their own Jewish laws.[12] The Codes, however, preserve
a law of Valentinian II that restricted this Jewish exemption
in 383, but justified the change with a reference to the with-
drawal of the immunities of Christian clerics by a decree of
371.[13]

A privilege that bore on a particularly sensitive point in
Judaism was freedom to celebrate both the weekly Sabbath
and the other holydays of the Hebrew calendar; the days
that remained as working days, the law asserted, ought to
suffice for business affairs and court cases, but it was stipu-
lated that Christians should suffer no inconvenience in consequence of this provision for the Jews.[14]

Synagogue Buildings

The question of constructing new synagogues was one
the popes would be glad to settle with a simple appeal to the
Christian Roman law.[15] On the one hand, the law declared it
illegal to confiscate or to burn down existing synagogues, but,
on the other, generally forbade the construction of new ones.
A fundamental text on this implies that there might be
localities in which such new construction would be tolerated,
but the conditions under which this might be so are not
specified, nor does the decree state by what procedure a
Jewish congregation might, in a given case, vindicate its
legal right to build a new synagogue under this law despite
the general prohibition. Such legislation is intelligible only

if there was both pressure from Jewish congregations to erect new buildings, and Christian resistance to this expansion, a resistance that threatened to go as far as arson; and indeed, Saint Ambrose had come into conflict with the Emperor over an instance of such illicit action on the part of Christians.

Should synagogues be erected illegally, after the law prohibiting their construction had gone into effect, this decree stated that a proportional decrease was to be made in the authorization of new ones in those localities where the law would otherwise have allowed them. As for endowments in favor of Jewish religious purposes that might have been confiscated in contradiction to the laws, these were to be returned. If confiscated items had been consecrated to Christian religious uses, however, the law acknowledged that this dedication was irreversible; justice was to be saved by making equivalent compensation to the defrauded Jews.[16]

Converts and Complaints

On no detail of Judaeo-Christian relations did the option of Roman officialdom in favor of Christianity work more openly to the disadvantage of Judaism than on the question of conversion from one faith to the other. A law to which the co-Emperors Honorius and Theodosius gave their names in 409 is particularly revealing in this respect. If "sky-worshipers," *coelicoli*, should fail to ask for Christian baptism within the year, they were pronounced subject to the laws against heretics since, the decree remarked, perhaps inspired by Luke 11 : 23, "Certainly whatever is out of harmony with the faith of Christianity is contrary to Christian law." Having imposed on these pagans the legal obligation of conversion to the Church, the decree turned to the Jews, on whom, it must be noted, no such obligation was imposed. Some Jews, "unmindful of their own lives and of the law," had dared to "force" Christians to pass over to Judaism, qualified here as a "perversity alien to the Roman Empire." Since "if anyone should be stained with Jewish disbelief, after having professed the Christian faith" this is "weightier than death and crueler than slaughter," the decree attempted to prevent such proselytism by subsuming the offense under the capital crime of treason, *maiestatis crimen*.[17]

Constantine himself had legislated against the violence shown by Jews against those of their number who had embraced the Church. The Jewish dignitaries to whom he addressed his decree found their community characterized as a "savage sect," *feralis secta,* and the punishment for resorting to stoning, or to other, similar violence against converts to Christianity, was death by fire for all concerned.[18] On the other hand, should anyone attempt to attract converts to the synagogue, he might expect the punishment his conduct merited.[19] Somewhat later, the same emperor signed a decree in more general terms, but to the same effect: It was not licit for Jews to "disquiet, or to do anything against the rights" of those from their community who became Christians; proportionate punishment would be inflicted on those who contravened the regulation.[20] In addition to restraining Jews from physical violence against the converts they could only consider apostates, imperial law forbade them to disinherit, indeed, forbade them to reduce the inheritances of convert sons or nephews. The same decree was directed against Samaritans as well as the Jews.[21]

The commitment of the emperors to Christianity was evidently interpreted by them as a decision that could not coexist with religious neutrality. As their pagan predecessors had been bound to the Pantheon, so they considered themselves bound to the Church. Judaism remained licit and there is no indication that they were tempted to withdraw that legal status granted to the Jews by the pagan emperors; unlike the *coelicoli,* Jews were not threatened with the sanctions for heresy in default of conversion to the official religion. Still, the emperors were not inclined to assume the posture of disengaged umpires while paganism, Judaism, and Christianity competed for converts. Within the limits of their legal tradition, including the rights which that tradition guaranteed the Jews, Christian emperors put their coercive legal power on the scales in favor of the Church. The Christian who became a Jew, far from receiving protection from the laws, as did the Jew who joined the Church, was subject to the confiscation of his goods.[22]

On only one detail do the Christian emperors seem to have been willing to extend more liberty to the Jews than would the popes of later years. Honorius and Theodosius heard that "to avoid incrimination, and for various neces-

sities," rather than in consequence of any internal acceptance
of the Christian faith, men of the Jewish religion had dis-
sembled the faith they did not hold and had presented themselves for baptism: It is the substance of the accusations
leveled against the fifteenth-century "Marranos" in Spain,
with all their dire consequences for Synagogue and Church.
To these emperors, but not to the popes, it seemed preferable,
less for the suspect converts' sake than for that of the Church,
to render licit the return to Judaism of "converts" whose
profession of Christianity had been a sham.[23]

Another anticipation of a later complaint is to be found
in a decree of 408. Jewish celebrations to commemorate the
deliverance of the Babylonian exiles when disaster overtook
Haman—hanged on the very gibbet he had raised for the
judicial murder of the Jew Mordecai (Esther 7)—were
alleged to include the burning of a cross "in contempt of the
Christian faith." Provincial governors were charged to prevent
this scandal: Jews were not to introduce "the sign of our
worship into their buffooneries," and they must be forced to
"restrain their rites, keeping them this side of contempt for
the Christian Law." Should the Jews fail to moderate their
illicit and sacrilegious abuses, they must expect to lose what
had hitherto been permitted them.[24] In some way this instance of friction anticipates that destined to mark the Holy
Week celebrations of the Christian Middle Ages, reflected,
for instance, in the decrees of the Fourth Lateran Council of
1215 against Jewish ridicule of Christian grief over their
executed Lord. The gallows of Haman and the cross of Jesus
may well have tempted militant Jews or sensitive Christians
to see in one a symbol of the other.

Mixed Marriages

Marriages between Jews and Christians attracted the
attention of the civil authority. A decree of 339 required that
women, formerly under imperial tutelage in that they had
been employed in the emperor's weaving establishments, but
who had married Jews, must be returned to those manu-
factories; the Jew who married a Christian woman in the
future would do so at the peril of his life.[25] This, however,
was mitigated in one direction, although rendered more
severe in another, by a decree of Theodosius in 388: The

marriage of a Jew to a Christian woman was still forbidden, but it was assimilated legally to the noncapital crime of adultery. On the other hand, the new law was more severe than prior statutes in that it provided for the denunciation of such unions by anyone, and no longer, therefore, by the relatives of the bride to the exclusion of all others.[26] Nor were Jews permitted to retain their own practice and law in the matter of marriage—a reference, perhaps, to the degrees of kinship within which marriage was forbidden. Neither could a Jew undertake at one time "diverse" marriage bonds.[27] The reluctance of Christian lawgivers to accede to mixed marriages is too well known to require comment; the canon law of our own day still counts disparity of worship and mixed religion as impediments. In the Christian Roman law, concern was manifested for the faith of Christian women, and the impression is that a woman was presumed to be incapable of resisting the prestige of the faith held by her husband. However this may be, the inferior status of slaves was certainly the motive for legislation against the holding of a Christian in bondage to a Jewish master.

Slaves

The mildest provision of the law with respect to Jews and their Christian slaves was that such masters must permit such slaves "to preserve their own religion," and that violations would count as sacrilege and so be punished.[28] But the same Emperors who had signed this decree in 415, two years later forbade any Jew to come into the possession of a Christian slave, even by gift. When in 423 they repeated their prohibition of all such transactions, these Emperors expressed the opinion that to stain Christian servants "religious in the extreme" with domination by purchasers "impious in the extreme" would be a piece of wickedness, and one to be punished without delay.[29] An earlier law (384) had forbidden the ownership of Christian slaves by Jews and had adverted in a particular way to the Judaizing of such slaves: If Christians should be found under the dominion of Jews, they were to be taken from their masters, who were to be subjected to penalties that matched their crime. The law provided, however, for the payment of a fair price by Christians for the redemption of such slaves from their "unworthy servitude," whether those slaves were Christians or former Christians Judaized by their masters.[30]

A law that in any sense gave recognition to the Jewish religion could not forbid Jews to circumcise their sons, even though Roman tradition was more than reserved with respect to that operation. The *Digesta* of Justinian preserves both attitudes in a comment on the *Lex Cornelia* concerning assassins and wizards: "By a rescript of the divine Pius, it is permitted to the Jews that they circumcise their own sons only; the penalty for one, not of this same religion, who shall have done this, is that inflicted on one guilty of castration. . . ."[31] Here the civil law posed a case of conscience for the observant Jewish slaveowner, for that a slave be circumcised was assumed to be a duty such that failure to fulfill it excluded the master from joining in the Passover liturgy.[32] As Christian law was to establish correlations between civil freedom and religion, so rabbinical law was willing to extend freedom to the slave sold out of Jewish control.[33] Furthermore, a pious Jew ought not to keep in his house a slave who refused persistently to be circumcised; after a year, he ought to be sold back to the idolators whose convictions he refused to relinquish.[34] Against this Jewish custom, Constantine had decreed as early as 335 that Jewish slaveholders who circumcised their slaves, whether these were Christian or "of any other sect," could no longer retain them in slavery; having borne the indignity of circumcision, such slaves were to obtain the "privileges of freedom."[35] Later legislation is even more severe. In 339, Constantius proclaimed that a Jew could possess no slave "of another sect or nation," and should he attempt to obtain one the slave was expropriated to the imperial treasury. If a Jew circumcised a slave he had bought, not only was he to suffer the financial consequences of losing a slave, but he also fell under capital punishment; if a Jew knowingly bought a Christian slave, all his possessions were to be forfeited.[36] The *Codex* of Justinian includes a decree of that Emperor, promulgated in Greek: "Anyone of non-orthodox faith, Greek or Jewish, or Samaritan, is incapable of owning a Christian slave; such a one is to be set free, and he who held him is to pay a fine of thirty pounds."[37] A decree of 423 fixed perpetual exile and the confiscation of goods as the penalty for the Jew who circumcised any Christian,[38] and the law that made the circumcision of a slave a capital offense remained in force.

Occupational Disabilities

If some aspects of Jewish privilege survived the Christianization of the Roman Empire and its law, many disabilities, which the Middle Ages were to echo and prolong, found a place in the collections that preserve the statutes of the Christian emperors. In an excess of optimism, still to be observed among some legislators, a decree of 439 proclaimed as "valid forever" a statute that declared Jews ineligible to hold any civil office that included power to judge or to pronounce sentence against Christians, and especially against the dignitaries of the Church, for this, it was stated, would be insulting to the faith of Christians. Besides, should a Jew attack the faith of a Christian with his own "perverse teaching" both his goods and his life were forfeit.[39] The Jews' privilege of bringing lawsuits before their own judges did not extend to causes that involved a Christian; such cases were not to be heard by Jewish elders, but by the "ordinary judges."[40]

To these civil and judicial disabilities was added one that blocked the possibility of a military career for a Jew. Both Jews and Samaritans, although they might cherish their continuing privilege to assume the sinister office of those confidential functionaries, the so-called *agentes in rebus*, were held to be unsuited to any military service.[41] There can be no doubt that the emperors held this restriction to be a heavy disability, and this is surely the way it must have appeared to young Jews in imperial times. Thus a decree of 418 provided that any Jews found among the *agentes in rebus*, a formation formerly open to them, or among the imperial guards, were to fulfill their enlistments, be paid off, and their service terminated. This generosity, the text warned, was not to be extended to cases that might arise in the future, nor would any appeal to past service be entertained in favor of relaxing these provisions. The Emperors who signed the law, Honorius and Theodosius, thought it right to remark that the Jews ought not to think this restriction too severe since the cultivation of the liberal arts and those honors of the civil service appropriate to their rank by birth remained open to them. The prohibition of military careers in the presence of such honorable alternatives, the text pointed out in an all too self-conscious disclaimer, is hardly worth mention: *pro nota non debent aestimare.*[42]

Not content with the extent of legal interference in Jewish life to be found in the statutes his experts had collected, the Emperor Justinian the Great undertook to regulate the language in which a Jew in his empire might read the Jewish Scriptures. It was the imperial pleasure that these might be read, not only in Hebrew, but also in Greek, or in another national tongue, as, for instance, the Latin in which the decree was written. If Greek were used, then the Septuagint version, "more certain than all others, and adjudged better than the others," must be given preference, although the Emperor did not exclude all others; in particular, he had a good word for that of Aquila: *Licentiam damus et Aquilae uti.* The so-called "Second Publication," the *Deuterōsis,* however, "We forbid, since it is not connected with the Sacred Books, nor handed down from the Prophets; rather is it an invention contrived by men, who speak only from earth, for they possess within themselves nothing of the Divine."[43] Such is the imperial precedent for the papal attempts to suppress Talmud in centuries to come.

The Law's Last Word

As is well known, it was the confused state of Roman legal materials that inspired the orderly collection of them under Theodosius. The *Novellae* of that Emperor, in their turn, contain, among other modifications of existing legislation, a brief statement of an attitude toward the building and repair of synagogues slightly at variance with the provisions of the older statutes: To build new synagogues remained illicit, to repair old ones remained permissible, but should a new one be built in violation of the laws, it became the property of the Catholic Church, and the loss of the building was rendered more damaging by the imposition of a fine of fifty gold pounds.[44]

In a more general way, two decrees bear citation here because both summarize the consistent attitude of the Christian emperors toward the Jews, and because they serve as a kind of commentary on the texts thus far adduced. The first, a law of 412 or 418, announced:

Let no one who has done no harm be molested on the ground that he is a Jew, nor let any aspect of his religion result in his exposure to contumely; in no place are their synagogues or dwellings to be set afire, or wantonly damaged, for, even if the case be otherwise and some one of them is implicated in criminal activities, obviously it is for precisely this that the vigor of the judiciary and the protection of public law have been instituted among us: That no one should have the right to permit himself private vengeance. But, just as it is Our will that this be the provision for those persons who are Jews, so too do We judge it opportune to warn the Jews that, elated, it may be, by their security, they must not become insolent and admit anything which is opposed to the reverence due to Christian worship.[45]

A law remains a dead letter unless the magistrates enforce it, and the laws with respect to the Jews, as well as those with respect to other non-Christian citizens, seemed to the emperors who promulgated them designed to further the Kingdom of God. Thus the duty of civic office wore a sacral aura, and the Law itself called Roman judges to their duty, conceived as a religious obligation:

Let not the Donatist, or any other heretical foolishness, or the error of those to whom the worship of the Catholic communion cannot be rendered persuasive, Jews alike and Gentiles—those commonly called "Pagans"—think that any tepidity has developed in what the laws have established against them. Let all judges realize that they must obey these precepts with faithful loyalty, and, foremost among these precepts, they must not falter in executing whatever We Ourselves have decreed against these men.[46]

The popes who merited the title "Fathers of the Church" had heard the voice of an empire at once Roman and, in its fashion, Christian; they could hardly fail to reflect in their own legislation the prestige of a law that had given so many evidences of permanent success in binding diverse races and religions into a polity that aspired, as did the Church herself, to be coextensive with the *oikoumenē*, the world inhabited by men.

III

AGE OF THE FATHERS

Although not counted, in the strict sense, among the Fathers of the Church, Pope Gelasius I (492–496) has a twofold claim to a place in their company, a claim reinforced from our point of view by his remarks on Jews. First, there is the juridical style of his formulation of the relationship between pontiffs and kings in a Christian commonwealth, and, second, the fact that his pontificate fell within the crucial last decade of the fifth century. For Gelasius shepherded the Church at a moment when Italy, and therefore Rome, had been governed for a generation by barbarian kings, in theory answerable to the Emperor at Constantinople. This solution was destined to break down in the chaos succeeding the Gothic War of the sixth century, and by the time of Pope Gregory I (590–604), the immense swathe of papal holdings across the center of the Italian peninsula and the great adjacent islands would know civic order only to the point that the Pope might enforce it. But when Gelasius was pope, an Ostrogoth king presided over an administration conducted by Roman senators and magistrates: Cassiodorus served King Theodoric as secretary, and Boethius, still young, had yet to achieve the honors of consul and *magister officiorum*, to say nothing of martyrdom. The Bishop of Rome still could, as did Pope Gelasius, expect that the Emperor at Constantinople would acknowledge him to be the mentor of kings with regard to the things of eternity.

Saint Gelasius I: Theory

Gelasius is the first pope to whom we are indebted for a statement of the embarrassing relationship between the

Church and an emperor who is also a Christian, as he is also the first pope to have left some texts on the less general, but scarcely less embarrassing, relationship between Jews and a polity officially Christian. From the Rome of Theodoric, Gelasius wrote to the Emperor Anastasius:

By two indeed, august Emperor, is this world chiefly ruled: The sacred authority of pontiffs, and the kingly power. Of these, the burden of the priests is the heavier in that, under divine scrutiny, they are to render the Lord an accounting for the very kings themselves.[1]

The Byzantine court where, within a generation, Justinian the Great was to commission a new collection of the materials that constitute "Roman Law," can have missed neither the distinction between the authority vindicated for bishops and the power conceded to kings,[2] nor the transfer to the plane of religious responsibility of what might have been seen as a merely juridical puzzle, as no more than a game to exercise the ingenuity of jurisconsults. The precision and balance of this celebrated formula on bishops and emperor reflect, in that wider context, the qualities that give this pope's words on the Jews a permanent value.

When Gelasius wrote his two letters on concrete problems that involved Jews, he brought to them his habitual understanding of Jews and Judaism; because he was Bishop and Pope, this understanding was grounded in his reading of Sacred Scripture, and especially in his reading of difficult passages that bear on the Jews. Nothing better prepares us to read his mention of Jews in official correspondence than a review of how he handled the Bible, on which his faith was founded.

On at least one occasion, Pope Gelasius permitted himself what seems at first reading an extreme of theological anti-Semitism. Explaining that, in biblical language, "the whole is often named from the part," he asserted that "Judas, concerning whom it was said: 'One of you is a devil' [John 6 : 71] for he was the devil's workman, without any doubt gives his name to all the race."[3]

But this estimate of a single line would be too summary as a characterization of the Pope's total position; he knew well that the mystery of Israel is not exhausted by a single instance of amateur etymology. Thus, for instance, he has remarked that the Bible speaks at times as if there were no repenting, no hope of recovery, when in fact there is; did not Isaiah proclaim a divine blinding of the Jewish people, lest they be converted? (Isa. 6 : 9–10) "Nevertheless," wrote the Pope, "we know that from this people the apostles and the primitive Church came forth; indeed, on a single day, a thousand [*sic*] men were saved by baptism" (Acts 2 : 41).[4]

When Saint Paul lamented the miseries of the human condition—"Miserable man that I am, who will deliver me from this body of death?" (Rom. 7 : 24)—he spoke neither as a Jew nor as a gentile, but simply as a man.[5] As this Pope read his text, the Apostle knew that human misery is not limited to one "race," to one group within the family of man. Because Gelasius was not a doctrinaire philo-Semite, he could recognize that his first predecessor at the head of the apostolic college, the Simon bar Jonah whom the Lord named Peter, the "Rock," had been wrong to go so far as to dissemble in his efforts to conciliate converts from Judaism (Gal. 2 : 11–21):

Saint Peter, we read, the first among the apostles, judging that the grace of the New Testament ought to be proclaimed in such wise that there would be no receding from the practices of the Old Law, conducted certain affairs, of interest to both Jews and Gentiles, by means of dissimulation. Are those doings of his to be imitated which his co-apostle disapproved when they were done, which he himself thereafter avoided, and are they to be taken up in the same way as are those saving truths which he preached, precisely in his character as the first of the apostles?[6]

Gelasius I: Practice

Two texts, as precious as they are rare, record two encounters of Pope Gelasius with Jews. In the first of these, writing to a Bishop Quinigesius, addressed, according to the chancery style of the day, as "Your Charity," the Pope commended to the good offices of this bishop the father of an eminent Jew, who was also his friend:

A very distinguished man from Telesia, although he may appear to be of the Jewish persuasion, has so striven to make himself approved by Us that We ought by rights to call him one of Our own; he has made a special plea in behalf of his parent, Antonius, with the result that We must commend him to Your Charity. And thus it is fitting, Brother, that you should so conduct yourself with respect to the aforesaid, in deference to Our will and Our commands, that not only should he in no way suffer oppression, but rather, in whatever way may be necessary for him, he should rejoice in the assistance of Your Charity.[7]

This text, to be sure, is not without its incidental obscurities. The word "appear," *videatur*, has led more than one historian to comment on what might seem a certain hesitation on the part of the Pope: As one has put it, he "prudently" mentioned that "it 'appears' Telesinus is a Jew."[8] Perhaps, too, it is the word "appear" that has prompted the editors of this letter to insert titles suggesting it is a demarche in favor of converts from Judaism. But it seems more probable that both father and son were Jews, first, because the Pope would hardly have neglected to urge a convert's faith as one more motive for assisting him (Gal. 6 : 10), and, second, the presence of the adversative "although." The force of "although" is to point up the exceptional quality that marked this friendship: the obvious Jewishness of the man from Telesia juxtaposed with the warmth of his relationship to the first Bishop of Christendom, so close that this Jew could all but be considered one of the Pope's own men. The term makes better sense if the Pope's friend was in fact as truly a Jew as his appearance suggested.

Unlike this glimpse of the Pope's personal friendship with two Jews, the second text is the only extant relic of an intervention by Gelasius in his official capacity as the juridical head of the Church in an affair in which the interests of a Jew were at stake. A man named Judah had complained to the Church authorities of Venafro that, although a Christian from his infancy, he had been circumcised by a former Jewish master. This allegation moved Gelasius to order an investigation by the competent bishops, lest "religion should suffer contempt," or a slave succeed in derogating "the legal rights" of a Jewish owner through a false accusation.[9] The impression is inescapable that the Pope was as little inclined to tolerate the latter outrage as he was to condone the former. Realistic enough to suspect that the plaintiff might be trying to use for his own purposes legislation intended to protect the right of a Christian slave to preserve his faith, the Pope was equally realistic in entertaining the possibility that a Jewish slaveholder might have complied with the rabbis' injunction to circumcise his slave, despite the prohibition of this by imperial law.[10]

Because he was no anti-Semite, this Pope could count Jews among his friends, and command a Bishop to protect, should there be need, a Jewish master against slander and fraud by an unscrupulous Christian slave. Sensitive to the claims of the Church, Gelasius was ready to defend the human rights and dignity of a Jew, or to concede that kingly power is a legitimate attribute of emperors.

Saint Gregory I

Pope Gregory the Great, in name as in fact a Father of the Church, on his election to the papacy in 590 inherited compounded chaos. Successor in part to the role long since transferred from the last of the western emperors, Gregory governed within the territories of the Church, the "Patrimony of Saint Peter," in the civil as in the ecclesiastical order; outside that jurisdiction, he possessed incomparable authority, but no coercive power. For a pope who faced armed barbarians, Catholic and Arian as well as pagan, and who had to contend with the rivalry of imperial Constantinople, the Jews can have accounted for only a minor part of his concerns; still, with respect to the Jews, as with everything else Pope Gregory touched, he is a founder of papal tradition, one of those great men who work for the future as they respond to the turmoil of present collapse. His routine solutions of specific cases, especially the text that is the germ of the celebrated medieval "Constitution on the Jews," cited by its opening words as *Sicut Judaeis non*—are characterized by the judicious Roman balance that makes for immortality. In a society that was to treasure "authoritative" texts as the guarantee of doctrinal and cultural continuity, the writings of Gregory the Great were called into council by each succeeding pope on every issue he had handled; for as long as popes held temporal power, Gregory's dossier on the Jews would never cease to prolong his influence.

From the more than 850 extant letters of Gregory I it is possible to compile a full documentation on his concern with the Jews.[11] These letters, without exception, are administrative responses to concrete situations that could never recur in precisely the same form, but both the reasons to which the Pope was accustomed to appeal in proposing his solutions, and the assumptions that can be discerned beneath those solutions, give his texts permanent value that justifies their status as "authorities" for later popes and canonists.

Through them run echoes of Gregory's woeful times. No longer could the popes leave power to Constantinople, as Gelasius had been willing to do; civic order demands the exercise of power, and who but the pope possessed an authority on which that exercise might be grounded? The ever-present threat of renewed war, for instance, provided a political motive for preserving civic peace between Jews and Christians: "At this time especially, when there is fear of the enemy, you must not have a divided populace."[12] At least once, the Pope demanded peace among Jewish and Christian citizens, alike afflicted by a barbarian onslaught: "Owing to the massacre that rages, the character of the time impels" civil harmony.[13] Within the frontiers of the patrimony, the Christianized Roman law could still be invoked, and the Pope's own officials, deacons, defensors, bishops, and prefects, charged to apply it. Outside the civil jurisdiction of the papacy, barbarian kings, Franks and Visigoths, shared the Pope's faith, but not always his civic traditions. By a paradox, those tribal chieftains must hear their duties reinforced by theological reasons that the Roman magistrates of the patrimony, trained to the law, would hardly require and which, in fact, they did not receive.

Gregory I: Theoretical Foundations

Saint Gregory's intentions and motives can be understood only in the perspective of his assumptions, both legal and theological. Meaningless from the point of view extolled by the men of the eighteenth-century Enlightenment and the univocal civic equality that was a battle cry for the French Revolution, Gregory's decisions postulate a human collectivity in which everything except human nature was diverse, and therefore unequal. Thus slaves and masters, although he acknowledged them to be equal participants in humanity, truly differed in the sight of the laws. Jews and Christians too, despite their common esteem for the Hebrew scriptures,

were by no means at one in the faith they extended to the
Law and the Prophets. True enough, a ruler can ignore such
disparate religious convictions as unimportant or, at least, as
irrelevant to his concerns as head of a civic order; detachment of this stripe recommended itself neither to the Pope
nor, we must assume, to the Jews who resided within his
jurisdiction. In the presence of the letter of Torah, Jews held
themselves bound, whereas Christians held themselves to be
free; owing to the very faiths that specify them, Jews and
Christians differ, and theologically they are unequal. If the
Christian faith is valid, and it would be hard to find any one
more deeply persuaded of this than was Gregory the Great,
then to just that point the Christian must count a Jew
deficient in faith. The technical theological language of the
time announced that the Jew is burdened with *perfidia*,[14] a
faith wrong because truncated, a distorted faith—indeed, a
disbelief. Not until our own day, alas, has this term, which
so long ago outgrew its intelligibility,[15] been banished from
the vocabulary of the very prayers Catholics offer for their
Jewish brothers.

Like most ages, that of Pope Gregory I was an outspoken
one; under his pen, terms for Jews and Judaism are nearly
always harsh. Only twice in his letters does he speak of the
faith of Israel as a religion, *religio*;[16] most often he calls
Judaism a superstition, *superstitio*,[17] and this in a letter in
which the term *religio* is also used. (A pejorative term, to
be sure, *"superstitio"* did not mean to Romans, whether pagan
or Christian, what "superstition" means to us; it referred to
the status of a cult outside the official religion, whether the
Pantheon of the pagans or the orthodox Church of the Christians.) This superstition, the Pope warned, would "pollute"
Christian faith and "deceive with sacrilegious seduction"
simple Christian peasants.[18] Indeed, Gregory did not think
it too much to term Judaism a disaster, *perditio*.[19] As he
reported them, some vagrant demons one day styled a Jew
from the Campagna who, in his fright at seeing them, had
made the sign of the cross, "an empty vessel but, alas, one
that has been signed," and in consequence beyond the reach
of their malevolence.[20] In the disciple John, who arrived
before Peter at the empty tomb of Jesus, but who waited and
entered second, Gregory saw a figure of the Jews. Like Peter,
the Gentiles arrived second, but entered first: At the end of

the world, the Jews too will see salvation as a people, thanks to the resurrection of Jesus.[21] To change the imagery, the Jews have been content to delay before externals, to gaze at what is but the vesture of Truth, unwilling thus far to adhere to that Truth through the understanding of love.[22]

To the relentless dialectic of dogma, Gregory added picturesque figures for what to him was the theological inadequacy of Judaism; anti-Jewish in their signification, his terms are not without precedents in the Hebrew scriptures. "Stone of darkness" and "shadow of death," "wild asses," "dragons for poisonous ideas," the "shaken reed" of Isaiah, glossed as a kingdom "gleaming without, but empty within," "their hearts the den of a beast"; these are but a part of the unpleasant lexicon that the book of Job inspired Pope Gregory to apply to the Jews.[23] Still, this Pope was hardly gentler in contriving figures to represent his own pagan forebears; compared to the Jews of old, he thought, they made a poor second:

Hence, let us recognize in the "sheep" the faithful and innocent people of Judaea, long nourished by the Law; let us recognize in the "camels" those simple men, coming to the faith from paganism. These latter were formerly under a sacrilegious ceremonial; owing to a kind of deformity of their members, that is, by the foulness of their vices, they were extremely ugly in appearance. . . . Again, Israelites can be taken as represented by the "oxen," broken to the yoke of the Law, whereas by "asses," as has been said, the pagan peoples are designated, for these were accustomed to prostrate themselves for the worship of stones, with never a disclaimer from their intelligence, stupidly bending their backs; with, as it were, sense fit for brutes, they kept doing service to idols of every sort![24]

It would be an error to burden the vocabulary of a sixth-century pope with more weight than it can bear. The acerbity of his language is but evidence that Gregory took prophet and psalmist for his models in expressing his own unshaken adherence to the faith preached by Jesus, and that he saw in paganism the abomination which Saint Paul, like any rabbi, had pilloried in the opening chapter of Romans. After the appearance of One he recognized as Messiah, Gregory could see in Judaism only a retrogression.[25] To put it as gently as possible, the fact that Gregory's solutions for the conflicts of interest between Christianity and Judaism, which came before him as Pope, presuppose his unqualified commitment to the former should occasion no surprise.

Gregory I: Practice

These conflicts center on three themes, at times intertwined: First, the religious liberty of Jews living among a Christian majority, defended by the Roman Law, under which the Christian name had once been proscribed; second, the desire of Christians to convert Jews to the Church; third, the tension—in that world both legally and theologically reprehensible—engendered when a Jewish master claimed dominion over a Christian slave.

Christian Slaves, Jewish Masters

Like Saint Paul, whose texts on the master-slave relationship inevitably commanded Christian reflection on slavery,[26] Saint Gregory saw that grim inheritance from paganism in the context of a faith that moves in a dimension that is neither that of the sociologist nor that of the revolutionary. Still, his response to what some Americans only a century ago were not ashamed to palliate as the "peculiar institution" makes no place for the pagan rationale, expounded with such devastating candor by Aristotle, of men condemned by nature to be the slaves, the objects, living tools, utilized by others. For this pope, master and slave are identical in nature: The servitude of the one is a sociological accident, recognized by the laws, and not without practical consequences that those laws will sustain, but an accident for all that:

Slaves must be admonished in one way, masters in another; the slaves, namely, so that they may regard at all times the lowliness of their condition, but masters in such wise that they be not unmindful of their own nature, in which, equally with slaves, they have been created.[27]

Saint Gregory's admonition that slaves ought always to have regard for their depressed status in a social order of pagan antecedents—antecedents not totally surpassed in our own days, let alone in the sixth century—is an extension of religious humility that the Christian conscience, after so many centuries of development, can only deplore.

On the other hand, Gregory's insistence that slaveholders acknowledge the radical equality of human nature proceeded from a perennially valid theological insight. He is neither the first nor the last theologian to be found defending, in the name of faith, that nature which the wise ones of this world, although they claim it as their province, are all too ready to demean. Aristotle's "slave by nature" reflects a philosophy of man that every biblical believer finds truncated; but does our common dignity fare better with, for instance, the wisdom of Gide?

Because Gregory's interest in slavery was primarily theological and legal, we shall not be dismayed to find that he was quick to see the value of encouraging the extension of civil freedom in order to parallel that freedom of the sons of God that faith perceives in every Christian, even though he wear chains. What is dismaying is to find protests by modern historians in behalf of slaveholders' interests, against the theological erosion of slavery; when all has been said, only theologically inspired reform has ever succeeded in eradicating the abomination of holding men as chattels. Saint Paul had used the analogy of manumission, the legal act of freeing a slave, to contrast the state of the Hebrew believer, still bound to the obligations of the Mosaic Law, with that of the "new creature," who begins a new religious life thanks to a faith in Christ that has its roots in that of Abraham.[28] In this perspective, Pope Gregory was only the more decisively opposed to the civil servitude of Christians, those theological freedmen, under Jews, who, on the same standard, remained the willing slaves of Torah. Add to this the reluctance of the Pope to expose the faith of Christian slaves to the daily pressure of its Jewish denial, embodied in masters whose social superiority might seem to reinforce the plausibility of their claims to religious superiority.

Pope Gregory's capacity for transcending the crude anti-Semitism of many of his contemporaries did not entail any compromise where the purity of the Christian faith, or the guarantee of the laws in behalf of Christian slaves were at stake. A letter to a Sicilian official shows the Pope commanding an investigation to ascertain the truth of certain charges, neglected by another official whose zeal for the law had been tempered, it was alleged, by bribes. These charges, laid against a Jew, accused him both of possessing Christian slaves and of alluring Christians to worship at an altar he had set up to venerate Elijah.[29]

Thus too, the Pope could send a tactful, but severe, rebuke to a bishop who had neglected to insist upon the enforcement of those laws, while Jewish masters, "less by persuasion than by virtue of their power" over Christian slaves, brought them to subserve "Jewish superstition."[30] Brunichilda, Queen of the Franks, tolerated more than one abuse for which the Pope took her to task, and among them was the fact that in her kingdom, she permitted Jewish masters to hold Christian slaves. To her Gregory addressed not legal but theological considerations against the practice; Roman Law did not run among the Franks:

For what are all Christians if not members of Christ? We all know that you faithfully pay honor to the Head of all the members, but what an inconsistency that Your Excellency should take thought to honor the Head, yet permit His members to be trampled by enemies! . . . may you show yourself a worthy worshipper of the Almighty Lord by freeing His faithful from His enemies![31]

In almost identical formulas, Gregory complained of a similar policy set by the Frankish kings Theodoric and Theodebert.[32] One of the early documents in the tragic history of Judaeo-Christian relations in Spain is a letter from Pope Gregory to Reccared the Visigoth, commending him for a law, a "constitution," enacted against the infidelity, *perfidia*, of the Jews, despite their efforts to block its promulgation with a bribe. In a situation in which the Catholicism of the Visigothic king represented a precarious option against powerful Arian interests, the Pope was ready to give the King fulsome praise for this evidence of his concern for Catholicism in his kingdom. David, the Pope recalled, had been unwilling to drink water for which the lives of three soldiers had been risked (1 Paralip. 11 : 15–19; otherwise Chron.); Reccared had renounced more than water in rejecting the offer of gold.[33]

His reproof mitigated by his customary reservation, "if it be true," Gregory wrote sharply to the Bishop of Catania with respect to the circumcision of pagan slaves by their Samaritan owners; the practice, he thundered, was "detestable to Us, and altogether hostile to the laws"; such slaves, he directed, were to be set free immediately and, far from receiving some reimbursement for them, the masters were to face the penalty of law.[34]

So too, in a letter to the Bishop of Syracuse, Pope Gregory ordered an investigation into a case that also involved Samaritans. The plaintiff had claimed that, although born of Christian parents, he had been given as a slaye to a Samaritan, a transaction which, the Pope held, neither "the provision of law, nor reverence for religion can admit." This case was complicated by the alleged conversion to Christianity of the owner's son, who then tried to reduce the slave to his former servile status, after he had vindicated his freedom under the Bishop's predecessor.[35] Needless to say, Roman law distinguished between Jews and Samaritans, but texts that make the distinction do not make different regulations for the two religions; both were inhibited in the same way and, in the end, for the same reasons.

To a priest, the Pope sent a letter by the hand of the brother of four Christians who were alleged to have been bought by Jewish merchants and detained at Narbonne. The priest was to investigate thoroughly the truth of this complaint, and if the facts should be as reported he was to undertake the redemption of the four slaves, secure in the Pope's promise that whatever he might spend in the matter would be credited to his accounts. "It is," wrote Gregory, "altogether unwholesome and accursed that Christians be in servitude to Jews."[36] Indeed, even the *intention* to pass over to Christianity, whether from Judaism or from paganism, put a slave under the protection of the Church, and among his immunities thus gained was the proviso that he could not be sold to a Jew. Pagan slaves, bought by speculators in foreign parts for resale on the slave market, required special provisions. If within three months such a slave should take refuge with the Church, or express his intention to do so, the master was obliged to proceed to sell him to a Christian buyer. If after three months the slave expressed this desire, then no one was to dare buy him, nor was the master to presume to sell him. The assumption of law was that the master had kept the slave for his own service rather than for the market.[37] In general, those who took refuge with the Church, both Christians of long standing and the newly baptized, were not to be restored to their Jewish owners; nor were those masters to be reimbursed.[38] The purchase of Christian slaves by Jews generated attempts to circumvent the legal prohibition of this practice. One Jewish slaveholder named Basil had managed, along with some others, to persuade judges to put pagan and Christian slaves on a par. Further, since his own sons were Christians, by giving such slaves to them Basil tried to retain real dominion over them through a merely nominal transfer of title, and thus to preclude their achieving freedom by conversion to the Church. Jewish slaveholders, Gregory ruled, were to dispose of Christian slaves to Christian masters within forty days, and gifts of slaves within a family were to be scrutinized for fraud: slaves given to sons ought not to remain in the "former" master's house.[39]

The Religious Liberties of Jews

An early representative of that long file of medieval, and even modern, converts from Judaism to Christianity, whose zeal for their new-found faith takes the form of a disconcerting severity toward the community they leave, engaged the attention of Gregory the Great. His intervention in this affair reveals both his concern to defend the legitimate religious liberties of Jews, and his recognition of the fact that the assent of faith cannot be the object of intimidation. A complaint had been lodged with him by a Jewish congregation from Cagliari, the first town of Sardinia, and the truth of their allegation had been borne out by the *magister militum* and other local notables. Against the express prohibition of the local bishop, a convert from Judaism named Peter had come on Easter Sunday, the very day after his baptism, to invade the synagogue, along with others as lawless as himself; there he had planted a cross, an image of Mary, and even his own baptismal robe. The circumstance that the Lombard king had ominously refused to renew a convention that seems to have been an armistice rather than a peace made harmony among the citizens of a town that might soon be under siege only the more pressing. But the Pope's instruction that the local bishop, who had done what he could to prevent the outrage, should restore the just pattern that violence had snatched away is not merely a piece of opportunism. The guarantee of this is the formulation by the Pope of his policy; he "canonized," so to speak, the existing civil law, and thus transcended the particularities of the episode at Cagliari:

As the determination of law does not permit the Jews to erect new synagogues, so also does it permit them to possess their old ones without disquietude.

As for such zealots as Peter:

Let them not answer that they have done this thing out of zeal for the faith, as if this constituted for them a compulsion for convert-making. They must be warned, for they ought to realize that they must rather use restraint, so that through them one might be drawn to choose, not to reject, and also that the unwilling are not to be compelled, for it is written: "Voluntarily will I sacrifice to You" [Ps 53(54) : 8], and: "Out of my will shall I praise Him" [Ps 27(28) : 7].[40]

Two of Pope Gregory's letters permit a glimpse of the gap between the commands of even so prestigious a ruler as he, and the execution of those commands as near home as the Roman Campagna. The first of the two is addressed to the Bishop of Terracina; it was sent to him by the hand of a Jew named Joseph, who had brought a complaint to the Pope. The Bishop, for a reason of which the letter makes no mention, but which we know from the second letter to have been the disturbance of Christian services by the sound of chanting in a nearby synagogue,[41] had expelled the Jews from their accustomed place of worship. Later the Bishop drove the Jews from a new location in which they had established themselves, although he had been aware of their project, and even had agreed to it:

But, if such be the case, We desire that Your Fraternity hold himself aloof from any quarrel of this sort, and that they be allowed to come together, as their custom is, in that very place which they acquired with your knowledge as a place of meeting.

As was so often his custom, here too Saint Gregory went from the concrete case to the general principle that justified his decision, and that would serve the future as a precedent:

For it is necessary to gather those who are at odds with the Christian religion into the unity of faith by meekness, by kindness, by admonishing, by persuading, lest these, whom the charm of preaching and a timely fear of the coming Judgment could invite to believe, should be repelled by threats and terrors. They ought, therefore, to come together to hear from you the Word of God in a kindly frame of mind, rather than stricken with dread, result of a harshness that goes beyond due limits.[42]

The second of these letters reveals how poor the compliance with the Pope's instructions had been, and how little inclined Gregory was to tolerate such insubordination. The Jews of Terracina, he wrote, had requested papal confirmation of their right to the synagogue they had possessed there, but word had come that the sound of Hebrew psalmody had interfered with the services in the local church; if such were indeed the case, then it was the Pope's will that the Jews leave that location, but he directed that they be granted an equally suitable place where there would be no such friction. The Bishop had evidently been less than cooperative, for Gregory then wrote to the Bishops Bacaude and Agnellus, making reference to his prior correspondence with Bishop Peter of Terracina. He charged the two bishops with the selection of an appropriate site within the city limits, and they were ordered to do this in such a way that future quarrels might be precluded. Gregory did not fail to conclude these practical dispositions with a statement of the principles from which he derived them:

We forbid that the aforesaid Hebrews be burdened or afflicted contrary to the order of reason; rather, just as they are permitted to live in accord with Roman statutes, they can, as they know, order their activities without hindrance, and to this Justice gives assent.[43]

Acting on a complaint received from the Jewish community of Rome, but on behalf of that in Palermo, Gregory sent a response that leaves us in the dark as to the precise nature of the conflict, except for the fact that it had to do with the expropriation of Jewish places of worship, since the Bishop was forbidden to consecrate places allegedly seized in contravention of law. But the letter is of incalculable importance because it contains the formula *Sicut Judaeis non,* destined to recur endlessly in papal documents concerning Jewish rights and disabilities throughout the Middle Ages:

Just as license ought not to be presumed for the Jews to do anything in their synagogues beyond what is permitted by law, so in those points conceded to them, they ought to suffer nothing prejudicial.[44]

To take over a synagogue and its guesthouse unreasonably and illegally counted as an act of injustice even—indeed especially—when done by a bishop: "Our brother has acted unsuitably." Nevertheless "inconsiderately and rashly to consecrate them" as Christian churches, the blunder committed by one clumsy bishop, precluded their restoration to non-Christian owners, as the civil law itself provided. Here we encounter, in the order of things rather than in that of persons, as was the case with baptized slaves, a Christian conviction fully grounded in the spirit as well as in the letter of the Pentateuch—namely, *What has been given to sacred uses cannot be withdrawn without sacrilege.* It must be noted further that here, as elsewhere, Pope Gregory could not confine himself to insisting that the Christianized Roman Law be applied; where the consecration was that of a person, the restriction was more acutely felt. In the matter of buildings, however, the Pope's solution was that of the law: The Bishop responsible must pay for the buildings, thus making them the legitimate property of the Church, and guaranteeing that the Jews "should in no way appear to be oppressed, or to suffer an injustice." As for the books and ornaments that had been taken with the expropriated synagogue, these were to be restored "without question" as to the Jews' right to them.[45] But if the Pope insisted that the lawful rights of Jews to their property, including their cult objects, be respected, he was no less sensitive to the air of sacrilege that surrounded the sale of objects sacred to the Christian faith to those who did not share that faith. Three officials of the church of Venafro a deacon and two clerics, so far "forgot the judgment to come" as to incur Gregory's wrath by selling ornaments of that church to a Jewish purchaser who, whatever his views as to Judgment Day, ought not to have been, as he was, "forgetful of the laws' vigor." The Pope demanded that the illegal sale be rescinded, and that the three guilty officials be bound over to do penance.[46] Here he is faithful in practice to the twofold principle he had formulated else-where:

Just as we ought not to lose things that belong to the Church, so, nevertheless, do We judge it unworthy of a civilized man to covet another's property.[47]

Perhaps it is less remarkable that Gregory was ready to defend the rights of a Jew whose boat, and other property, had been attached by his creditors without the delivery of a proper bond: The competent official was ordered to ascertain the truth, and to compose the matter in such a way that no further quarrels would arise.[48]

The Conversion of the Jews

To the Bishop of Naples, Pope Gregory wrote, appealing chiefly to pastoral considerations, in favor of permitting there the celebration of Jewish rites. The Jews, he thought, were more likely to be attracted to the Church by reasoning and meekness than by an ill-advised opposition calculated to repel. Whoever acted otherwise, said the Pope, made it clear that he put his own intentions ahead of God's. It is useless to forbid their feasts and holydays in the hope that this will lead to their conversion; far better to show them that what we say is from their own Holy Writ: *ex eorum codicibus*. With the help of God, we may then be able to change them. In any case, the Bishop was no longer to permit that the Jews of Naples be disturbed in holding their solemnities, long carried out by them and by their forebears: "Let them enjoy their lawful liberty."[49]

On at least one occasion the Pope found it necessary to write a letter for the protection of a woman who had turned to the Church from Judaism. She had married a Christian, and was said to have suffered certain unspecified inconveniences in consequence of her conversion. A subdeacon was charged by the Pope to investigate whether she had received equitable judgment, and if so, to see to it that the judgment be carried out, "For it is clear that she has chosen the better part, and she ought not to be harassed by the cavilling of the wicked."[50] He had also to charge the deacon who represented his authority in Sicily to protect a woman against a Jew who, not without collusion on the part of certain churchmen in Messina, had so shown himself her enemy that he had attempted to injure her "by the iniquity of wizards."[51]

Jews who might wish to become Christians, Gregory thought, ought to be attracted in ways that may find some justification in psychology, perhaps even in the sincerity of the Pope's zeal for the salvation he had been elected to announce. But these methods square badly with the theology of the human person, and his inviolable freedom from undue pressures, for how can Gregory's devices be discriminated from bribery? If manual workers, for instance, were prospective converts, the daily stint of work was to be reduced so that, with the kindling of desire for this relief, an occasion might be provided for another, more spiritual desire—that is, the desire for baptism.[52] Jews living in places under the civil authority of the papacy might expect a reduction in their taxes should they enter the Church. Always practical, Gregory had a word of caution for over-generous officials. If "the burden of the convert were reduced," the reduction must be moderate: "The resources of the Church are not to be pared down by heavy expenses." Recognizing that converts who were motivated by such earthly considerations might be less faithful than could be desired, the Pope consoled his correspondent with the hope that their children would be better.[53]

A distressing outburst by Duns Scotus, centuries later, on how he thought a Christian prince ought to deal with Jews and their children, was to recall the letter, but flout the spirit of this conception of the Pope:

The Prince not only may, but he ought, to take the little ones away from the control of parents who wish to rear them in a way contrary to the worship of God, the supreme and most worthy Lord, and he ought to steer them to divine worship. . . . What is more, if these parents are forced by threats and terrors to receive baptism, and after it has been received, to live up to it, I would consider this to have been religiously done. . . .[54]

It has been noted that a Jewish slave had but to declare his intention of accepting baptism and Gregory would refuse his master the right to sell him; for the same reason, a comparable regulation held in the case of a pagan slave.[55]

As for those who had left Judaism for Christianity, the

Pope was willing to go so far as to grant an annual pension in some cases, lest poverty be the result of this step.[56] Prospective Jewish converts might also enjoy some exemptions from the usual delays of the catechumenate, especially onerous in times so evil, when massacre by invading barbarians was always to be feared: "The long delay might be enough—may this be far from them!—to reverse their intentions." An official was sent to confer with one local bishop on this point, and he was given authority to reduce the preparation of the converts to a minimum, and to choose a Sunday, or some important feast, as the day for their baptism, rather than insist upon waiting for Easter Eve, although, if desired, this traditional date might be retained. Furthermore, the official was instructed to supply baptismal robes for those too poor to pay for them, an expense to be credited to the bishop's accounts.[57]

For all his concern to promote conversion, however, Gregory forbade forced baptism. In a letter to the Bishops of Arles and Marseilles with respect to a complaint that Jews in their territories were led to the font by force rather than by preaching, the Pope conceded that the policy might proceed from good intentions, but forbade its continuance with all possible firmness, this time adverting to the consideration that it invited relapse. A bishop, he wrote, ought to replace force by his preaching, and trust that a harvest might be forthcoming, a harvest "as numerous as God might grant."[58] If we wish to assign this great pope to the category that most becomes him, we shall count Saint Gregory less a theologian than a bishop, less a theorist than a pastor. One of his comments on the role of a bishop in a world that put force at the disposal of the Church, found its way into Gratian's *Decretum*; thus his text entered the effective magisterium of the medieval Church. Addressing John, Patriarch of Constantinople, Gregory wrote:

Your Fraternity knows well what the canons say concerning bishops who wish to be feared for their blows: We have been constituted shepherds, not persecutors. And that outstanding preacher says: "Argue, instruct, admonish, with all patience and doctrine" (2 Tim. 4 : 2). A novelty, indeed a thing unheard of, is this doctrine that extorts faith through blows![59]

Faiths and Reason

Unauthorized preachers in the city of Rome provoked a
letter in which Pope Gregory expressed his views on still
another aspect of the relationship between Jews and Christians. The odd doctrine of those amateur canonists was that
work ought to be omitted both on the Jewish Sabbath and
on the Christian Lord's Day. Indeed, they held, even to
bathe on Sunday would violate the sanctity of the day. Gregory saw in their program the spirit of Antichrist, and he was
convinced that not only could he unmask that deceiver, but
he could expose his strategy as well. If the Pope was right,
Antichrist maintained the observance of the Christian Sunday
in order to simulate the death and resurrection of the authentic Messiah; in order to increase his credit with the Jews,
Antichrist would promote Sabbath observance in exterior
fulfillment of the Old Law, thus Judaizing the whole population. In the name of a spiritual interpretation of the Mosaic
Law, no longer binding according to the letter, Saint Gregory
rejected this return to Jewish practice. As for bathing on
Sunday, his decision was that this could be sinful only if
indulged in for some wicked motive; no one familiar with
the pagan institution of the baths will find his distinction an
empty one. The foolishness of these preachers, Gregory held,
ought to be put to the test: "Weigh it on the scale of reason,"
in rationis trutina pensate.[60] Gregory here bore witness to
the patristic conviction beneath the development of Christian
theology: Reason is so little profane that *Logos*, Word and
Thought, can serve as a divine Name.

IV

INTERIM

Between the pontificate of Saint Gregory the Great and the Crusades at the end of the eleventh century, papal intervention in the affairs of the Jews seems to have been relatively rare, confined to a few localized conflicts, particularly in Spain, but also in Carolingian Gaul, and in German lands.

Jews and Moslems in Spain

The Church in Spain knew violence in the name of faith from an early date. The Visigoths, who settled there on the heels of the Vandals, were Arians, quick to repress dissent by force, and thus the universal Church early counted her Spanish martyrs. Catholicism had hardly triumphed over that Christian heresy, and at the price of the rigor that inevitably accompanies internal disorders, when the Islamic armies crossed the Strait of Gibraltar and, soon after, the Pyrenees. From that moment forward, until the expulsions of 1492, the confrontation in Spain of Jew and Christian, intricate enough in itself, would be rendered no simpler by the stupefying phenomenon of Islam.

If the Moslems, who seemed to threaten all Gaul when they faced Charles Martel at Tours in 732, were no more than raiders in force, the Saracens were already so well-rooted south of the passes that to expel them was to require a Christian counterattack, prolonged through seven embittering centuries and as relentless as the Moslem Holy War itself. Jews and Christians entered upon a period of complication with Islam that would do nothing to ease the tensions between Church and Synagogue. On the contrary, Spanish Christians were persuaded that the Moslem invader had been welcome to the Jews, and that he had been assisted by them, with all that this implied for the national and religious life of Spain. The Judaeo-Moslem symbiosis that characterizes most of the period of the Arab occupation gives considerable plausibility to the view of the Christians that in these two communities, alien both in faith and at law, their province of Christendom faced an unfriendly alliance. Still, it ought not to be forgotten that "Jew" and "Moslem" are by no means univocal terms, nor were the two communities always inclined to cooperate; at times there were not unimportant frictions between them. There were Moslems, the zealot Almohades of Morocco, for instance, to drive the family of Moses Ben Maimon into African exile; so little monolithic was Islam that the great Aristotelian commentator Ibn Roschd, the "Averroes" of the Latin translators and the very incarnation of the threat posed to Christianity by Greco-Arabian thought, was obliged to take flight from persecution inspired by indignant Moslem theologians. As for the internal diversity of the Jewish community, it is enough to mention the ideological warfare of Maimonists and anti-Maimonists that was to set Jew against Jew for generations after the great rabbi's death. Until the end of the Reconquest, the Jews of Spain were suspected of treachery in the civil order, and were subject to varying degrees of repression as an insupportable threat to the Christian faith and to the national life in which that faith found societal expression. Thus the Seventeenth Council of Toledo could proclaim in 694:

As for the impious Jews dwelling within the frontiers of our Kingdom . . . they have entered into a plot with those other Hebrews in regions beyond the seas, in order that they might act as one against the Christian race . . . through their crimes, they would not only throw the Church into confusion, but, indeed, by their attempted tyranny, have essayed to bring ruin to the Fatherland and to all the population.[1]

Without wishing to multiply texts to establish the existence of a conviction so evidently widespread as to require no proof, we may adduce one more line of documentation in order to convey something of the atmosphere within which Spanish Christians lived and sought solutions for a pluralism at once political and religious. The *Anales Bertinianos* record the loss of Barcelona to the Moors in 852:

Jews having played the traitor, Moors capture Barcelona and, nearly all the Christians having been killed, and the city devastated, they retire unpunished.[2]

Any collusion by the Jews with Islam in Spain could count only as treasonable cooperation with a religious deviation, the more dangerous to the Church because embedded in the technically and culturally advanced Islamic civilization, heir as it was, thanks to conquest in the Near East, to the Greek scientific and philosophical tradition that had been all but lost to the Latins.

The Covenant of 'Umar

Obscure though the affiliation may be, some striking details of Christian legislation regarding the Jews find their parallels, if not their patterns, in Islamic law with respect to those whom the Koran, in a phrase said to derive from the period before "The Recitation" was committed to writing, calls the "People of the Book." By this expression, the Koran refers both to Jews and to Christians,[3] for the attachment of both communities to Sacred Scripture had made a profound impression on the first Moslems. As is well known, the Koran reflects both favor and disfavor for Jews and Christians. Loyal Moslems are warned on religious grounds against intimacy with them,[4] but their designation as "People of the Book"—devotees, therefore, of prophets and patriarchs esteemed by Mohammed—is already at least a limited approval. The often-cited line on the respect due to Christians thanks to their monks, priests, and a freedom from pride that renders them "nearest those who believe"[5] mitigates the harshness of their exclusion from full participation in Islamic society.

The "Covenant of 'Umar," which may be a report on practice in the early Islamic world rather than a fragment of legislation,[6] lists restrictions that will not fail to remind us of those enforced against the Jews in Christian circles. However problematic their direction, cross-influences must surely have been at work in medieval society, and this text reveals some of the points at which a host community in that world, deeply conscious of its debt to the faith that had formed it, would fear for its security if left open to assault by an unrestricted, dissident minority. Nevertheless, a community based on religious aspirations could not willingly disavow all concern with justice for the alien. Consequently, the law recognized the carefully circumscribed rights of the un-believing minority, but always with the disclaimer that these infidels were not to threaten the superior status of the faith professed by the host peoples.

According to this Moslem document, Christians and their families had "come among" the faithful; they were, therefore, in the posture of guests, who might demand and receive protection, but who could not reasonably refuse certain con-sequences of their inferiority: they must expect to pay taxes and "to be humiliated," an expression that seems to echo the "perpetual servitude" so often assigned to the Jews in Christendom. Conversions to the dominant faith must remain an inviting possibility, and propaganda designed to divert the current of conversion to the contrary direction could not be tolerated. On this, the Covenant descends to detail. Noise connected with church services, the beating of a wooden board—habitual among Eastern Christians to call the people to church in a way analogous to the bells of those in the West—and the chanting of offices, must be minimal. No new ecclesiastical buildings were to be constructed, nor were any old ones to be repaired. External marks must show forth unmistakably the religious commitment of each mem-ber of the community, lest apostasy approach by stealth or by deception; dress and accoutrements affected by unbelievers are not to resemble those customary with the Moslems. Last, slaves formerly owned by Moslems cannot be acquired by Christians or by Jews.

Force, Freedom, and Fidelity

One issue, especially acute in Spain, that required the attention of medieval popes was the propriety of forcing baptism on the unwilling adult Jew, or on his child. No doubt the most effective destruction of theological dissent is the conversion of one's opponent, but, on the other hand, no threat to the inner security of a community, a community unified by religious belief above all others, is more sinister than infiltration by false brethren. It is no accident that Spain, with her perennial civil war in the name of competing re-ligious faiths, has been the scene of forced baptism and of its consequences. Not a single papal text supports the sacrilegious tactic of destroying a Jew precisely as a Jew by impugning his freedom of conscience as a man. Catholic personalities have forced Jews into the Church, or argued that it is just to do so, but not one pope has been found among their number.

Still, in the historical situation, the problem had its complexities, and these are visible in papal remarks on specific cases. First among the data of the problem is the practice of the Church never to repeat the sacrament of baptism. Theologians early taught that baptism must be held to leave ineffaceable traces, analogous in the order of the spirit to the ineffaceable brands and tattoos of slaves and soldiers; not even wilful apostasy, it was concluded, could render the repetition of the sacrament appropriate; the permanence of its effect is absolute. Provided always that the sacrament had been administered validly, its effect follows inevitably. A chief consequence of this state of affairs is that an obligation falls upon the baptized to carry out the religious duties prescribed by the Church of which the baptized is now a member. The popes were as consistent in requiring the fulfillment of these obligations on the part of validly baptized Jews as they were in condemning the intemperate zeal that would force the sacrament on an unwilling Jewish adult or on his child.

Second among the elements of this awkward problem is the fact that, at times, Jews did accept baptism under threat of violence. Freedom, as theologians were ready to concede, is diminished, and may even be totally destroyed, by force or by the fear of force. Since freedom is required for valid baptism, what attitude ought the Church take with respect to the "convert" who has come to the font with a raging mob at his heels? Further, with the disappearance of such pressure, a baptized Jew might wish to revert to Judaism; ought he to be compelled to remain faithful to obligations assumed under duress? Since just such claims were often made, ought not the Church to refuse requests for baptism from candidates so likely to relapse? This double issue grew to immense proportions in Spain. The Christian reconquest of the land made the baptism of "new Christians," converts from Judaism or from Islam, progressively more numerous, but this multiplied too the instances of relapse, on the ground that force or fear, in a situation of warfare and reprisals, made the acceptance of baptism a piece of dissembling that was considered legitimate because necessary.

One result of this was that all new Christians fell under suspicion as unreliable, both as Christians and as citizens. Some local bishops were persuaded that neither Jews nor Moslems could safely be entrusted with the grace of baptism, not even at their own request. This suspicion begot a growing esteem in Spain for "pure blood," a family line that counted neither Jews nor Moslems among its members. Needless to say, no authentically Christian belief justifies this esteem; pressed to the letter, it would disclaim the Church of Pentecost.

Such pressures could not fail to require from theologians and canonists a theoretical solution for the problem posed by this dialectic of force and freedom. The common doctrine distinguished between force that was "absolute" and force that was "conditioned." Absolute force implied a physical compulsion so intense as to overcome all capacity of the recalcitrant candidate to resist; it would invalidate the rite. But no lesser degree of violence renders consent totally involuntary, nor, in consequence, would such lesser, conditioned force render the baptized immune to the rigors of canonical penalties should he fail to practice his new religion. At this point it is not useless to introduce the remarks of a later theologian and canonist, expounding the doctrine that was to dominate the field:

Indeed, although Jews cannot be forced to accept baptism, still, if they have in fact received it owing to force, they cannot now evade the penalties of heretics. For, although the man who placed the act may have done so under force, forced though he was he willed it; a will that is forced remains a will . . . provided, however, that the force was not absolute . . . for, if any one should accept baptism owing to force that is not conditioned but absolute, he cannot be called a Christian and, in consequence, cannot be forced to serve that faith as if he were such.[7]

Two disparate reactions by local bishops were to provoke papal intervention in this problem. A pope might find it necessary to protect the human freedom of Jews against the excessive, and inauthentic, zeal of a bishop who saw in forced conversion a simple way to dissolve pluralist tensions in his jurisdiction. On other occasions, the right of sincere Jewish applicants for admission into the Church might require papal pressure on a bishop who was inordinately hesitant to receive converts he thought unreliable in principle. No doubt it was the first of these that constituted the more pressing problem, and it is the one that speaks most exigently to the modern conscience. The most conspicuous advocates of violence in order to "convert" Jews were the Spanish kings Reccared and Sisebut. If Pope Gregory IV would later refer to Sisebut as "that most religious of princes" in a letter disclaiming his policy on this matter,[8] Saint Isidore, Archbishop of Seville, had already distinguished between the king's good intention and the deplorable means he chose to achieve it: "He had zeal, but not zeal in conformity with knowledge [Rom. 10 : 2], for he compelled by means of power those whom he ought to have invited to the faith by reasoning."[9]

Pope Honorius I

Not only did his position as Supreme Pontiff fail to protect Honorius I (625–638) from posthumous condemnation by the Sixth Ecumenical Council (Third Constantinople, 680–682), this unfortunate pope was familiar in his own lifetime with the disenchanting experience of queries from his subordinates concerning his orthodoxy. Among these was one from the Fathers of the Sixth Council of Toledo with respect to a rumor; Saint Braulio, Bishop of Saragossa, wrote in the name of the Council to express the dismay, indeed the disbelief, of the Spanish prelates when confronted with reports on how the Roman pontiff had dealt with converted, but inconstant, Jews:

For this too has been conveyed to us—a thing, however, incredible to us, nor has it been believed at all—that it has been permitted baptized Jews, by the official responses of the Venerable Roman Prince, that they revert to the superstitions of their own religion; how false this is, Your Holiness will know better than any![10]

Without more documents than we possess, this text can hardly be clarified fully, but it must reflect in some way the theological-canonical concern to save both freedom and validity in baptism when Jews receive that sacrament. Needless to say, the conception of freedom, and of the degree of pressure compatible with validity, could well be open to discussion. Nothing in our text suggests that Pope and Council were at odds on theory. The uncertainty expressed by Braulio, then, seems to bear on the Pope's procedure in some specific case where the facts surrounding a putative baptism did not seem clear to the Council, or perhaps it is a formula of rhetoric, intended to open the door for a face-saving escape. The dissent between Pope and Council thus would center on the factual issue: Had the Jewish convert or converts at stake been subjected to a pressure so strong as to destroy real freedom and, consequently, to invalidate a sacrament that requires freedom for validity?

Pope Hadrian I

Yet another instance of conflict between a Council and a pope on the baptism of Jewish converts is provided by the opposition between Pope Hadrian I (772–795) and the Second Council of Nicaea in 787. The Fathers of that Council refer to those Jews who "pretend to become Christians . . . secretly and in hiding keeping the Sabbath," but also to others who enter the Church "out of a sincere heart and faith." Canon 8 of the conciliar decrees enjoined that the first "ought to be received neither in communion nor in prayer nor in the Church . . . nor should their children be baptized nor their slaves bought or acquired," for the excellent reason that, from the point of view of religion, they "are obviously Hebrews."[11] This sweeping provision failed to obtain papal approval. In refusing to sign this canon into law, Pope Hadrian is at one with the traditional Roman policy: valid baptism, pressure short of absolute force notwithstanding, makes the Christian; once a Christian, the baptized convert is morally and legally bound to live as a Christian. Later theological discussion might make the point more clearly, but it remains the same point. A letter of Gregory IV (827–844) to the Bishops of Gaul and Germany in 828 underlies a canon of the Fourth Council of Toledo that has found a place in Gratian's *Decretum*:

With respect to Jews, however, the Sacred Synod commands that henceforth no one bring force to bear in order that they must believe: "Thus He shows mercy where it is His will,

and where it is His will, He hardens men's hearts" [Rom.
9 : 18]. For such are not to be saved unwilling, but willing,
so that the form of justice might be undiminished. Now, just
as man met disaster, obedient to the serpent as he was of his
own willing choice, so too is each one, the grace of God
calling him, to be saved by believing, thanks to a conversion
of his own mind. Therefore must they be persuaded, not
compelled, in order that they might be converted by their
own free faculty of choice. Those, however, who long ago
were forced to Christianity, as happened in the times of that
most religious of princes, Sisebut, since now it is obvious
that they have been associated in the divine mysteries, and
have received the grace of baptism, and have been anointed
with the chrism, and have taken their share in the Body of
the Lord, it is necessary that they be obliged to hold the
faith which they received by violence or by necessity, lest
the Name of the Lord be blasphemed, and the faith which
they have received be appraised vile and worthy of contempt.[12]

Here it is to be noted that the consideration of public scandal
outweighed all others in the cases of long-standing conversion.

To return to Pope Hadrian, he also protested against
those Catholics who claimed that they could live in common
with Jews or pagans without guilt. He reminded them that it
is licit for no one to be yoked with the unbelieving, an echo
of Saint Paul (1 Cor. 5 : 9–13), often cited to discourage
mixed marriages, but here adduced against sharing food and
drink, and thus against all social contact between the two
communities.[13]

Pope Nicholas I

Saint Nicholas, pope from 858 to 867, had occasion to
deal with a question that bears on another aspect of sacra-
mental theology, namely, the validity of baptism conferred
by one of unknown religious beliefs, perhaps Jewish or pagan
ones. Although the Pope was obliged to hear the case and
to pronounce judgment, he was not obliged to provide a
solution for the theoretical issue; this had been settled long
since by no less an authority than Saint Augustine, who had
formulated the position of the Church with all the cogency
customary with him. Theological deficiencies on the part of

the minister of a sacrament have no adverse effect on its validity.[14]

Pope Leo VII

Spain was not the only province of Christendom in which the forced baptism of Jews seemed to some local bishops an appropriate solution of religious tensions. In 936–937, Frederick, Archbishop of Mayence, asked Leo VII (936–939) whether he ought to force baptism upon Jews living under his rule as an alternative to exile. Astonishing though it is that an archbishop should have considered forced baptism his conscientious duty, given the consistent tradition we have already seen developing through the years, still, his century was the "leaden" tenth century, and just such facts have justified this characterization. The Pope responded with word that the Archbishop's first duty with respect to the Jews was "to preach without ceasing, with sagacity, with the prudent counsel of God, and with reverence, faith in the Holy Trinity and faith in the mystery of the Lord's putting on flesh," thus emphasizing the two doctrines that are at once the most fundamental to Christianity and those over which dissent between Jews and Christians is most acute. If the result of such preaching should be that the Jews come to believe, and to desire baptism, then, wrote the Pope, "with praises beyond counting, we return thanks to the omnipotent Lord." If, on the other hand, the Jews should still refuse to believe, then, with the support of papal authority, the Archbishop was to expel them from his cities. To the text: "You must not consent to be yoke-fellows with unbelievers. What has innocence to do with lawlessness? What is there in common between light and darkness? How can a believer throw in his lot with an infidel?" (2 Cor. 6 : 14–15), Pope Leo VII added that of Matthew: "You must not give that which is holy to dogs. Do not cast your pearls before swine [7 : 6]."[15]

Defenders of the Faith

The current of conversion can run in two directions, and the popes were no less concerned to safeguard the faith of Christians than they were to deal with issues raised by the baptism of Jews in the presence of violence or of its threat.

Pope Zachary I

In 743, for instance, a canon of the First Council of
Rome, the decrees of which were signed by the Pope, Saint
Zachary (741–752), restated the familiar prohibitions of
Roman Law against marriage with a Jew and, indeed, against
marriage with a convert from Judaism "unless he should
believe completely," as well as those other prohibitions
against the sale of a slave or handmaid by a Christian to a
Jew.[16]

Saint Zachary has also responded to an inquiry addressed
to a Roman synod, and in his reply has anticipated the legal
reasoning that, centuries later, would bring under the jurisdiction of the Inquisition, in certain circumstances, Jews who,
as such, were admittedly outside the scope of ecclesiastical
tribunals. The occasion for this Pope's response was the
delation to Rome of a bishop named Clement; he was accused
of several disorders, among them that he had been guilty of
"inducing to Judaism" through teaching that a Christian
might marry, if he wished, the widow of his brother, thus
entering with the Bishop's approval a "levirate marriage," as
presented in Deuteronomy 25 : 5–10. Pope Zachary qualified
Clement as a heretic on this account,[17] that is to say, ruled
that the man who induces a member of the Church to violate
the marriage laws defended by the Church is himself guilty
of the violation he recommends. In the thirteenth century,
canonists would reason that, although the Church can claim
no jurisdiction over the unbaptized Jew in normal circumstances, should a Jew induce a Christian to embrace Judaism,
that Jew is answerable, along with the apostate Christian, to
the courts of the Inquisition. Outside the purview of the
anti-heresy legislation of the Church by reason of his status
as an unbaptized Jew, in these circumstances a Jew fell under
the competence of the Inquisition by reason of his illegal
proselytizing.[18]

The concern of popes and of local bishops to protect the
religious security of simple Christians in the presence of those
who held other faiths, and who enjoyed a superior social
status, is not difficult to understand. Despite her conviction
that the faith she preaches is beyond questioning, the Church
must be prepared at all times to find the children of darkness

wiser than the children of the light (Luke 16 : 8); she counts it her duty to discourage unwarranted theological inferences from such a state of affairs. Gregory the Great, as we have seen, reacted to threats in this order,[19] and there is a somewhat enigmatic testimony to the attraction exercised by Judaism on certain Christians in a letter of an even earlier Pope, Saint John I (523–526). This contemporary of Boethius and Cassiodorus—like the first, a victim of the Arian Theodoric—wrote to the bishops and priests of Scotia concerning a report to the effect that there were some among them who had attempted to celebrate the Fourteenth Moon with the Hebrews, thus opposing to the new and correct faith a heresy constructed from one that Christians must consider antiquated.[20]

Pope Stephen IV

In this spirit, Pope Stephen IV (768–772), not without rhetoric, expressed his dismay at certain aspects of Jewish prosperity in the Frankish kingdom:

For this reason are We touched by sorrow, anxious even unto death, since We have known through you that the Jewish people, ever rebellious against God and derogatory of our rites, within the frontiers and territories of Christians, thanks to some rules or other of the Kings of the Franks, own hereditary estates in the villages and suburbs, as if they were Christian residents; for they are the Lord's enemies. . . . Christian men cultivate their vines and fields, and Christian men and women, living with those same deceivers, both in town and out of town, are day and night stained by expressions of blasphemy. . . . What was sworn to and handed over to those unbelievers by the Lord himself . . . has been taken away deservedly, in vengeance for the crucified Savior.[21]

Christian Frankish serfs, like the slaves of Gregory's day, ought not to be exposed to the steady pressure of Jewish masters whose faith would profit by an irrelevant social superiority. Perhaps too, in the reference to Jewish ownership of the land, there is an echo of concern over the loss of feudal dues and Church tithes. Finally, this letter was addressed to the Archbishop of Narbonne, who had jurisdiction over Catalonia, the Christian bastion from which the reconquest of Spain was to be launched. As in the rest of Gaul, the tensions between Jew and Christian in the Spanish March around Narbonne seem to have arisen less from a fear of insincere Jewish converts, who might undermine the Church from within, than from a fear that Christians might succumb to extracredal advantages enjoyed by prosperous Jews. Still, the fact that evidence of conflict in Gaul is rare bears witness to the normally good relationship that prevailed there, and the burden of the complaints by personalities in the Church makes it clear that in their judgment the people were only too friendly with Jews.

A text of the monastic scholar Hrabanus Maurus, on the prophet Jeremiah, is an illustration of the tendency of Frankish Christians to Judaize. He referred to "our Judaizers" who joined the Jews in expecting that certain prophecies, already fulfilled if the Church is right, would come to pass only at the end of the world. Hrabanus conceded readily to the Jews that those prophecies had not been fulfilled in the time of Zorobabel, but if read "spiritually" they would be understood to have found fulfillment in the Christian dispensation. Could Hrabanus have spoken of "our Judaizers" if they had not been a group eminent enough to be well known to his readers, even if not very numerous? His reasoning helps us to see how the religious problem was posed for Jews and Christians in ninth-century Gaul when he drew a summary distinction between the variant interpretations of the prophets proposed by the two communities, a distinction he was sure he could support on the authority of the apostles and the evangelists—above all, on that of Saint Paul:

Whatever is promised according to the flesh to the people of Israel, we show to have been brought to completion spiritually in us, and to be fulfilled today. Nor is there any quarrel between Jews and Christians other than this: Although they, and we, believe that Messiah, the Son of God, has been promised, those things that are to come to pass under Messiah are by us pronounced to have been fulfilled, but by them, yet to be fulfilled.[22]

Bodo the Deacon

The most celebrated defection of a Christian to Judaism in ninth-century Gaul, however, was not that of a "simple" believer but, to the consternation and scandal of the Church, that of a court cleric, Bodo the Deacon. Despite its length, we can hardly provide a better account of the distressing event than this one of a contemporary:

The Deacon, Bodo, born of the German race, imbued almost from his swaddling clothes with the Christian religion and, to a degree, with an education in divine and humane literature suitable for one who frequented the palace, a man too, who, the year before, had sought the permission of Their Majesties to hasten to Rome for the sake of prayer, a man, also, enriched with the many gifts he had requested—enticed by the Enemy of the human race, he has spurned Christianity, and has betaken himself to Judaism!

First, having planned with the Jews this betrayal, his ruin, he has not trembled to plot in crafty fashion the sale to pagans of those he brought with him; but they say that these were taken from him and he keeps by him only his nephew.

Then, having denied the faith of Christ, he has professed himself a Jew—it is with tears that we recount this! Now, circumcised, hair and beard long, his name changed, or better, the name Eleazar usurped, a soldier's belt buckled on, he has linked himself in marriage with the daughter of some Jew, and the nephew mentioned has been forced in like manner to go over to Judaism. Finally, undone by base avarice, he entered Saragossa, a city of Spain, along with the Jews in the month of August. What a sorrow for Their Majesties, and for all those redeemed by the grace of the Christian faith! The difficulty this has been for the Emperor is clear to every one; he could not be persuaded easily that the thing must be believed.[23]

Hrabanus Maurus too has noted this apostasy, but his account adds nothing to the long text cited;[24] one from Spain, however, merits inclusion, since it records how the event was received by Christians in that crucial region:

Bodo, who some years ago deserted Christian truth and passed over to the disbelief of the Jews, advanced so far in evil that he determined to stir up the animosity of the Saracens, King and people alike, against all the Christians living in Spain: Either they must abandon the practice of the Christian faith, and become converts to the insanity of Jews or to the madness of Saracens, else all should certainly be killed.[25]

Pope Gregory VII

Hildebrand, as Pope Gregory VII (1073–1085), made
it his task to reform the Church; in so doing he laid foundations for the astonishing papal power that soon would be
revealed in the Crusades. He is remembered without pleasure
by historians of Judaism owing to a letter he addressed to
Alphonso VI, King of Spain, in 1081. In substance, this letter
does no more than insist on the long-standing exclusion of
Jews from offices in which they might exercise political or
judicial power over Christians, a point of law that had been
restated by a Roman synod in 1078:

We are compelled out of duty to warn Your Affection, that
you ought not permit Jews in your land to be lords over
Christians, or to wield any power over them any longer. For
what is it to set Christians beneath Jews, and to make the
former subject to the judgment of the latter, except to oppress
the Church and to exalt the Synagogue of Satan, and, while
you desire to please the enemies of Christ, to contemn Christ
himself?[26]

His language, to be sure, was careless of Jewish sensibilities,
and to remark that it echoes Scripture hardly mitigates its
acrimony. Nor is this the only place in his *Register* where
Gregory's references to Jews are not such as would conciliate
them. When superstitious Danes blamed their priests for bad
weather, for example, the Pope rebuked them with an a
fortiori argument in defense of the Catholic clergy: Jesus
had shown a certain respect "even to Jewish priests" when
he sent the cleansed lepers to them (Luke 17 : 14); "yours,
however they may act, are still far better than those!"[27]
Gregory's talent for reprimand was such that he could ex-
coriate in the same breath both the noble lords of Christendom and the Jews to whom he compared them:

Among the secular princes, I know of none who would give
God's honor and justice precedence over their own gain.
Those among whom I live, Romans, namely, Longobards,
and Normans, I arraign often as in some way worse than
Jews and pagans.[28]

V

THE CRUSADES

With the Crusades against the Moslems in Palestine, as distinguished from Christian resistance and reconquest in Spain, a new and tragic element appeared in Jewish-Christian relations, for now Jewish communities in Germany and France too were engulfed by the massive violence of armies that had been mustered in the name of the Church and on papal initiative to fight in the Holy Land. This is not the place to pursue the motivations, patent and obscured, of the Crusades, those convulsive efforts to open and to maintain by military force safe pilgrim routes to the shrines of Palestine. The announced goal of those expeditions was to meet the challenge of the infidel, and the infidel against whom was preached the right and the duty to take up arms was not the Jew, but the Moslem, that perennial invader and besieger of Christendom. There were Christians, nevertheless, who proclaimed that the Jews too were "infidels," and nearer home than Palestine. Their failure to believe in Jesus, culpable as it was supposed, had been the occasion, not to say the cause, of the Passion that in Christian eyes had given the Land of Promise a new and more profound title to holiness. The passing centuries had not improved the reputation of the Jews; had they not welcomed the Saracen to Christian Spain, traded with him, even to the point of supplying him with armaments to use against the Cross? The ill-disciplined feudal levees, which constituted the crusading armies, were not notably adept at distinguishing between the alien formations encountered on their pathway to Jerusalem; Jew and Greek Christian, before the Moslem, knew the edge of the Crusader's sword.

66

Pope Urban II (1088–1099) launched the First Crusade at Clermont in 1095, and the spring of 1096 was to see the first Jewish massacres by Crusaders in the Rhineland cities. These disasters had their remote anticipations throughout the eleventh century. In its first decade, for instance, Limoges was the scene of a month-long series of conferences intended to convert Jews to Christianity.[1] No doubt Christians were bewildered and chagrined that an apostolic effort inspired by a friendly desire to share the truth with Jews should meet with no success; Jews regularly resisted all such overtures as clumsy invitations to apostasy. Meanwhile, as this failure occurred in France, an episode in Jerusalem itself foreshadowed the horrors to come. According to Latin chroniclers of the period, one Robert, a fugitive serf from a monastery in France, was bribed by the Jews of Orleans to incite the Caliph Hakim, styled "The Admirable" and "Prince of Babylon," against the Christians in his realm. Robert is said to have brought Hebrew letters with him to warn the Caliph of a Frankish army that threatened to deprive him of throne and kingdom.[2] One recounts that he responded to this warning by demolishing the church constructed on the site of the Holy Sepulcher; according to another, he not only dismantled the church, but unleashed a full-scale persecution of Christians as well. Faced with the choice of death or Islam, "innumerable" Christians apostasized to "Saracen Law"; only the Patriarch of Jerusalem and two young brothers in Egypt were found to shed their blood for the faith.[3] In reprisal, there was a general expulsion of the Jews from cities and feudal holdings throughout the "Roman" world. The expulsion was accompanied by massacre, and by the grim phenomenon, familiar in Jewish history, of suicide rather than death at the hands of persecutors. Bishops forbade all commerce with Jews, and although some accepted baptism these soon reverted to their abandoned faith. The fugitive monk Robert was identified and apprehended; royal officers executed him by fire outside the city limits.[4] Five years later, Jewish survivors began to reappear in the cities from which they had been driven, and this, the chronicler remarked (employing a stereotyped explanation for the survival of the Jews despite trials that made even survival improbable), could be tolerated because thus they bore their providential testimony to the blood of Christ.[5] Christian-Moslem hostility in Palestine was already focused on the Holy Sepulcher, and collusion with Islam already ascribed to Jewish communities in the Christian territories from which the Crusaders would be recruited.

Fifty years later, papal texts were to bear witness to the precarious situation of Jews in Provence, in the kingdom of Sicily, and in Spain, for a pope's praise of a ruler who protected Jews is as ominous as his rebuke of another who persecuted them without cause. Both notes were struck by Pope Alexander II (1061–1073).

Pope Alexander II

In 1063, Alexander II wrote to commend the Archbishop of Narbonne because he had refused to burden the Jews unjustly, but also to instruct the Archbishop that this must remain his policy in the future, should it be necessary to face a similar crisis again:

All laws, ecclesiastical and secular alike, condemn the shedding of human blood, unless it happen that they punish one adjudged guilty of crimes, or, perhaps, as is the case with respect to the Saracens, a hostile attack is actually threatened.[6]

The same Pope, in congratulating the lay lord Berengar, Viscount of Narbonne, for having protected the Jews of that territory, gave felicitous expression to the reason on which he based his praise:

God has no joy in the pouring forth of blood, nor is He rendered happy by the ruin of men, not even by that of evil ones [cf. Wisd. 1 : 13].[7]

On the other hand, Pope Alexander found it necessary to moderate the pseudo zeal for bringing Jews to Christianity that had been manifested by Landulf, Prince of Benevento:

Our Lord Jesus Christ, we read, forced no one into his service by violence, but rather by humble exhortation, freedom of choice for each one guarded, and he called back from error whomsoever he had predestined to eternal life, not by judging, but by pouring out his own blood.

The Pope supplemented this impeccable exegesis of the Gospel with a reference to the practice of his predecessor, Gregory the Great:

Blessed Gregory forbids, in a certain epistle of his [I, 45; see Notes, Chap. III, n. 58], that this same race be dragged to the faith by violence.[8]

Finally, in a letter addressed to the Bishops of Spain who, like the Archbishop of Narbonne, had protected the Jews, Alexander gave full expression to points already made in the texts cited:

Pleasing to Us has been the account We have lately heard in your regard, concerning the way you have protected the Jews who dwell in your midst lest they be destroyed by those who are setting out against the Saracens in Spain. For, moved by stupid ignorance or, it may be, blinded by avarice, these wished to play the savage unto the destruction of those whom divine paternal love may well have predestined to salvation. Thus too did blessed Gregory forbid some who were on fire to wipe them out, denouncing it as an impious thing to desire to wipe out those who have been preserved by the mercy of God, with the result that, their own father-land lost, their penance prolonged, owing to that prior judgment of their fathers unto the pouring out of the Saviour's blood, they live in dispersal throughout the regions of this earthly globe. For disparate indeed is the case of the Jews and that of the Saracens. Against the latter, who persecute Christians, and drive them from their own towns and estates, warfare is just; the first, however, are everywhere ready to do service. He also forbade a certain Bishop who wished to demolish a synagogue of theirs.[9]

Preliminary Massacres

Even though there are no papal texts concerning the Jews in connection with the first great Crusade, nevertheless, as Saint Bernard was later to insist, the Crusades were first and last a papal enterprise. Hence, without suggesting that any pope foresaw, and still less intended, extemporaneous forays against the Jewish quarters of cities in Europe by those armies, we cannot here remain silent on the atrocities perpetrated by Crusaders against the Jews in 1096 and 1146. Both Jewish and Christian accounts record brutal massacres, especially in the Rhineland and in France during the spring and summer of 1096, by warriors who had taken up arms and had set forth under the sign of their faith. Having enlisted to meet with force the armed enemies of Christendom in Palestine, the Crusaders turned first to the helpless Jews at home; in the words of a Christian source:

Although they ought to have traveled the road undertaken for Christ, remembering divine commands and maintaining the discipline of the Gospel, they turned to madness, and shamefully and wantonly cut down with cruelty the Jewish people in the cities and towns through which their passage lay.[10]

By this violence the Crusaders made inevitable not only the heroism of authentic martyrs, but also the baptism by policy and the persistent tendency to relapse from Christianity, which is recounted without a hint of sympathy for the victims by one chronicler of that tragic year:

And, throughout the cities through which they were passing, they wiped out completely, as enemies internal to the Church, the execrable Jewish remnants, or forced them to the refuge of baptism—but many of these later reverted, like dogs to their vomit.[11]

On no important point are the Jewish and the Christian accounts in disagreement, but the Christian ones are excessively brief, whereas no less than five detailed Hebrew reports of Jewish persecutions connected with the first Crusades are extant; three of these contain a mass of information on the events of 1096. Not only the scope of the Hebrew accounts but also their value as human and religious documents recommends them. That of Salomo bar Simeon, for example, is the work of a writer who was able to question eyewitnesses of the terrors that had occurred forty-four years before the time of writing:

In the year 900 [1140] I, Salomo bar Simeon, described these events at Mayence. There I inquired into the affair from the elders and, in accord with their depositions, I set down each thing in proper order; this hallowing they recounted to me.[12]

Ephraim bar Jacob, who has told the story of the slaughter that accompanied the Second Crusade in 1146 and 1147, was himself an eyewitness:

And I, the insignificant writer, at that time a thirteen-year-old boy, found myself in the Fortress of Wolkenburg with my relatives, for the most part belonging to the family of my mother—may she rest in Paradise![13]

The third of the three chroniclers of the 1096 massacres, Elieser bar Nathan, has included the dates and the places of the first major outbreaks of 1096: Speyer, May 3; Worms, May 24 and May 25; Mayence, May 27; Cologne, July 1.[14]

Here is the cry, repeated in place after place by Crusaders or by popular preachers, that set off the massacres, and it is one of the innumerable details on which the agreement of Jewish and Christian writers provides total certitude:

Look you! We set out on a long road in order to reach the Burial Place, and to revenge ourselves on the Ishmaelites, and behold! here are Jews, dwelling in our midst, men whose fathers killed Him, all guiltless, and crucified Him. Let us, therefore, take our revenge first on them, and extirpate them from among the nations, so that the name of Israel will no longer be mentioned; else they must become the same as we are, and profess our faith.[15]

Still another significant agreement is that on the role of Count Emicho of Leisingen. Jews and Christians alike ascribe a major role in the Rhineland massacres to his initiative, and both characterize him as a notorious malefactor. Ekkehard, whom we have seen write of the victims with detachment, not to say disdain, did not flatter Count Emicho:

There rose up in those days a certain military man, Emicho by name, Count of those regions that lie about the Rhine, and long infamous in the extreme, owing to his tyrannical behavior. Then, so the story went, called to religion in this guise by divine revelations like a second Saul, he usurped for himself the leadership of nearly 12,000 who had taken the Sign. These then were led through the cities on the Rhine, the Main, and the Danube, and even in that they ministered to their zeal for Christianity, for they made it their concern, wherever the execrable Jewish people were found, either to wipe them out completely, or to force them within the bosom of the Church.[16]

Several elements that recur in other anti-Jewish disorders of 1096 are already present in the first outbreak. On May 3, Emicho appeared at the head of his Crusaders to face the Jews of Speyer with the classic choice of baptism or death. The Jews fled for refuge to the Bishop of the city, and he undertook, not without suffering the accusation of both Jews and Christians that Jewish money assisted him in the decision, first to defend the Jews, and second, to punish those guilty of the outrage. At Speyer too, the phenomenon of suicide, forbidden by Christian moral teaching, was remarked by chroniclers whose accounts are so brief that only the most noteworthy details are recounted. Since, with the exception of the important item that the Bishop managed to prevent the slaughter of more than ten or eleven victims, the massacre at Speyer counts as a paradigm of those in other Rhineland towns, it merits telling in the precise words of a Hebrew report:

On the Sabbath, the 8th Jjar, the enemy fell upon the community of Speyer, and killed eleven saintly persons. These were the first who hallowed their Creator on that holy Sabbath Day, because they would not allow themselves to be baptized. Among them was a distinguished, pious lady, who slew herself for the hallowing of the divine Name; she was the first of those in all communities who slew themselves or were slain. The survivors, as has been written above, were rescued by the Bishop, without having to change their faith.[17]

Juxtaposition of a Christian's report of the same tragedy will serve to exhibit the substantial agreement that marks our sources for these events:

In certain cities this year Jews were slain in a great massacre by those who sought Jerusalem, in such wise, I say, that taking refuge in the palace of the King and of the Bishop at Speyer, even though they fought back, and this with the help of John the Bishop, they could scarcely defend themselves. Afterwards, he was moved with wrath at this, and, bought by the Jews' money, caused some Christians to suffer amputation.[18]

Unhappily, we must now engage in a comparative accounting of human lives that would be unforgivable if it were not also unavoidable, and remark that the disaster at Speyer with its ten or eleven victims was but a curtain raiser for the horrors to follow. Fifteen days later, there occurred the first of two successive outbreaks at Worms, where half the Jews remained in their houses, but the rest fled to the Bishop. On that first day, the Crusaders broke into the homes and looted them, trampled on the Torah scrolls they found, and

slaughtered young and old alike.[19] The emphasis on plunder
in the Hebrew account is more than borne out by Christian
complaints that anti-Jewish "zeal" in the name of faith has
often been a transparent mask for avarice, and the frenzy
of the Crusaders against the Hebrew scrolls is an additional
characteristic many times to be repeated. Once more we
have recourse to a Christian account, this time, however,
because it narrates with a kind of innocence both the dis-
appointing response of a bishop—whose theology of baptism
did not permit him to rise above exploiting the necessities of
the terror-stricken Jews—and the consternation felt by Christians at the Jewish propensity for martyrdom by suicide:

At Worms too, the Jews, flying from the persecuting Christians, hastened to the Bishop. Since he promised them rescue
only on the condition that they be baptized, they begged a
truce for consultation. They entered into the Bishop's cham-
ber at that same hour, and while our people waited outside
for what answer they were going to make, they, persuaded
by the devil and by their own callousness, killed themselves![20]

The same Hebrew report cited above distinguished carefully between the events of the eighteenth of May and the
suicides on the twenty-fifth by those who had put their hope
in the Bishop, and, perhaps, in the security of his palace and
his attendants. Some allowed their heads to be struck off,
others killed each other—fathers their own sons, the bride-
groom his bride—to the number of eight hundred.

One more aspect of those woeful days must be noted.
Civil officials as well as the bishops seem to have opposed
the lawlessness in varying degrees. It is not difficult to
imagine that, in the face of odds so overwhelming—an army
ranged against the handful of men-at-arms sufficient only
for the normal threats against the peace—the municipal
officers were helpless. One of the Hebrew reports assures us,
for instance, that the chief municipal officer of Mörs first
promised his best efforts to keep order, but on June 30 was
compelled to make the following proclamation, which, three
times translated and more than nine hundred years old, still
conveys the ring of authenticity:

"Listen to me, you Jews! At the beginning I promised you
that I would shield and protect you so long as one Jew lives
in this world; these promises I gave you, and so I acted,

keeping my promise! But from now on, in the face of all these people, I can no longer do anything for your rescue. Consider now what you want to do. You know well that if you do not do thus and so, the city will be devastated; therefore, it is better that I deliver you to their violence than that they come upon me with a siege and level the castle." To this they all, from small to great, answered: "We are ready to stretch forth our throats to death for the sake of our faith in our Creator, and in the unity of His Name!"[21]

Comparable scenes took place in Cologne, Neuss, Altenahr, Kerpen, Wevelinghofen, Kanten, Trier, Metz, and Regensburg. Nor, as is well known, were the Crusaders any more humane to the Jews after they had fought their way into Jerusalem; the Jews of the Holy City were burned within the chief synagogue there. At Haifa their armed resistance was crushed, and there too they were exterminated. In 1104, French cities—Orleans, Blois, Loches, Paris, Sens, and Tours— witnessed the massacre of Jews by Crusaders; all are listed in the account of Salomo bar Simeon.[23]

The persecutions in 1146, associated with the Second Crusade, are noteworthy owing to the personalities who roused and repressed the passions of the Crusaders. This time a monk named Rudolph was responsible for the Jewish agonies. According to Otto of Freising, Rudolph "cleverly imitating religious austerity," preached the Crusade in those regions of Gaul that border on the Rhine, and he managed to induce many thousands from Cologne, Mayence, Worms, Speyer, and Strassburg to assume the Cross. But, in the course of his preaching, Rudolph carelessly asserted that the Jews resident in the towns and cities of Christendom ought to be wiped out as enemies of the Christian religion. The sedition stirred up against them forced immense numbers of Jews, not without losses, to take refuge "under the wings of the Prince of the Romans" in his capital "Nourenberk," as well as in other imperial cities;[24] thus Otto of Freising. Against this monk, Saint Bernard, himself the official preacher of the Crusade, finally prevailed in defense of the Jews:

The aforesaid Abbot of Clairvaux, teaching them to avoid that propaganda, directed messengers or letters to the people of Gaul and Germany in which he skilfully demonstrated from the authority of the Sacred Page that the Jews ought not to die in consequence of the immensity of their crimes, but rather to suffer the Diaspora. . . . And when he came to Mayence, there he found Rudolph dwelling, and enjoying the greatest popularity. Still, having summoned him and admonished him that he ought not, against the rule of monks, presume to preach the Word, wandering over the globe, on his own authority, with the result that he induced this fellow, having promised obedience, to go back to his monastery, even though the people were highly indignant, even ready to start a rebellion, had they not been restrained by the consideration of his sanctity.[24]

Saint Bernard on the Jews

Bernard's scriptural exegesis, to which Otto alluded, is reported by Ephraim bar Jacob:

It is noble of you to wish to go forth against the Ishmaelites; still, whoever touches a Jew so as to lay hands on his life, does something as sinful as if he laid hands on Jesus himself! My disciple, Rudolph, who has spoken against them to exterminate them, has preached only unrighteousness, for, concerning them it stands written in the Books of Psalms: "Do not kill them, let my people not be forgotten!" [Ps. 58 (59) : 12].[25]

The accuracy of this report is borne out by a comparison with the language of Bernard's famous letter to the clergy and people of eastern France:

We have heard, and we are gladdened, that the zeal of God renders you fervent, but it is absolutely necessary that the moderating rule of knowledge be not lacking. The Jews must not be persecuted, they must not be slain, they are not even to be put to flight. Put your queries to those divine pages: I have known what is read in the Psalm as a prophecy concerning the Jews, says the Church: "As for my enemies, do not kill them, let my people not be forgotten" [Ps. 58 (59) : 12].[26]

The ill-famed Rudolph was, unfortunately, not the only one, not even the only monk, to preach a zeal that Saint Bernard would count as deficient in the moderation that accompanies true knowledge:

Because Peter, the Abbot of Cluny, reproached them in his elegant style, [hatred for the Jews] grew all the more, to the point that an excuse was provided for announcing that all Jews ought to be killed, which we have just seen repressed by Saint Bernard.[27]

This remark is only too well founded. To the distress of his admirers, whose admiration has so much justification on other grounds, Peter the Venerable had words on the Jews that differ perhaps in elegance, but not one whit in their effect, from the summons to massacre already heard in the Rhineland in 1096:

What does it profit to track down and to persecute enemies of the Christian hope outside, indeed far beyond, the frontiers, if the evil, blaspheming Jews, far worse than Saracens, not at a distance, but in our midst, so freely and audaciously blaspheme, trample underfoot, deface with impunity Christ and all Christian mysteries?[28]

The Abbot of Cluny did not recommend massacre, to be sure: "My admonition is not that they be killed, but I exhort that they be penalized in a mode that suits their wickedness." The Jews, he assured the King of France, are neither farmers, nor lawyers, nor do they cultivate any respectable and useful occupation; their wealth comes from the trickery they exercise against Christians. Hence, his solution was expropriation:

Let their life be safeguarded, let their money be taken away. Thus, by the right hand of Christians, aided with the funds of the blaspheming Jews, the audacity of the unbelieving Saracens might be conquered.[29]

Quite apart from his intervention against Rudolph, Saint Bernard merits a place in any discussion of how medieval popes saw their duties, for, like the rest of Latin Christendom, the popes of his time were attentive to the freely proffered advice of the Abbot of Clairvaux. Before his election to the papacy, Eugene III had been a monk at Clairvaux, and Saint Bernard's dedication to him of the *De consideratione* bears massive witness to the fact that even after Eugene's promotion to the summit of Christendom, the great abbot still counted the former monk among his disciples. On one point at least, Eugene III was a disciple of Peter the Venerable, for in 1145 this pope, who ruled from that year until 1153, gave the force of law to just such a regulation as Peter had proposed. All those willing to take the Cross were granted an exemption from their obligation to pay usury on loans, even though they had been bound by oath or contract to do so;[30] needless to say, Jewish moneylenders were seriously affected. This economic exercise of the "power of the Keys" was reinforced in 1147 by a ruling of the King of France, reported by Ephraim bar Jacob:

The King of France then allowed an order to be published to the effect that one who resolved to go to Jerusalem on the Crusade must be forgiven his debts to Jews. Most of the loans made by French Jews, however, were made on mere credit; through this they lost their fortunes.[31]

Eugene heard from Bernard that the conversion of the Jews cannot be hurried: The Gentiles must come first—labor enough for the most zealous apostle!—and since the time has been set by God, patience is justified, even though it resemble delay.[32]

The Bible dominates the preaching of Saint Bernard and biblical language can be harsh enough, a trait that has always had its effect on statements concerning the Jews. Well aware of this, Bernard thought his own words on the Chosen People gentler than those of Isaiah:

A Jew might complain, perhaps, that I go too far in baiting him when I term his understanding "ox-like." But let him read Isaiah, and he will hear what goes farther than "ox-like"! "The ox," he says, "knows his owner, and the ass his master's crib: Israel has not known Me, My people had no understanding" [Isa. 1 : 3]. You see, O Jew, I am milder than your own prophet: I put you on a par with the beasts, he puts you beneath them![33]

Quick to condemn the faults of Jews, Saint Bernard was evenhanded in dispensing his thunders against Gentile failures. The Canticle of Canticles unfolds against the background of a mystical night and, like every interpreter, Bernard felt called upon to explain what this "night" might be:

This world has its nights, and they are by no means few. What am I saying? That the world "has" nights? The world itself is almost totally a night, always and totally reeling in shadows! Jewish disbelief is a night, the ignorance of pagans is a night, the wickedness of heretics is a night, and a night, too, is the fleshy or bestial way of life led by Catholics.[34]

Saint Bernard applied the term "to play the Jew" to those Catholics who took usury; they ought to be called, he claimed, not Christians but "baptized Jews,"[35] and he interpreted Jewish misfortunes, which he had observed vividly enough, as a device to teach the Church her faith:

For us, they are living pen-strokes, *vivi apices*, rendering the Lord's passion present. On this account, they have been dispersed . . . sustain their harsh captivity under Christian princes.[36]

Only if the Jews should offer violence against Christians, Saint Bernard held, would it be right to say that force must match force. But these people, whose dolorous servitude has no equal, make a claim on Christian piety to show mercy to the weak rather than a zeal suitable for exercise against the proud. It would be difficult to improve upon the reasons that Saint Bernard considered the peculiar warrants of the Jewish people for Christian goodwill. From them, he recalled, has come the Law of the Promise, from them the Patriarchs who are our fathers as well as theirs, from them, according to the flesh, has Christ Himself come forth. The Abbot of Clairvaux was armored against the sophism that would identify a triumph for Christianity with a massacre of Jews; on the contrary, the only real victory for the Church in their regard is to gain the triumph that remains, in our day as in Saint Bernard's, the object of the Good Friday prayer:

In the case of the Jews, does the Church not triumph more when, day after day, she persuades them, or converts them, than if on a single occasion and all at once, she should devour them with the maw of the sword? Else would not that prayer of the universal Church, which is offered for the unbelieving Jews—*pro perfidis Judaeis*—be established to no purpose?[37]

Before the day of Eugene III, a descendant of Jewish converts, Peter Petri Leonis, was illegally elected Pope by a handful of Cardinals in opposition to the newly elected Innocent II. Saint Bernard supported Innocent, and his wry reference to the anti-pope's Jewish ancestry must be recorded as another instance of tactless language, even on the lips of one who had so effectively defended the Jews; Christian readers will not miss his evocation of the threat expressed by the leaders of the mob to Pontius Pilate at the trial of Jesus (John 18 : 12):

As it is obviously against the rights of Christ that a Jewish sprout has occupied the Chair of Peter, so let there be no doubt that anyone who makes himself a king in Sicily is in contradiction to Caesar![38]

The Torah Scroll Ceremony

The election of Cardinal Petri Leonis, styled Anacletus, forced Innocent II to leave Rome and to take refuge with Abbot Suger in the Abbey of Saint Denis at Paris. There he celebrated the Easter liturgy in 1131, and there received from the Jews of Paris a "veiled scroll of the Law" as was customary in the ceremonial for papal coronations.[39] Few items in the history of the popes and the Jews are more thoroughly "medieval" than this ritual detail. The newly elected Pope, entering Rome to receive the civil as well as the religious fealty of the population, was met by a delegation of distinguished Jews, the authorized representatives of their "corporation." A Torah scroll, magnificently executed, and veiled out of reverence, was at once their most characteristic and most precious possession as Jews. The Pope received the scroll from their hands with ceremony to symbolize the fact that the Jews have provided Christians with this essential part of their inheritance. Lest the real distinction between Judaism and Christianity be submerged in this proclamation of their continuity, the Pope recited a formula to express his acceptance of the Hebrew scriptures, but also his simultaneous rejection of the interpretation given them by normative Judaism. This ceremony, still performed in the nineteenth century, is one more reason for counting as "Middle Ages" for the Jews who lived in the patrimony of Saint Peter the period that ended with the loss of the popes' temporal power.

Alexander III and the Third Lateran Council

At a date between 1159 and 1167, Rabbi Benjamin of Tudela visited Rome in the course of a pilgrimage he was making to the Holy Land. He had the happy inspiration to record his experiences and observations on this journey,

noting in particular the condition of Jewish congregations in
the various cities through which he passed. His comments
are precise, and generally held to be reliable; on the state
of Jewish affairs in the Rome of Alexander III (1159–1181)
we have no better source of information than Rabbi Benjamin's account. He qualified Rome as the "large city, metrop-
olis of all Christendom" and remarked that the two hundred
Jews who lived there were held in high esteem—indeed, they
paid tribute to no one. Still more noteworthy, Jews were to
be found in the service of the Pope himself, the "principal
ecclesiastic of the Christian Church." The most eminent of the
Roman Jews were a Rabbi Daniel and a Rabbi Jechiel, the
second of whom was one of those in the Pope's service,
habitually received in the papal palace for he was set over
the household and the property of the Pope himself.[40] But
it would be wrong to conclude from this report that harmony
between Jews and the Church was total in that pontificate.
Both use by the Pope of financial support to encourage converts from Judaism to persevere, and the provisions of the
Third Lateran Council, held under his eye and authority,
can be cited against any temptation to extend the success
of Rabbi Jechiel in the Roman Curia to a golden age in
Judaeo-Christian relations.

The economic necessities of a converted Jew named Peter
merited the attention of Pope Alexander, and the spirit in
which such help was proffered had been traditional from the
days of Gregory I. This convert had a distinguished and
influential godmother, the Abbess of Saint Peter's at Reims,
and she, with the assent of the whole Chapter there, had
granted her protégé a prebendary for his support. But, Peter
complained, after a considerable time in peaceful possession,
he had lost his benefice at the instigation of Archbishop
Henry. The Pope's letter that deals with this complaint has
all the marks of skillful administration. It refers to the facility
with which a Jewish convert might lose hope, and to the
consequent obligation of Christians to treat him "humanely
and kindly," but also to the cause, "just, as We trust," on
account of which the Archbishop had taken his action. These
face-saving considerations duly noted, the Pope commanded
that either Peter's original income be restored, or that some
other, equivalent office be granted him, lest the convert
return, owing to poverty, "like a dog to his vomit."[41]

Much of what the Third Lateran Council of 1179 decreed with respect to the Jews was already traditional policy of many years' standing. Jews were not to possess Christian slaves and servants—specifically, neither nurses nor midwives. Compulsion was not to be used in order to convert Jews, but sincere converts from Judaism were to be received without calumny. Jews were to suffer neither in their persons nor in their goods, apart from lawful trial and sentence; no one was to disturb their religious ceremonials. They were not to drag clerics before secular judges, and Christians could give testimony against Jews in court trials; to give preference to Jewish witnesses fell under the penalty of excommunication. What frictions, we may wonder, impelled the Fathers of the Council to vindicate the competence of Christian witnesses in the courts of Christendom? And what conception of civic rights and duties prompted the Council to remark that it was "necessary that Jews be subject to Christians, and yet be fostered by them, for the sake of humanity only." Is it possible to see in this expression an appeal to our common human quality as the ultimate foundation for the hospitality Jews deserve to find among Christians, a canonization of natural law jurisprudence, benign enough so far as it goes, but strangely silent on the special role of Jews in the designs of Providence preached by Christians? Saint Bernard, we cannot help remarking, would surely have improved the statement of the Council. Furthermore, Jews were not to obtain control over Christian churches, to the contempt of God and the loss of revenue. Last, a corollary to the venerable prohibition against the servitude of Christians to Jews: feudal homage could not be sworn to a Jew.[42] The long constitution in which most of these provisions occur is the oldest extant form of the famous *Sicut Judaeis non,* already mentioned and to recur regularly in the future.[43]

The power to call up crusades is evidence of a new degree of papal power, for what is the supreme act within the scope of political power if not to declare and to wage war? With the Crusades to reclaim the Holy Land, conceived by and, to a point, directed from Rome, faith had become the last justification of all communal action. In such a perspective, the position of the Jews could only appear anomalous. True enough, the Scriptures all Christians esteem record their glories, including the promises that no progress in revelation invalidates, but it seemed equally clear to medieval Christians that in their very reading of their own Scriptures the Jews were clinging to a stage of faith long since rendered obsolete by the mercy of God, to which they had been blind. The kernel, in a stereotyped metaphor, remained hidden from the Jews under the shell which is the letter of the sacred text. Christian lawgivers—popes chief among them— would think it their duty to use their authority and their power to make manifest in the legal institutions of Christendom the credal deficiencies of Israel. Providence is patient— the fields burgeon until the harvest with growth both good and bad—but human legislators feel compelled to act more quickly. Popes capable of defying and challenging Moslem military strength did not fail to promulgate laws designed to give the theologically inferior status of the Jews dispersed through Christendom a detailed expression in canon law and councils.

VI

THE PONTIFICATE OF INNOCENT III

Medieval papacy, as apex of a feudal pyramid, was most fully itself between the pontificate of Innocent III (1198–1217), who wielded the maximum of papal strength as the thirteenth century opened, and that of Boniface VIII (1295–1303), at the end of the same century. Despite the most profound dissent as to the value of his reign for the world or for the Church, few would dispute the estimate that makes Innocent III the incarnation of medieval papacy at its zenith.[1] Possessed of undeniable personal talents, Innocent was elected to guide the Church at a climactic moment, when the twelfth century was flowering in the new movements and institutions of the thirteenth.

The enormously widened perspectives of a Christendom which, at long last, was beginning to roll back Islam in Spain, a Christendom newly instructed in philosophy and science by a deluge of Greek and Arabic texts, found in this Pope a man of affairs, ready to make good use of the feudal overlordship enjoyed by the papacy in coordinating the energies of Europe in common tasks. Two such tasks, he believed, imposed themselves upon him: "Among all the desires of Our heart, We have principally two aims in this life: That We might be able to undertake with success the recovery of the Holy Land, and the restoration of her form to the universal Church."[2] Innocent was not unwilling to make peaceful overtures to the Sultan of Damascus and Babylon, to the end that "the condition of our people among you be not worse than the condition of your people among us,"[3] but he had small hope that anything would come of these courtesies unless preparations for a Crusade strike the

Sultan's heart with terror.[4] The means Innocent thought best calculated to achieve both goals was the convocation of a General Council, the time-honored custom of his predecessors in times of crisis, for "these matters pertain to the common welfare of all the faithful."[5]

Developments that might have tended to diminish the power of the Holy See under this Pope tended rather to strengthen her. The charismatic dynamism of the new mendicant orders, Franciscan and Dominican, far from threatening the institutional Church, were placed by their founders at the disposition of the Pope, and Innocent III, trained in canon law, was sufficiently percipient to recognize the apostolic value of these unexpected auxiliaries. More superficial observers——the secular masters of Paris, for instance—confused the passionate devotion of the friars for the ideal of the Gospel with apocalyptic sectarianism. Social organization in this Pope's day was characterized by chartered guilds, including those guilds of intellect, the universities; the papacy would not be slow to favor their development, and to exploit their resources. From below, the urban populations, thanks to their charters of liberty, diminished the centrifugal authoritarianism of the lay lords; from above, an emperor—Frederick II was Innocent's infelicitous choice—gave to the secular order a unity in principle that corresponded to that of the Church in the order of the spirit. Over this turbulent and transitional polity, Innocent presided, enforcing in a mode impossible for any of his predecessors, and for most of his successors, an exalted conception of his papal office.

Innocent III on the Papacy

Although the theological expertise of Pope Innocent has been contested, and not without reason,[6] his doctrinal positions have an interest quite apart from their intrinsic validity, and on no subject are they more significant than on the dignity of the Roman Pontiff and his See. One place to look for Innocent's conception of Rome's grandeur is in his sermons for the feasts of Saints Peter and Paul, patrons of Christian Rome. Thanks to Peter, Innocent proclaimed, the Rome that was once the fountainhead of error has become the teacher of truth. The measure of Rome's profit, in exchanging her imperial state for that of the apostolic teaching

office, is that the emperor himself, in the Christian dispensation, is subject to that teaching function. Earthly power has
given way to heavenly authority, and what papal Rome
decrees on earth runs in heaven (Matt. 16 : 19; 18 : 18).
The mark of heaven's favor toward her is her manifold
dignity, at once "priestly and royal, imperial and apostolic,
possessing and exercising, not only dominion over bodies, but
mastery over souls."[7]

Innocent did not shrink from drawing the most extreme
conclusions from what he conceived to be the double depend-
ence of emperor on pope. Did not the renewed western
Empire owe its origin to the intervention of the Holy See,
undertaken for her own better defense? Thus "in origin,"
principaliter, the imperial dignity depended upon the See of
Peter. The same is true of the end of the affair; the emperor
is an emperor "in the end," *finaliter*, owing to his benediction,
crowning, and investiture by the Supreme Pontiff.[8] Superior
to the emperor, to whom could the pope be inferior? Less
than God, to be sure, the pope occupies a unique position,
and no one can venture to express Innocent's daring conception better than he did himself:

Now, therefore, see who this servant is: A servant given
preeminence over the family! Truly he is vicar of Jesus
Christ, successor of Peter, the Anointed of the Lord, the god
of Pharaoh! Set in the midst, between God and man, this
side of God, but beyond man, less than God, but greater
than man, he is judge of all, and by no one is he judged,
proclaiming through the voice of the Apostle: "He who
judges me is the Lord" [1 Cor. 4 : 4].[9]

Never a man to despise the advantages that feudalism
might provide where feudal right failed him, Innocent could
appeal to the even more universal bonds of sin to justify his
intervention in public affairs. All authentically human activity
brings with it the risk of sin and, as preachers make sure
their congregations know, few among us escape its peril.
The just man of Scripture sins seven times a day (Prov. 24 :
16), and who could gainsay a thirteenth-century pope's
claim that to him, if to anyone, belonged the censuring of
sin? Surely not Philip Augustus of France, who in 1204
received a papal letter that conceded to the King his feudal
right in an affair that interested the Pope, but undercut the

royal right in the name of the higher, papal right to pass judgment on sin:

In conformity with the admonition of the aforesaid Abbot, or rather, Our own, indeed, with that of God, do you establish a solid truce, or enter upon suitable arrangements for a truce . . . so that the aforesaid Abbot, with Our venerable son, the Archbishop of Bourges, may have full knowledge of it, not by reason of feudal right, the judgment of which does belong to you, but because of the incidence of sin, the censuring of which, without any doubt, belongs to Us.[10]

Innocent was the first pope to make habitual use of the title "Vicar of Christ"; until his day, the popes had been content to style themselves "Vicars of Peter."[11] In a panegyric on Saint Sylvester I, pope from 314 until 325, Innocent referred to his predecessor as "Vicar of Him concerning whom the Apostle said: 'God was in Christ, reconciling the world to Himself'" (2 Cor. 5 : 19).[12] A *Dialogue Between God and a Sinner* allowed Innocent to put words on the lips of both, and he ascribed to God the remark: "The pope, my vicar, whom I have established in my own place as your judge on earth. . . ."[13] His commentary on the rubrics prescribed for mass celebrated by the pope, which comes to us under the title *Concerning the Roman Pontiff*, appeals to the pope's status as Vicar of Christ to account for the direction that deacon and subdeacon kiss the foot of the pontiff rather than his hand: Is not the pope vicar of him whose feet the woman, a sinner in the city, had not ceased to kiss? (Luke 7 : 37–48).[14] So too, the rubric that governs a detail in the ceremonial of the pope's communion: He breaks the bread at the altar, but communicates at the throne. In the absence of an authoritative text to support his interpretation, Innocent thought it better not to give this admittedly obscure direction a "historical" explanation, but, persuaded that profound mysteries underlie the rite, he ventured an "allegorical" one. This ceremony, peculiar to the pope, is a ritual imitation of the circumstances that the Lord broke bread before the two disciples at Emmaus, whereas he ate in the presence of the eleven at Jerusalem.[15] Even the human lapse of Peter in the Garden of Gethsemane impressed Innocent as a testimony to his primacy among the apostles, worth listing along with the traditional texts that buttress that doctrine: "Peter

alone unsheathed a sword, struck the servant of the High
Priest, and cut off his right ear" (Luke 22 : 50).[16] Jesus had
been more severe in his judgment of this first apostolic appeal
to the secular arm (Matt. 26 : 52; Luke 23 : 50–51; John
18 : 10–11), and Saint Bernard, for one, even in the midst
of preaching a crusade, had known how to apply the Lord's
teaching. Because our concern is with Innocent's response
to the mystery of Israel, we join to his doctrine on the role
of popes some indications of how he conceived of the Jews
and what place he thought was theirs in the Christian world.

Innocent III on Judaism

The Pope who headed a Christendom so deeply conscious
of her expanding possibilities, who was as conscious of his
own dignity at the head of that highly unitary world, could
only consider the Jews, that unassimilated minority, an embarrassment and an irritant. Innocent saw his world as one
without neutrals; to the point that Jews were not fully a part
of that world, they were thought of as its enemies. In any
case, the ascendancy of the papacy in the person of this most
eminent of medieval popes has been counted the very nadir
of Jewish fortunes. In the estimate of at least one Jewish
historian, the pontificate of Innocent and the death in his
time of the great Rabbi Moses Ben Maimon deserve to be
coupled as twin disasters.[17] To judge with what reason the
reign of Innocent III can be thought the extreme humiliation
of medieval Jewry requires an examination not only of the
theories and initiatives of the Pope, but also of the legislation
enacted with respect to the Jews by the Fourth Lateran
Council, which he convoked and dominated. Legal dispositions presuppose more fundamental convictions and, in the
end, those of a Christian derive from his reading of the Bible
in the light of ecclesiastical experience.

The Jews According to Scripture

The distinction between Jew and Gentile, bipartite source
of the Christian people, seemed to Pope Innocent the ultimate burden of certain scriptural passages, and his exegesis
of these texts reveals important aspects of his conception of
the Jewish people. More than once in a sermon, for instance,

Ephesians 2 : 14 ff. is adduced to explain that Jesus is the cornerstone that unites the two walls which are the two peoples, Jews and Gentiles.[18] This union is a work of peace, and implies that the enclosures that formerly separated the pagans with their idolatries from the Hebrews with their ceremonial have now been broken down; Jesus is our peace because he is the cornerstone (Ps. 118 : 22), because he has made of what were two something one, so joined the two walls that there is now but one sheepfold (John 10 : 16). Because "he was born in the manger of ox and ass," Jesus is peace restored between man and man, for the ox represents the Jewish and the ass the Gentile peoples.[19] To vary the figure, Christ is the mediator between the two peoples in the way that the cross on an altar stands between two candelabra; he took his place between the shepherds from Judaea, and the Magi from the pagan East.[20]

If Jews would be little inclined to thank Innocent for associating their ceremonies with the idolatries of the heathen, superseded in the new dispensation, still less would the Jews have been pleased by the Pope's view that peace on earth is one fruit of the firm faith in Christ that they had been invited to share with the sons of just those pagans. The choice offered by Pilate, "Whom do you wish that I release to you? Barabbas, or Jesus who is called Christ?" (Matt. 27 : 17), was "posed to the Jewish people in order that our question might be posed to the Christian people: Good or evil? Truth or vanity? Iniquity or justice?"[21]

In general, Innocent taught, the Mosaic Law promised temporal and earthly delights, a land flowing with milk and honey, the law of the talion, conjugal joy, and a numerous progeny. Against all this, the law of the Gospel extolls poverty, invokes a blessing in answer to a curse, venerates virginity—heavy burdens, to be sure, but to those moved by love they seem light.[22] The Old Law was characterized by the active life and by the five senses which make it possible: "Such are the carnal Jews, who seek only what sense perceives, who delight in the corporeal senses alone,"[23] and this despite the fact that their own prophets "spoke, not carnally, but spiritually."[24] Isaiah called the Child whose birth he foretold "God substantially, according to nature," the Pope explained in a Christmas sermon, appealing to both Testaments, "so that the heretic might be confounded, and the

Jews put to shame."[25] The psalmist's cry, "Night unto night transmits knowledge" [Ps. 18 (19) : 3], became in his interpretation an ironic line: "Judas, who was a night, harsh and shadowy, handed over to the night of the Jews the Knowledge of God, that is, the Son of God."[26] Innocent understood well enough why Jews withheld faith in Jesus:

Until today, in truth, the Jews are scandalized when they hear that God was scourged, was crucified, and that He died, holding it unworthy so much as to hear that God endured things unworthy.[27]

Innocent was unwilling to excuse Jewish disbelief on the ground of ignorance: "The Jew who denies that Messiah has come, and that he is God, lies."[28] Nor is this the limit of the Pope's invective: "Herod is the devil, the Jews demons; that one is King of the Jews, this one the King of demons. . . ."[29] The Lord abandoned those who failed to believe, and had recourse to those who had faith, "condemned the Synagogue because of her disbelief, and chose the Church because of her obedience"; the fever-ridden mother-in-law of Simon Peter (Luke 4 : 38–39) is a figure of the Synagogue, whereas Peter's wife is the Church, born of the Synagogue. This instance of typology in no way strains historic fact, nor does the Pope's use of the text "Salvation is from the Jews" (John 4 : 22). Still, the Synagogue labors under the twin fevers of envy and of error: "It was winter," wrote Saint John (John 10 : 12); if the Pope was right, the Beloved Disciple meant that the winter of Jewish error, of disbelief, of ignorance, prevailed.[30]

The Synagogue has reasons enough for envy: Her most precious possessions have been inherited by the Church. Kingdom and priesthood—it is Innocent III who writes, a priest who claims the right to determine the imperial succession—temple and altar, Law and prophecy, all this Hebrew wealth is now in the hands of the Church. Perhaps without perfect consistency, the Pope observed that the Synagogue is hardly aware of her manifold present disabilities: "By so great an error is she detained, she does not even understand the truth this way." Innocent's next lines are somewhat more sympathetic, but—and this is the ultimate obstacle to the unity of Jew and Christian—his very concern to share with Jews the faith he counts his best possession can only appear an enticement to apostasy, if the Jews he addressed considered themselves bound by the decision of the Sanhedrin of Annas and Caiphas. Those who constitute the household of the true faith pray for the Synagogue in order that God might remove the veil from Jewish hearts, that she might acknowledge Jesus who is Truth, Jesus who healed the whole sufferer on the Sabbath (John 7 : 23), this marvel a remote figure of the Day when all Israel will be saved (Rom. 4 : 1–13; 9 : 3–24; Jer. 33 : 6–26).[31]

No text of Scripture has inspired more speculation, whether among Jews or Christians, than has the line of Exodus (3 : 14) that contains the four letters of the mysterious and ineffable Divine Name, the Tetragrammaton. We ought not be surprised to find that Pope Innocent has undertaken some comments on this strange passage, nor is it unexpected that his exegesis leaves something to be desired. The four letters of the Name, he told his congregation, "as the most learned from among the Hebrews assert, are Joth, He, Vau, and Heth," and there was a Hebrew custom of writing the Name one way, but of pronouncing it another: "written I, E, V, E, it is pronounced 'Adonai.' " The Latins, so Innocent thought, did something similar: "Jesus," the letters of which in the Pope's opinion coincided with those of the Tetragrammaton, is pronounced, but the letters I, H, S, are written.[32] Innocent does not seem to have realized that the familiar IHS monogram is a Latin approximation of the first three letters of "Jesus" as written in the Greek alphabet.

With all his contemporaries, Innocent III held that the Bible is susceptible of four interpretations, four "theological understandings."[33] The least dramatic of these is also the least instructive, but, alas, it is the one with which Innocent judged the Jews to be content. This is the "literal" or "historical" sense, and the Pope used the banal analogy of seeking "beneath the shell for the kernel" to describe the wiser search by Christians for the vivifying spirit, contained in, but also hidden and protected by, the letter of the sacred text. For the percipient reader, the letter of Scripture is like a portrait; what is of interest is less the tablet to which paint has been applied than the picturing the artist has contrived, less the "history," so often inadequate to the burden of revelation, than the "allegory," which will instruct us on one occasion as to what is good through an account of evil, and on another, through an account of what is good, signify to us what is evil.[34]

Despite the limitations of his biblical science, Pope Innocent's comments on the Gospel make it clear that his opposition to the Jews was far from the racist bias of the modern anti-Semite. Fully cognizant of the Jewish origin of the Church, his reservations on the Jews in his own world were religious reservations, directly or indirectly reducible to the theological option taken by the Jews against receiving Jesus as Messiah; he never forgot that Jesus is a Jew. The faith of Israel, the Pope believed, is a progressive one; from a time of relative darkness, the Jews had advanced to the Mosaic Law, carved on stone tablets. Mary Magdalene, for instance, when she came early in the morning to the tomb of Jesus, a tomb sealed with a stone, and thus a figure of the Sinaitic Law, can be understood as a figure of the Synagogue before the time of Moses.[35] The first faithful Christians were "of the circumcision," and, truly, "salvation is from the Jews," but the fullness of faith required that the rocks be split, the monuments opened, the stone rolled back from the door of the tomb. At the preaching of the Gospel, the Synagogue could learn that the Law is to be understood, not literally, but spiritually, and those who thus understood it were precisely the first Christians.[36]

Despite a certain grandeur in the Pope's vision of their history, Jews must have been dismayed by the role his trinitarian typology assigned them. Chosen for the worship of the One God, the Jews were presented by Pope Innocent as the mystical type of him who is from no one, who, in the scholastic term derived from the Gospel, receives no "mission;" the Jews are, in short, a terrestrial figure of God the Father, first Person of the Trinity. The two Persons who are from that One, and who from that One receive their respective "missions" are the Latin and the Greek Christian Churches. The first is a type of the Son, for it is to this people that His vicar, Peter, has been given, whereas the second, which glories in the devotion of her monks, and to whom Saint John was given, is an earthly type of the Spirit, who seeks out and cherishes all who are spiritual.[37] The Pope had a word, too, on the dispute between the theologians of the East and the West on whether the Spirit proceeds not only from the Father but also from the Son, *filioque*. Does the Spirit proceed from the Father? Humbly receptive of doctrine from the Jews, as Innocent put it, careless of how a rabbi would respond to this commendation of Judaism as a source of trinitarian theology, the Greeks were willing to concede that the Son proceeds from the Father. "But, until the present, they disdain to show themselves receptive with respect to the Latins who, in this matter, possess a similitude with God the Son." At the tomb of Jesus, the Synagogue, in the person of Mary Magdalene, stood outside, gazed on the exterior shell which is the letter; in the person of John, the Greeks attained to the interior pith, although, like the Jews, they unfortunately have not yet fully realized that the letter is dead and that the Spirit is also the Spirit of Jesus.[38] Thus did Innocent account, in a way as offensive to the sensibilities of Greek Christians as to those of Jews, for the use of the verb "proceed" in John 15 : 25, with respect to the relation of origin of the Spirit to the Father.

Jewish-Christian Frictions

A measure of the deficiency of Jewish faith, in the eyes of Pope Innocent III, was that the Saracens, persecutors of the Catholic faith and unbelievers in their own fashion, could not tolerate Jews within their territories, but were accustomed to drive them into exile.[39] But it is difficult to give ethical weight to his a fortiori reasoning; the sole comfort a Christian reader can find in the line is the clear evidence that here "disbelief," *perfidia,* juxtaposed with "Catholic faith," *fides catholica,* can only refer to a credal discrepancy between Jews and Christians, and not to an alleged universal treachery on the part of Jews.

Two letters of Innocent III—one of 1204, addressed to the King of the Franks, and the other directed to the Count of Nevers in 1207—taken together constitute a fairly complete budget of the Pope's complaints against the Jews.[40]

The first of these letters opens with a statement of theological background, against which Innocent viewed the situation of the Jews in a Christian nation. By a providential dispensation, he asserted, the Diaspora of Israel, *dispersio Judaeorum,* lives under the sway of Catholic kings and Christian princes in a state of temporary servitude. Their slavery is temporary because a remnant of their number has been predestined for salvation, and there will be a time when Israel will dwell in the security of a mutual trust, *cum habitaverit confidenter* (Ezechiel 38 : 14), a trust that will be a shared faith such as Samuel knew (1 Sam. 12 : 11). Meanwhile, the Jews carry the burden of a corporate disability, consequent upon their corporate responsibility for the crucifixion of the Messiah. The Pauline analogy between the children of Abraham by his bondwoman, and those by Sarah, the Patriarch's lawful wife, served the Pope to account for the disparate inheritances of Jew and Gentile (Galatians 4 : 21–31).

Needless to say, this application to the ordinances of the earthly city of an allegory on the mysteries of predestination is a suspiciously facile justification of medieval social and religious groupings; only an excessively hardy exegesis of Saint Paul's reflections on Abraham's children can pretend to see in those insights directives for the formulation of public law. We cannot help remarking, however, that it is only in our own day that the concept of a corporate and, in fact, universal Jewish responsibility, first for the rejection of Jesus' teaching, and second, for his execution, has been scrutinized with a penetration commensurate to the historical and theological realities at stake.[41] Until the day before yesterday, medieval interpreters of the parables of rejection and of the Passion narratives, still had descendants whose exegesis of those texts had advanced not an inch. Exegetes still saw in the unjust husbandman a figure of the total Jewish community, still saw in the cabal of scribes and Pharisees, of Sadducees and of hereditary priests, the authorized representatives of the whole Hebrew people, those as yet unborn not excluded. Jesus himself had been unwilling to honor the more than suspect credentials of those worthies (Matt. 23 : 1–12), for how does the Gospel present them if not as a conspiracy of clerks, a minority for whom the vast majority of Jews, the "People of the Land," were obnoxious, and irredeemably sinful? Entrenched officials, His enemies were fearful lest all the world follow the Nazarene, only too willing that one man should die, not so much for the nation, as for their place at that nation's head (John 11 : 47–53). The too summary biblical theology of Innocent III on the point could hardly be defended before the Pontifical Biblical Institute today, but how lately was it common doctrine! No less inadequate because so commonly and so uncritically held, Innocent's thesis was long accepted, and that perennial acceptance, like other awkward facts, is a datum that the historian is not free to ignore when he essays the evaluation of the responses it has occasioned.

In the presence of a theological reduction so clumsy, it is no surprise that the Pope was scandalized to hear that Jews were conspicuously successful in finance, and this at the expense of Christians. Jews in France, so the Pope had heard, were accustomed to extort, not only usury, but "usury on usury," a fiscal compounding that led to the alienation of even Church property. If the application of a text of Jeremiah (Lam. 5 : 2) to the loss of ecclesiastical goods goes more than a little beyond the literal sense of the prophet himself, Innocent was on firmer ground in citing the legislation of the Third Lateran Council against the holding of Christian slaves by Jewish masters. The section at issue[42] refers to a provision of law already venerable in the days of Gregory the Great, and it had been renewed by the Council with respect especially to the presence of Christian nurses in Jewish households. But it was Innocent III who asserted that abuses too shameful to specify attended the violation of those ancient laws. The remark on ineffably shameful episodes is not a casual one, for the Pope made the same observation in a letter addressed to the Archbishop of Sens and the Bishop of Paris. According to that text, one abuse not too shameful to recount was that for three days after the paschal communion—a custom the Fourth Lateran Council was to render obligatory—Christian nurses were obliged by their Jewish employers to dispose of their milk in the latrine,[43] a practice that would argue a notion of the eucharistic Presence considerably more extreme than any proposed by the theologians. Other regulations of the Third Lateran Council were recalled, but it is not useful to repeat them here.[44]

A curious detail in this litany of complaints is the protest Innocent made with respect to litigation over interest on loans. More credence was placed in a document that an unwary debtor had deposited with his creditor, and carelessly failed to reclaim on payment, than in the witnesses he might later adduce to establish the fact that he had paid his debt. Can this be anything but an echo of the bewilderment felt by the children of a culture still largely oral, and with a little developed economy, a naïve people dismayed by the relentless efficiency of bankers adept at documentation? Why should those notes, cheaply appraised and incautiously signed by the financially embarrassed, be so esteemed by these sophisticated aliens? As Renaissance savants were destined to discover, the same society produced, with a kind of innocence, forged charters to color traditional claims, and one symptom that the Middle Ages were shading into modern times was to be the novel concern of scholars to prune the excessively luxuriant bibliographies so long ascribed to Aristotle, to Dionysius, to Saint Augustine. Men who forged monastery charters and theological treatises with childlike simplicity could hardly bring themselves to honor indefinitely a written promise to pay against the oath of a Christian man that he had paid but had neglected to procure a receipt.

The Jews at Sens, like those noted by Pope Gregory the Great,[45] had gone so far as to build a synagogue, not only near, but notably more lofty than the venerable local church; far from celebrating their rites in a low tone of voice, a courtesy long customary, the Jewish cantors raised such a clamor that they interfered with services in the adjacent church. Worse, Jews were guilty of blaspheming the Lord's Name, and of insulting Christians as worshipers of "a mere rustic, gibbeted by the Jewish people." True enough, Innocent wrote, Jesus died on a tree, victim of our sins, but neither in His address nor by birth was He a rustic. The Lord—and the Pope believed no Jew could deny it—was of priestly and royal descent; his manners, the aristocratic Innocent affirmed, were outstanding and correct, *mores ejus praeclari fuerunt et honesti.* On Good Friday, contrary to ancient law and custom, the Jews had taken to rioting through the streets and squares, ridiculing Christians for adoring One nailed to a cross, and this in the hope of diverting Christians from their religious obligations. The Jews were accused of leaving their gates unlocked until midnight for the convenience of thieves, and no one, the letter claimed, ever succeeded in recovering stolen property from among them. Jewish abuse of the hospitality extended them by the King's forebearance went so far, a recent report had it, as to include the murder of an impecunious scholar, for his body had been discovered in one of their latrines. Here, it must be noted, the reference is to a rumor of casual homicide, and nothing in

the text permits us to read it as an accusation of ritual murder, preferred against the Jews by the Pope. All these abuses
the Pope ascribed to the presumption of the Jews, and their
repression by means of secular law, he proclaimed, would
redound to the remission of sin and to zeal for God. Remembering that not all religious dissent was Jewish, the prosecu-
tion of heretics too, Innocent concluded, would be a measure
of the King's fervor for the faith.

The second text, a letter to the count of Nevers, begins
with another biblical analogy; like the fugitive Cain, who
bore a sign imposed upon him by the Lord—a tremor of his
head—which served at once to mark his guilt and to protect
him against merely human vengeance, so the Jews, dispersed
over the earth bear an appearance of ignominy which must
must protect them in their wanderings. They are not to be
killed, for their role is to remind Christians of the divine
law; but the princes, far from assisting the Jews to oppress
Christians, ought to enforce their servitude, the just lot of
men who laid violent hands on the Messiah who had come
to bring them liberty.

But certain lay lords, so the Pope had heard, with no
eye for God, were welcoming Jews to their manors and
towns, in order to promote the exaction of usury from the
Church of God, from the poor of Christ, from the widow and
the orphan. With the connivance of these same lay lords,
ruinous usury was enforced with all the apparatus of forfeited security pledges and the debtor's prison. In addition
to the question of usury, there was that of the support of
churches in a feudalized society. Any alienation of Church
property to Jewish owners led to the impoverishment of the
parishes, since thus they lost their accustomed tithes. No
small scandal too, the Pope felt, attended the observance by
Jews of their dietary laws. By the favor of the princes, Jews
slaughtered animals in accordance with their own rite, for
they held cattle butchered by Christians to be ritually unclean. Then the Jews took what they wished and sold the
leavings to Christians, a precedent matched by Jewish wet
nurses, who provided Christian infants with the milk that
Jewish babies did not need. As for wine: shod in linen shoes,
Jews trod out the grapes for their wine, retained what they
wanted for their own use, and the residue went to Christians,
among whom it might come to serve for the Sacrament. **Last,**

no Christian witnesses, not even those of the best reputation, were ever admitted by Jews to testify against them, and this because they were sure they could count on the favor of the powerful to enforce the privilege they claimed.

The Bishop of Auxerre, wrote the Pope, had done his best against these scandals, and had proceeded in the approved canonical fashion. Having taken the advice of prudent men, the Bishop had imposed in solemn synod the penalty of excommunication to reinforce his prohibitions. Many of the faithful showed themselves ready to keep clear of all such abominations, but certain of the nobles and other men of influence, along with their lackeys, had been subverted by Jewish bribery. Using the fear inspired by threats and contumely, these were compelling the continuance of whatever the Jews desired, and, not content with that, were attempting to frustrate ecclesiastical discipline by an appeal to the Holy See itself against the excommunication. Meanwhile, the Jews were delighted by the sentences of excommunication that had fallen on certain of the Christians—now Christian harps were hung on the willows of Babylon (Ps. 136 (137) : 1–2), and Christians were deprived of their priests' assistance. As for the Count himself, an evil report had reached the Pope; one who ought to have used his position as a Catholic man, and Christ's servant, to block "Jewish superstitions" had in fact been a principal offender. To him the Pope addressed a crescendo of precisely graduated phrases: "We beg," "We warn," "We exhort," "We command" the end of all such abuses. Finally, he capped them with a naked threat: "Lest We be forced to set Our hands to their correction."

Sicut Judaeis non

No text manifests more clearly the continuity of the medieval papal attitude toward the Jews than does the Constitution known from the first phrase of the line that also sets its theme as the *Sicut Judaeis non,* and we have already several times adverted to it, an inheritance, as it is, from Pope Gregory the Great.[46] Between the versions from the pontificate of Alexander III and that of Celestine III (1191–1198), the variants in this text are trivial changes in word order, the suppression or addition of unimportant terms, but Innocent III was hardly the man to follow in the footsteps

of other popes without leaving clear evidence that the strong-
est of popes had passed that way. Here, his method has been
to add an introduction and a conclusion to the substance of
the Constitution.[47]

According to Innocent's Introduction, there are many
reasons for taking issue with Jewish disbelief, but, owing to
the paradoxical role of the Jews as unwitting witnesses to the
truth of the Christian faith, they must not be oppressed
gravely by Christians. True enough, the Jews fail to understand the import of their own Books, but it ought not be
forgotten, Innocent wrote, that these same Jews have provided those Scriptures for the Christians, who do understand
them. Then follow the familiar admonitions: No Christian
is to compel an unwilling Jew by force to accept baptism,
but the Jew who freely manifests a desire for baptism is to
be christened "without calumny." Apart from lawful judicial
sentences, no Christian is wickedly to injure their persons or
violently to confiscate their possessions; no one is to change
the good customs they have in any given region. No one is
to disturb their rites with clubs and stones, uncouth weapons
of the street brawler, and no one is to attempt to extract from
Jews service unsanctioned by custom. Their cemeteries, and
the bodies therein, are to be respected.

To these provisions, already of long standing, and to be
reformulated for centuries to come, Pope Innocent added a
concluding qualification which many a succeeding pope
would make his own: This manifold protection is intended
to shield only those Jews who have not been guilty of plotting to subvert the Christian faith.

Crusaders and Interest

Innocent III had claimed no more profound ambition
than to mount a successful Crusade to recover the Holy
Land,[48] and he was as fully committed to that of Simon de
Montfort against the Albigensian heretics of Provence.[49]
Naturally, he did not deprive himself of so simple a way of
making enlistment attractive as the traditional practice of a
moratorium on the payment of charges for the use of borrowed money in favor of Crusaders. Not only the "immoderate" usuries that were to be forbidden by the Fourth
Lateran Council, but all usury whatever levied against men

who were willing to take the Cross was suspended, and this relief was to be guaranteed by the secular arm. Thus a letter announcing both Council and Crusade,[50] and another addressed to King Philip of France.[51] A similar letter to the Archbishop of Tours, and to the Bishops of Paris and Nevers, fails to specify Jews as the moneylenders affected; on the other hand, it does specify that the period of grace for the Crusaders ought to be two years.[52] The "power of the Keys," in virtue of which authority in the Church is held competent to remit bonds contrived by men, seems to have been the theoretical justification for the instructions Innocent addressed to local ordinaries, charging them with forcing creditors to release debtors from their engagements, made under oath, to pay usury, should this be an obstacle to their taking the Cross.

Pope Innocent was not blind to another side of the Jews' relationship with Crusaders; although the text of the apposite letter is not extant, a notation of its content has survived:

Command is given to the Archbishops and Bishops appointed throughout the Kingdom of France that they restrain all Christians, Crusaders especially, lest they molest Jews or their families.[53]

Converts

Papal concern for the welfare of converts from Judaism, already clear in Gregory the Great if not in Gelasius I, is present in Innocent III. A convert could count on apostolic letters to procure his welcome by a local bishop, a welcome that might include food and clothing for his family. Should the bishop be cool to the project, and thus apt to induce the danger of relapse on the part of a poverty-stricken convert, the Pope did not hesitate to threaten canonical penalties against a bishop so little zealous, and to charge neighboring authorities with carrying out his mandate. That one Jew and his family had been converted by a miracle did not dissuade the Pope from providing the new Christian with a letter of recommendation to the Archbishop of Sens for temporal support; miracles do not render normal precautions superfluous.[54]

An incidental point is that, according to Innocent, the marriages of unbelievers were to be respected after their baptism, and that this provision included the marriages of

Jews is evident from the way the Pope cited the Gospel text forbidding man to put asunder what God has joined (Matt. 19 : 6); it was the Lord's response to a question posed by Jews, and "through it He was showing that marriage exists among them." If such converts were already bound by the levirate marriage, sanctioned and, indeed, commanded by the Law of Moses, although not tolerated by the Church, Innocent was willing to favor the interest of their new, and presumably delicate, faith to the extent of permitting them to continue in such unions; no such marriage could be contracted after baptism.[55]

The conviction that the Jews will enter the Church at the end of time led Innocent to an unexpected exegesis of the promise Jesus made to Peter after the miraculous draught of fishes (Mark 1 : 17). When the Lord told Peter that he could expect to catch men in the future, the Pope saw in "fish" a type of Christians. Fish, after all, live in water, and Christians are those who have been reborn of water and the Spirit. Men, on the other hand, live on the earth, and thus signify those who seek and cling to terrestrial things, those multitudes outside the Christian faith. Perhaps not altogether felicitous, still, this typology is intelligible in a letter that was addressed to the bishops, abbots, and other clergy of Constantinople in 1204. In the great work of uniting all men, the reunion of East and West was the first goal the Pope had set. The separated Christians had been reborn truly; the Spirit did move among them; they were not of the earth earthy, and hence precedence must be given them over all others, Jews included. "When all Christians shall have returned to the obedience of the Apostolic See, then will the multitudinous races enter into the Faith, and thus all Israel shall be saved."[56]

Conversion had its repercussions on the institution of slavery. A pastor had the right and the duty, enforced by the sanction of excommunication, to compel slaves converted to Christianity to leave Jewish households, lest Judaism succeed in reducing them "from the grace of liberty to the opprobrium of slavery."[57] It is incontrovertible that here the "slavery" to which such converts might fear reduction is Judaism, and not a civil status.

A letter of 1205, addressed to Alphonsus VIII of Castile, lists violations of such provisions with respect to slaves that the Pope could complain "the Synagogue increased, as the Church decreased; the bondwoman took precedence over the free woman."[58] The King had many failures for which to atone. Capriciously changing his mind, for example, he had taxed the clergy after exempting them; a bishop in his kingdom had complained that he had been forced to pay a Jewish master whatever he claimed a converted slave was worth; the Bishop of Burgos had thus paid two hundred gold solidi for a Saracen girl worth, in the Bishop's judgment, hardly ten. Jews and Saracens were exempt from tithes, and thus were in a better position than were Christians. Not all the King's faults involved philo-Semitism; the same bishop, owing to royal interference, had lost one of the richer churches in his diocese to a Cistercian abbess, and the King had repossessed the church of Saint Julian for which the Bishop's precedessors had paid. Alphonsus himself did not pay the tithes his ancestors were accustomed to pay, and he had given support to an abbot and other clerics who rebelled against this same unfortunate bishop.

Because Spain and Portugal have ever been exceptionally sensitive provinces with respect to Judaeo-Christian-Moslem tensions, it would be a mistake to ignore the small echo of an episode in which a Christian widow, victim of unjust pressure to remarry, was aided first by a Jew, who hid her for three weeks in his house, then by a local church where she stayed in hiding for six weeks, until finally she was obliged to seek the help of the Pope against her enemies.[59] More typical of the tensions is the regulation the Pope felt it right to make with respect to Jewish or Saracen slaves who wished to become Christians: their masters, whether Jewish or Christian, were commanded to put no obstacle in the way of their conversion out of fear of temporal loss.[60]

The "Judgment of the Jews"

No weapon of the Church against a lawless Christian can be more effective than is excommunication in the case of an individual, and interdict in the case of a community; but both are in the order of the spirit and useless, as such, against those who do not share her faith. For the unbaptized—pagan, Jew, or Moslem—these penalties are irrelevant, except by indirection; when applied indirectly, the procedure was called

in the Middle Ages the "judgment of the Jews." In one letter
of Innocent III, a bishop was advised on how he ought to
deal with a Jew who had laid violent hands on a priest, an
offense punishable according to canonical regulation by excommunication. First, the Bishop was to appeal to the feudal
lord who had civil jurisdiction over the culprit in order that
a suitable fine "or other temporal penalty" might be imposed
upon him. Should the lord neglect his duty, then the Bishop
was to proceed to isolate the Jew by forbidding all Christians
to have any dealings with him and to enforce this by the
threat of excommunication against the Christians who might
not comply.[61] Thus, indirectly, the penalty of excommunication would bring a lawless unbeliever to book. It could have
other effects as well. In the Spanish kingdom of Leon, the
excommunication and interdict consequent upon the marriage
of the king and queen within forbidden degrees of kinship
had meant that, since the clergy could no longer provide the
laity with services in the order of the soul, laymen were
declining to provide them with support in the order of the
body. These clerics had fallen, not only to the evangelical
indignity of begging and of digging, but were also forced
"to serve Jews, to the disgrace of the Church, and of all
Christendom."[62] The most imperial of popes could hardly
be expected to tolerate this unintended consequence of
canonical sanctions, and hence his letter to protest it.

VII

THIRTEENTH-CENTURY POPES

Papal concern with the Jews during the thirteenth-century pontificates that followed that of Innocent III is marked not only by a relentless effort to render effective the provisions of the Great Council of 1215–1216, the Fourth Lateran, but also by certain novel elements that appeared as succeeding pontiffs came to grips with new developments.

The Fourth Lateran Council and the Jews

Whether the legislation on the Jews by the Fourth Lateran Council reflects a direct intervention by Pope Innocent III seems to be a question impossible of determination. Since the apposite titles of the conciliar decrees are consistent with Innocent's personal statements, perhaps the question is not worth raising;[1] in any case, among the numerous provisions of the Ecumenical Council of 1215, four are concerned with the status of the Jews in Christendom.

The first of these (title 67[2]) gave expression to the fear that Christian resources would be exhausted shortly, owing to the usury on which the Jews, despite their misbelief, had been permitted to batten. In order to mend the evil, the Synod ordered that in the future "immoderate usuries" should no longer be extorted, and that Christians, under pain of ecclesiastical censure and with no right of appeal, must avoid association with Jews until they should have conformed to the regulations of the Council on the matter. The princes were commanded to do their best to inhibit the Jews, rather than to show themselves hostile to Christians by enforcing collection of those charges. Under the same heading, Jews were ordered to continue the tithes and rents owed to churches on property held formerly by Christians, lest the churches suffer through the transfer of ownership.

To this economic ordinance was added one on clothing (title 68[3]), often spoken of by historians as imposing the "badge," although, taken to the letter, it refers simply to identifiable garb, and perhaps most of all to a total costume, characteristic of the Jews. Whatever the truth as to this detail may be, the purpose of the decree was that Jews (and Saracens) in Christian lands appear at all times in public in distinctive apparel, lest Christians have some excuse to explain their attachments to infidels by claiming ignorance of their religious affiliations. The Council remarked that, for the Jews at least, Moses himself had anticipated its legislation (Lev. 19 : 19), and we have seen that a comparable conception is to be found in the Islamic tradition.[4] The fact that this ruling bound Moslems as well as Jews makes it clear that it was inspired by a positive concern with the care of souls and not by a merely anti-Jewish bias. The Church legislated with equal vigor on the garb and tonsure of clerics; it was on her own men that she imposed shaven pate and sober robes, whereas the costumes of the Levant, characteristic of Moslems and of Jews, were marked by a magnificence that prompted Latins, Frederick II and his court, for instance, to imitation. In this context, protests that the insistence on a distinctive garb was a device to humiliate, or to degrade, the Jews require qualification. Complaints by Jews against wearing even a badge, and the occasional dispensations from this requirement, granted as a mark of favor, leave no doubt that such was the effect of the regulation. But the intention of the Council was the pastoral concern to preclude mixed marriages, unions as unwelcome to the devout Jew as to Christian ecclesiastics. Except for laws against impersonating the police and the military, our day knows no such interventions by public authority on comparable matters, but classic society had its toga for the citizen, breeches for barbarians, distinctive cloaks for philosophers; the Middle Ages were no less attached to the symbolic possibilities of clothing, and there is a long tradition of legislation to the same effect within the Jewish communities of medieval Europe.[5] Jewish sumptuary regulations, for instance, continued on their statute books long after our period ended; among Christians, in Tudor and above all in Puritan England, it was generally held, and enforced at law, that if clothes do not make the man what he is neither ought they make him appear to be what he is not.

Joined to this under the same title (68) is the familiar provision—part accusation, part police regulation—that Jews keep out of public view during Holy Week. Council Fathers had heard that some Jews were accustomed to express their disdain for the sufferings of Jesus by attire more festive than that usually worn, and by making game of the Christians and their sorrow during those solemn days. Neither accusation nor the reaction by the Council was new;[6] secular princes were engaged to enforce the decree.

A third title on the Jews (69) is a restatement of the classical provision of the provincial Council of Toledo, forbidding public office to Jews.[7] This General Council extended the prohibition to pagans as well, together with the instruction that non-Christian officials were to be denied all communication with Christians until they had contributed to the poor whatever profits they might have gained from the exercise of such illegal offices. "Exceedingly absurd" it would be, in the language of the Council, that a "blasphemer of Christ" wield power over His worshipers. With austere logic these juridical formulations were derived from dogmatic positions: the Jew or pagan was considered to be, by that fact and necessarily, a "blasphemer" against the Messiah he declined to acknowledge. In a sacral community, thirsting for the peace that hierarchical order and unity were credited with guaranteeing, there was no thought of separating "Church" and "State." The distinction meaningful then was between laity and clergy, the first often enough given to poaching on sacred grounds, but forming, with the clergy, the structure constituted of two walls that met on the cornerstone that is Christ the Lord. Where in such a sacred congregation, latter-day version of the *qehal* YHWH, could the unbeliever find a place? Since the puzzle, in principle, is insoluble, we must see in ecclesiastical statutes the piecemeal adjustment of the law to facts for which prevailing theological-political theory could give, at best, but a partial account.

Yet another report to the Council had inspired a fourth title on the Jews. Title 70 adverted to the allegation that converts from Judaism to Christianity were relapsing into their former persuasion, at least in the sense that they were retaining certain vestiges of Jewish practice.[8] What these may have been is not specified, and it would be perilous to insist that the expression "remanents of the former rite" necessarily refers to properly religious, as opposed to merely cultural, customs. Whatever the Council may have heard, the Judaism at issue was adjudged incompatible with the purity of Christian commitment. The reference in this text to the liberty with which the convert binds himself to the Church is an invitation to read the title in conjunction with the consistent refusal of responsible authorities in the Church to force baptism on Jews or on their children. Once the choice had been made, however, compulsion to live up to it was considered salutary for the man who had made it, and the duty of Christian power to enforce.

Pope Honorius III

The first pope to follow Innocent III has left confusing traces in that it is possible to ask whether variations in the Jewish policy of Honorius III (1216–1227) ought to be understood as evidence of inconsistency, or as sensitive adjustments to varied circumstances. Our first information is the remark that in 1220 Honorius charged three bishops to enforce in Spain the restrictive Jewish legislation of the Fourth Lateran Council, in particular that requiring a distinct garb to distinguish Jews from Christians; in the same year, in a letter to the universal Church,[9] he is said to have defended the Jews against forced baptism and against interference in the celebration of their feast days. Only one obsessed with categorizing popes into those "favorable" and those "unfavorable" to the Jews would find it difficult to recognize that these interventions are compatible, but within a few years Honorius thought it right to mitigate the instruction he had sent to Spain:

Jews living in the Kingdom of Castile consider what has been established in the General Council concerning their wearing badges so burdensome that some would choose flight to the Moors rather than wear badges of this sort. Elsewhere, on provocation of this kind, they are forming conspiracies and plots. . . . We order you to suspend, for as long as you understand it to be expedient, the execution of the Constitution mentioned above.[10]

Thus too, with respect to a Jewish medical practitioner of Barcelona, Isaac Beneviste, described as "alien to usury, and devoted to Catholics," Honorius showed himself lenient; in 1220 the Pope gave Isaac his patronage, along with a document that justified with considerable candor his proselytizing intention:

The Apostolic See, a kind mother, sometimes in her devoted kindness offers the breasts of charity, with which she nourishes her own children, to others whom she strives to bring to birth in the faith, widening the space within her tent so that, if drawn, perchance, in some way to emulation, they might arrive at the adoption of sons, and that Christ be formed in them, and they be conformed to Him whom they formerly decried.[11]

The Archbishop of Tarragona was commanded to shield Isaac from annoyance; he was also forbidden to compel Jews to wear "unaccustomed" badges.[12] At the same time, the Pope rebuked the King for employing Jewish legates to the Moslem authorities; it was unlikely, the Pope reasoned, that those to whom the Christian faith is abhorrent would keep faith with Christians. Several Spanish bishops received written instructions to urge this consideration on the Kings of Leon, Castile, and Navarre.[13] In 1221, Honorius was imposing more stringent penalties on Jews who failed to wear badges.[14] Finally, Pope Honorius has left one of the rare, but significant, papal texts in favor of tolerance in the practical order among members of diverse religions. The Pope wrote to a Moslem authority:

Since We, to whom Christ has committed His flock and sheepfold, even though unworthy, suffer an uncounted multitude of men of your Law to practice their rites among Christians, in order that in this the condition of Our people and of yours be not disparate, but rather that from this there be an equal, humane solace, it is not right that you be discovered to be difficult, but rather favorable and open.[15]

Pope Gregory IX

Saint Raymond Penafort, under the authority of Pope Gregory IX (1227–1241), made one of the canonical collections that constitute medieval Church law. Two canons of this collection, which bear on the Jews, have their immediate source in the same Pope's letters. One refers to the traditional exclusion of Jews from public offices, and insists that where a property transfer to Jews or pagans might diminish the rights of Christians, some trustworthy Christian ought to oversee the transaction. The other holds that no baptized Jew, nor any prospective convert from Judaism, can remain in slavery; the redemption of such slaves, if they were bought for the market, was fixed at twelve solidi, and three months' possession gave a presumption of law that they had not been bought for that purpose.[16]

A document of Gregory addressed to the hierarchy of Germany in 1232, *Sufficere debuerat,* conveys the atmosphere of perplexity generated among Christians by Jewish resistance to what seemed to those who exercised it notable generosity: "simply for humanity's sake, they received and nourished" Jews, men whom other religious communities would not even allow to live among them. In spite of this, the Jews of Germany were far from conceding the propriety of "perpetual serfdom," allotted to them by their host society. On the contrary, Jews proselytized actively and not without success, broke all the regulations in regard to them that stemmed from the Council of Toledo, and ignored the Jewish legislation of the Fourth Lateran Council. As might be expected of a pope who figures prominently in the history of canon law, Gregory ordered that all canonical regulations for the life of Jews in Christian lands be held in honor, and he added another order: Lest the simple be ensnared by Jewish apologists, Jews were forbidden to engage in theological discussions with Christians.[17]

In the same spirit, Gregory underwrote a campaign against the Talmud and other Jewish books that was to be continued by his successors, and especially by Innocent IV; in Gregory's time, it is recorded, there was an immense burning of Jewish books at Paris.[18]

One of the most frequent subjects of Gregory's concern as it affected the Jews was the problem of the usury owed Jewish moneylenders by Crusaders; although in some texts he is represented as doing nothing more than continuing traditional policy, his responses contain some noteworthy details. His general formula was that local bishops ought to compel Jews to remit their charges on loans to Crusaders, and that

this ought to be pressed home by invoking the "judgment of
the Jews" until they had complied. As for the loan itself,
should a Crusader be unable to pay it off before leaving on
the Expedition, then the incurring of any more usury must
be suspended until his death or his return. Further, the
Jewish moneylender must credit income from any pledge he
retained against the principal owed, but he had the right to
deduct from such income his own necessary expenses in the
affair.[19] In a letter of 1235, the Pope pointed out that Florentine merchants were not bound by laws formulated for the
Jewish bankers, and stated the general principle that their
affairs ought to be settled in such wise that neither the
Crusade nor justice suffered.[20]

Like so many other popes, Gregory IX had occasion to
complain of violations of the laws on the Jews in Spain and
Portugal. His objections range from "immoderate usury," the
holding of public offices, haling clerics into secular courts,
the Jews' bad practice of claiming they could be convicted
only if a Jewish, as well as a Christian, witness testified
against them, failure by Jews to wear badges to losses
suffered by the Church when Jews came into possession of
property on which Christians had paid tithes.[21] That this last
was not an unusual situation is clear from a letter in which
this Pope defended Franciscan friars in several French dioceses against property owners who "strove to extort tithes
from them, even on the houses of the brethren, as on the
houses of Jews."[22] Evidently it was accepted practice that
the mendicant friars, under vows of poverty for the sake of
religious perfection, were exempt from tithes formerly paid
on the houses in which they lived, but it was also accepted
practice that Jewish owners assume the obligation of tithes
when they assumed ownership of Christian property.

Still, in pressing for the rights of the Church wherever
he felt they might have been infringed by Jews, Pope Gregory
was anxious to save values on both sides; in the words of an
annalist, "He wished their crimes to be repressed in such a
way that no crime would be committed in their prosecu-
tion."[23] Above all, when Jews had recourse to him for protection, Gregory showed himself benign, issuing in his turn the
basic papal Constitution on the Jews, *Sicut Judaeis non*,[24]
as well as many documents dealing with particular cases.

For instance, the Pope sent a detailed letter to the hierarchy of France, which reveals in how theological a mode he saw the Jews:

Although the disbelief of the Jews must be reproved, it is, nevertheless, useful and necessary for Christians to have dealings with these same men, for they possess the image of our Saviour, they have been created by the Creator of all, and they must not be destroyed by His own creatures, namely, by those who believe in Christ: It is the Lord who forbids it! Now, to whatever point their median group may be perverse, their fathers were rendered friends of God, and their remnants will be saved.[25]

In the striking conception of the Pope, the Church faces the mysterious middle period of Judaism, flanked by the evident sanctity of their patristic period, and the final period of Judaism, foretold by Scripture, during which their remnants will achieve salvation. What is more to the point, Pope Gregory wished contemporary Judaism to be seen in this context of a holy beginning and a holy end, despite all frictions. He then went on to recount the oppression of the Jews in France; first, the Jews were defrauded by some sharp practice in connection with a four-year moratorium on the payment of debts owed them. When the four years had elapsed, the Jews were arrested and imprisoned until they consented to write off the debts that had come due; worse yet, the most revolting tortures were employed in this sorry business by certain of France's noble lords—nails torn out, teeth extracted. The Jews had appealed to the Pope, and Gregory's thunders concluded with a line that deserves to be remembered: "That brand of kindness ought to be shown the Jews by Christians which we wish shown Christians who live in heathendom."[26]

Nor was this Gregory's only intervention to prevent atrocities against the Jews in France. Fourteen bishops and archbishops, as well as the King, received his vehement protest against "an unheard of, unwonted excess of cruelty" by Crusaders, in which two thousand five hundred Jews had died. Once more it was the Pope to whom the Jews had turned in their extremity.[27]

In Gregory's *Register* there appears a new case of conscience in connection with usury, a problem to be posed often enough to future popes. The King of France had come to realize that revenues derived from Jews might well represent money accumulated through immoral usury; no pious ruler would wish to share in the guilt attached to such ill-gotten gains. The direction consistently given by the popes to assuage this scruple is the time-honored solution of giving to some "pious cause" money that could not be restored to its original and rightful owner since he could no longer be identified. The pious cause recommended by Gregory IX in 1237 was the support of the Eastern Empire, and in three letters of 1238, either the Crusade in the Holy Land or that against the Albigensian heretics, or, once more, Constantinople.[28]

Like all popes, Gregory was zealous to promote conversions to Christianity from Judaism, and he wrote to two Jewish converts, Nivello and Anselm, that their house was under the protection of Saint Peter, not only for their own sake but also for other Jewish converts, or for Jews who might wish to become converts to the Church. Further, they were authorized explicitly to retain after baptism all they had possessed before, despite the illegal feudal practice according to which a local lord might confiscate the possessions of a converted Jew on the occasion of his baptism. Already provided for by the Third Lateran Council, this elementary right of Jewish converts would long require the defense of the papacy.[29]

Pope Innocent IV

Like his immediate predecessor, Gregory IX, Pope Innocent IV (1243–1254) joined a severity against Jews on the plane of theology and canon law to an alacrity in defending their rights as men chosen by God for a unique role in the history of salvation.

No instance of the first is more conspicuous than his renewal in 1244 of Gregory's anti-Talmud legislation, a detail of Christian jurisprudence that recommended itself strongly to the interest of Saint Louis, King of France.[30] Letters of the Pope on this subject went out to the Archbishops of France and England, Castile and Leon, Navarre and Portugal; to the Bishop of Paris, to the Prior of the Dominicans, and to the Minister of the Franciscans in that university city.[31] We shall know we are in another world when we read the com-

plaints that popes were moved to register against the Talmud.
The Jews, Innocent IV asserted, were:

Ungrateful to the Lord Jesus Christ who, His forebearance
overflowing, patiently awaits their conversion; they manifest
no shame for their guilt, nor do they reverence the dignity
of the Christian faith. Omitting or contemning the Mosaic
Law and the prophets, they follow certain traditions of their
elders, the very ones for which the Lord took them to task
in the Gospel, saying: "Why is it that you yourselves violate
the commandment of God with your traditions?" [Matt.
15 : 3]. It is traditions of this stripe—in Hebrew they call
them "Thalamuth," and an immense book it is, exceeding the
text of the Bible in size, and in it are blasphemies against
God and His Christ, and against the blessed Virgin, fables
that are manifestly beyond all explanation, erroneous abuses,
and unheard-of stupidities—yet this is what they teach and
feed their children . . . and render them totally alien to the
teaching of the Law and the prophets, fearing lest the Truth,
which is understood in the same Law and Prophets, bearing
patent testimony to the only-begotten Son of God, who was
to come in flesh, they be converted to the faith, and return
humbly to their Redeemer.[32]

For reasons such as these, the University of Paris had been
enjoined by Gregory IX to examine the Talmud and, since
this estimate seemed accurate enough on examination, to
commit it to the flames, while the men-at-arms of Saint Louis
stood guard to repress the tumultuous Jews. Needless to say,
these remarks on the nature of the Talmud reveal more of
the puzzled Latin censors than of the work they describe.

Like the *Summa* ascribed to Master Alexander of Hales,
the Talmud is arraigned on the strange ground that it is so
big, bigger than a Bible, much as Brother Alexander's work
was decried as more than the load one horse could carry.[33]
The enthusiasm of thirteenth-century Latins for the summary
treatment and the brief discussion, for *summa* and *brevilo-
quium,* may have had many motives to explain them, including the cost of parchment and the scribe's stipend, but it
seems harsh that a canonist, accustomed to draw distinctions
between the substantial and the accidental, should pillory a
work on a quantitative basis. There is more excuse for the
dismay of Latins, schooled in a tradition in which logic had
long held pride of place, when faced with the record of

rabbinical dispute and anecdote, couched in literary modes
alien to minds formed by the seven liberal arts. Even if Latin
censors had come to their task with real sympathy, it would
have been all but impossible for them to evaluate talmudic
tales. When we remember that Jewish converts to Christianity
seem always to have been in the forefront of those who
denounced the Talmud as intolerable in a Christian society,
the task appears totally impossible. In the opposite direction,
a glance at Christian exegesis of Scripture in the Middle
Ages will make clear how arbitrary the "allegorical sense,"
beloved of the theologians, must have appeared to the rabbis,
here accused of wilfully concealing clear proofs of Christianity, and of blinding each generation of Jews with interminable
and unintelligible talmudic lore. Jew and Christian alike
claimed his religious position was in continuity with the Law
and the Prophets, but it was psychologically impossible for
either one to understand the other.

Yet another episode in which Saint Louis the King and
Pope Innocent IV were associated in severity against Jews
was the King's edict of 1253, which exiled all Jews except
those who exercised "mechanical arts."[34] A letter from the
Pope to the Archbishop of Vienne added papal sanction to
the expulsion of Jews from Provence, a sanction that sprang,
so the letter assured the Archbishop, from the Pope's total
dedication to the salvation of souls; scandal given by Jews
and their disregard of prior edicts of the Holy See, the letter
asserted, counted as justification for expulsion.[35] An instance
of what the Pope may have considered such disregard merited
a letter from Innocent to a bishop in 1248, in which he complained that Jews who wore full, round capes were confused
with clerics, and received the marks of honor due the latter;
he ordered that Jews wear what would distinguish them
from both the clergy and the Christian laity.[36] It goes without
saying that Innocent maintained the standard regulations on
nurses and servants, on Crusaders, debts, and usury. To the
last, he added the refinement that Crusaders ought not to be
dragged before extraordinary judges, not even before dele-
gates of the Holy See, provided they were willing to state
their cases before their ordinaries and diocesans.[37] At least
twice, this Pope's concern to guarantee the financial support
of converts from Judaism has left traces in his *Register*: In

July, 1250, on behalf of a woman named Mary, from the diocese of Reims, and in November of the same year for a cleric named John, recommended by the Pope to the Prior of Saint Nicholas at Nevers.[38]

Against this background of interventions unwelcome to convinced Jews, the significance of Pope Innocent's three major documents in their defense against the horrifying accusation of ritual murder is only the more striking. Despite its intrinsic implausibility, and despite its affinity to one of the calumnies leveled against Christians by pagan Roman persecutors, the claim that Jewish ritual demands human sacrifice, and that, in order to provide victims, Jews kidnapped and slaughtered Christian children, has a history that extends at least to the last years of the nineteenth century. From the beginning, popes have raised their voices in protest against this fatuous libel, and the climax of their efforts, outside our period, is the celebrated report made by Lorenzo Cardinal Ganganelli, who was later elected to the papacy and assumed the name Clement XIV (1769–1774). His superbly documented and argued investigation is the definitive study and refutation of the calumny;[39] Innocent IV provided important texts for Cardinal Ganganelli's dossier. On the twenty-eighth of May, 1247, he directed two letters to the Archbishop of Vienne. One, *Si diligenter attenderet*,[40] was directed precisely against the accusation of ritual murder; the other, *Divina justitia nequaquam*,[41] speaks of the charge of kidnapping. But Innocent's most important contribution to the long list of papal texts in defense of the Jews in this matter is one addressed to the Archbishops and Bishops of Germany and France, the *Lacrymabilem Judaeorum Alemanniae*:

To the Archbishops and Bishops
appointed throughout Germany:

We have received from the Jews of Germany a tearful complaint: Certain princes, ecclesiastics as well as laymen, and other nobles and lords of cities and dioceses, in order unjustly to seize and to usurp their goods, are plotting wicked schemes against them, and contriving varied and diverse pretexts. Far from giving prudent consideration to the fact that it is, as it were, from their archives that the evidences of the Christian faith proceed, and that, among other commands of the Law, Sacred Scripture proclaims: "Thou shalt not kill" [Exod. 20 : 13; Deut. 5 : 17], and imposes this prohibition upon them, that during the solemnity of the Pasch they must have no contact with anything dead [Num. 5 : 2; 9 : 6; 19 : 11–16; cf. Agg. 2 : 13], believing that the Law itself commands what is clearly contrary to the Law, they charge falsely that these same men hold a communion rite in that very solemnity with the heart of a murdered child, and, should the cadaver of a dead man happen to be found anywhere, they maliciously lay it to their charge. Raging against them by means of this, and by many another fraud, in opposition to the special laws, *privilegia*, granted them with clemency by the Apostolic See, in opposition to God, and to justice, they despoil them of all their goods, even though they have never been indicted, never have confessed, never have been convicted! Furthermore, they oppress them by depriving them of food, with imprisonment, and indeed, with so many troubles, with burdens so great, afflicting them with penalties of diverse sorts, and condemning very many of them to the most shameful kind of death, that these same Jews, living under the dominion of the aforesaid princes, nobles, and lords, in a state that is all but worse than that of their fathers under Pharaoh in Egypt, are forced to go miserably into exile from places inhabited by them and by their forebears from time beyond memory.

Hence it is that, fearing their extermination, they have had recourse to the discretion of the Apostolic See. Unwilling, therefore, that the aforesaid Jews be harassed unjustly, since the merciful Lord awaits their conversion, and since our faith holds, on the Prophet's testimony [Isa. 4 : 2–3; Jer. 23 : 5–6], that remnants of them are destined for salvation, We command that you prove yourselves so favorable and so benign in their regard that whatever of the aforesaid you discover to have been undertaken rashly against those same Jews by the aforesaid prelates, nobles, and lords, be restored to due order in accord with the laws, and that you shall no longer permit that they be harassed undeservedly in these or in comparable ways by anyone whomsoever, inhibiting by ecclesiastical censure, the right of appeal denied, those who thus harass them.

Given at Lyon, the third day before the Nones of July, in the fifth year [of Our pontificate, 1247].

In the same sense to the Archbishops and Bishops appointed throughout the Kingdom of France.[42]

Pope Alexander IV

No problem concerning the Jews seems to have troubled Pope Alexander IV except that of the support of Jewish converts in the area of Paris. These besought the intervention of the Holy See because local authorities were reluctant to provide them with the necessities of life.[43] Although there is, to my knowledge, no indication that this pope so much as heard of the incident, it was during his pontificate, in the year 1255, that Christian annalists, both Catholic and Protestant, record the death of Hugh of Lincoln, an eight-year-old Christian boy whose death was to become the most celebrated, although not the first, instance of the ritual-murder accusation.[44] Repercussions would be felt in folklore, as witness its presence in a popular ballad[45] and in the tale told by Chaucer's Prioress.[46]

Pope Urban IV

References to the Jews are rare in the records of the pontificate of Urban IV (1261–1264), as well, but there are a few. Writing to Cistercians who had complaints to register against local bishops, Urban IV restated the monks' problem:

They in some way excommunicate you when they do not allow the faithful to communicate with you; from this arises the incongruity that, inasmuch as this is concerned, you seem to be "judged by the judgment of Jews."[47]

Asked to rule in a case of conscience with respect to money derived ultimately from usury charged by Jews—the same type that had been brought to Gregory IX—Urban's answer was similar: that money such as this can be donated with a good conscience to pious causes—in the case under discussion, one hundred pounds to a Cistercian abbot.[48] As for usury owed by Crusaders, the provisions of the Fourth Lateran Council seemed adequate to Urban, but he made it explicit that not only Jews but also Christians, and indeed clerics, were to be compelled to comply with that legislation. In a general letter on the Crusade, issued in 1263, he ordered that Jews be forced by the secular power to remit usurious charges, and he applied the "judgment of the Jews":

Until they remit these, communion with all the faithful of Christ is to be denied them, under sentence of excommunication.[49]

A last mention of Jews occurred in a command Urban sent to the Patriarch of Jerusalem; the Patriarch was to provide support for prospective converts from Judaism and from Islam on the days when they might assist at religious instructions.[50]

Pope Clement IV

This pope too (1265–1268), thought it right to maintain the usual policy on the financial arrangements of Crusaders, to the disadvantage of the Jews from whom they had borrowed money,[51] and more than once Clement IV intervened to bar Saracens and Jews from public office.[52] But Clement's place in the history of papal-Jewish relations is not confined within the limits of these familiar tensions. In listing his complaints on abuses current in Portugal, Pope Clement made reference to magnates who had married unsuitable wives, and among these he counted women "who traced their origin from Saracens or Jews."[53] For James I, King of Aragon, he had severe words: The King was not to divorce the wife who he claimed was infected with leprosy,[54] nor was he to maintain a substitute in concubinage,[55] he ought not to allow Saracens to remain within his frontiers at all, and he was to "repress Jewish mischief," especially as manifested by the Jew who first had carried on a religious "disputation with Brother Paul of the Order of Preachers in the King's presence, and then composed a book full of flagrant lies" about it.[56] Here the Pope alluded to the famous Disputation of Barcelona, in which Rabbi Moses Ben Naḥman (Bonastruc da Porta) faced the Dominican convert from Judaism Pablo Cristia. Brother Pablo had undertaken to show the messianic mission of Jesus from Jewish sources, and the distinguished Rabbi from Gerona had been constrained by the King himself to present the Jewish point of view. Both sides published versions of the debate, and that of Rabbi Moses, despite the safe-conduct he had been granted, led to his trial and sentence to a fine and exile.[57] It is probable that the vigor of the Pope's most important contribution to the corpus of papal documentation on the Jews, his *Turbato corde*, owes something to the impression made on him, if not by the simple fact that the disputation had taken place, then by the publication of the Rabbi's report, asserting that the Christian apologist had failed to fulfill his promise to give a Jewish demonstration that Judaism had become obsolete.

In any case, with the bull *Turbato corde* the Inquisition was given jurisdiction over Jews who induced Christians to adopt Judaism; new as a legal instrument, this text is but an official expression of a papal viewpoint with a long history.[58] Like other documents of its type, *Turbato corde* was to be renewed by succeeding popes as they judged it necessary, and it is important, both as a revelation of papal policy and as evidence of Jewish proselytizing, since it would be unintelligible apart from the Jewish successes to which the opening paragraph refers:

With Our heart in turmoil We have heard, and We now recount, that exceedingly numerous reprobate Christians, denying the truth of the Catholic faith, have gone over, in a way worthy of damnation, to the rite of the Jews. This is realized to be the more reprobate in that thus the most holy Name of Christ is the more heedlessly blasphemed by a kind of enmity within the family!

Since, however, it is right to block this plague that makes for damnation, and which, as We hear, is growing outrageously with, of course, the subversion of the aforesaid faith, and that this be done with remedies both suitable and prompt, through these Apostolic documents, We command your organization, *universitas*, that, to the limit of the terms designated for you by the authority of the Apostolic See with respect to holding inquiry against heretics, concerning the aforesaid, whether done by Christians, or even by Jews, having diligently and faithfully sought out the truth of the matter, you are to proceed against Christians whom you shall have discovered to have committed such things in the same way as against heretics; Jews, however, whom you shall have discovered inducing Christians of either sex into their execrable rite, before this, or in the future, these you are to punish with due penalty, curbing by ecclesiastical censure those who contradict this, appeal being denied, and the help of the secular arm, if need be, invoked for this purpose.

Given at Viterbo, the seventh day before the Kalends of August, in the third year of Our pontificate.[59]

Instructions to the Inquisitor in Portugal make mention of the "judgment of the Jews" as a device against those who obstruct the work of the tribunal, and three articles in a long list referred to abuses that involved Jews. As usual, office-holding by Jews was deplored, but both Saracens and Jews were arraigned for less banal offenses: they had dragged from churches those who had sought sanctuary there, and had not feared to harass the clergy.[60]

In July, 1267, Pope Clement IV requested that James of Aragon collect all copies of the Talmud, with its additions and commentaries, as well as all other Jewish books, and that these be submitted for examination to the Archbishop of Tarragona.[61] More explicit instructions under the same date to the Archbishop himself specify that copies of the Bible, or of any other works in which there is no question of "error or blasphemy," were to be returned to the Jews, whereas the rest were to be deposited under seal in a safe place.[62]

Pope Nicholas III

Papal protection of the Jews against the accusation of ritual murder was continued by Pope Gregory X (1272–1276) in a suitably adjusted version of *Sicut Judaeis non*,[63] but Nicholas III (1277–1280) provided a new item for the papal dossier on the Jews. This is one that stirred their resentment; called *Vinea Soreth velut*, it prescribed "sermons and other means for the conversion of the Jews" as part of the apostolate of the two great mendicant orders, the Franciscans and the Dominicans. The Pope's *Register* records that copies were sent on the fourth of August, 1278, to the Minister of the Franciscans in the Austrian Province, and to the Provincial Prior of the Dominicans in Lombardy; in December of the same year, this instruction was directed to the Franciscan Minister in Sicily.[64] According to this document, converted Jews ought to be treated with the utmost courtesy, but those who might resist the proclamation of the Gospel were to be reported to the Apostolic See:

Concerning these, if any such you find, do not fail to report to Us in what places, and under whose dominion, they dwell, in order that We might take thought with respect to those stubborn in this fashion concerning their salutary cure, as

We shall deem it expedient. As satisfaction may be given to Our ardent plans, however, in accord with Our desires, be careful to intimate to Us frequently how the business confided to you is prospering.[65]

Although no pope of any period has thought it permissible to force a Jew to accept baptism, medieval popes did not include in their conception of force the most extreme moral and psychological pressures, nor did they exclude the use of naked force to compel the attendance of Jews at sermons designed to convert them, in fulfillment of the provisions of *Vinea Soreth sicut.* It must be concluded that, for medieval men, such sermons did not count as assaults on freedom, and one standard commentator on papal and canon laws has put it this way:

To compel belief, and to compel the hearing of the Word of God, are totally different . . . the second is persuasion, rather than constraint.

But the same commentator made a wry report on the effectiveness of this device:

We everywhere see Hebrews obstinate in their disbelief, even though they have many times been present at preaching.[66]

Nicholas too, in his turn, complained that Jews held civil offices in the Kingdom of Castile, and was persuaded that many ills came to pass in consequence of this violation of traditional policy.[67] The most exceptional episode in the record of his dealing with Jews, however, was the initiative of a rabbi whose zeal for Judaism prompted him to attempt the conversion of the Pope. Abraham Abulafia of Saragossa, a man of mystical and ascetic inclinations who had studied Kabbala, philosophy, and Talmud, had earlier devoted himself to an equally improbable venture: he had searched for the ten lost tribes on the banks of a river with only mythical indications to recommend it as their location. Fortunately for himself, as the event proved, he arrived in Rome on his mission during the last days of the Pope's life, for he was promptly apprehended, and as promptly condemned to death. But since the Pope died first, Rabbi Abraham was released to vary the tedium of chronicle with yet another imaginative project: he announced that redemption would come in the year 1290, that he was himself Messiah, and organized his followers for a journey to the Holy Land.[68]

Pope Martin IV

A series of articles specifying reforms for Portugal was issued by Pope Martin IV (1281–1285) in 1284, and it is noteworthy for some new complaints against Jews, Saracens, and Christians alike. All three communities had produced men to violate the right of sanctuary; the old feudal practice of confiscating the goods of converted Jews and Saracens, long since condemned, was still practiced; and when property passed from the hands of Christians into those of Jews or Saracens, the Church lost her tithes. Both complaints on property, if the allegation of the King of Portugal in his reply can be believed, lacked foundation.[69] The same pope wrote in behalf of the Inquisition to the Archbishops and Bishops of France to deny the right of sanctuary to heretics and to lapsed Jewish converts—both those who were simply guilty and those who were the objects of notable suspicion, in the case of heretics as such, whereas in the case of convert Jews, both those who had lapsed openly and those on whom there were plausible indications.[70] According to this jurisprudence, grave preliminary suspicion was highly prejudicial, for we have seen this Pope's predecessor, Clement IV, defend the right of sanctuary against alleged violations by Saracens and Jews.[71]

Pope Honorius IV

The name of Honorius IV (1285–1287) is associated with an important letter addressed by him to the Primate of England and to his suffragans in 1286, thus anticipating in time, as in its complaints, the expulsion of the Jews from England a few years later, which was to perdure beyond the end of the Middle Ages until the time of Cromwell. *Nimis in partibus Anglicanis*,[72] the text at issue, asserted that the Jews of England, studious readers of Talmud rather than of Moses, were attempting to seduce Catholics to Judaism and Jewish converts to relapse. In order to effect this, the text further charged, the Jews of England lived with, and corrupted, Christians; they induced converted Jews to live in localities where they were not known and where, therefore, it would be safe to return to their former allegiance (roundly qualified by the Pope as *perfidia*). Among the techniques they used was that of inviting Christians to their synagogues where Torah would be venerated by all present, including the Christian guests; another was to keep their Christian servants busy with servile labor on days of precept, thus preparing the way for failures against the faith on the part of Christian women by first inducing them to moral failure; in general, English Jews used social contacts to prepare apostasy. Finally, the Jews daily cursed Christians in their "supplications, or more precisely, imprecations." The English hierarchy, so the Pope berated them, had often been instructed to remedy the situation, but their negligence required the present letter; it ended with the command that they report on what steps they were taking to remove such abuses.

Not content to react against Jewish initiatives, Honorius continued a positive policy of Innocent IV, Alexander IV, Clement IV, and Gregory X in using the resources of Paris, premier university of Christendom, to provide for the training of clergy from the East—Arabs and others—who might be expected to return to their own nations and there proclaim the Gospel; thus Parisian theology might speak in the tongues of the East.[73]

Pope Nicholas IV

In August of 1288, Nicholas IV (1288–1292) wrote to the Emperor Rudolph on behalf of the Jew Mehir de Ruthenburth, who had been imprisoned by royal mandate without reasonable cause, so the Pope claimed, demanding that he be set at liberty.[74] The next year, he repeated the articles for reform that had been directed to Portugal by Clement IV, one of which specified violations of the laws respecting Jews; they held offices, wore no badges, and paid no tithes.[75] In 1290, Nicholas wrote to the Franciscan Inquisitors, ordering them to take steps against both Jews and Christians in several jurisdictions in connection with Judaizing practices. Christians who suffered illness, or other misfortunes, had taken to visiting synagogues, where, with lighted lamps and candles, they made donations, and venerated Torah scrolls to the point of idolatry.[76]

On the other hand, Nicholas IV forbade the molesting of Jews resident in Rome.[77] Like more than one predecessor, he was consulted on the disposition of money received from Jews who had amassed it through usury charged borrowers who could no longer be identified; Queen Margaret of France suffered the scruple this time, and she received the standard solution: the money could be used with good conscience to support the current Crusade.[78]

Pope Boniface VIII

From 1295 until 1302, Pope Boniface VIII (1295–1303) issued no less than eight letters to inhibit a fault on the part of Christians that has frequently been imputed to the Jews. This was the provision of supplies, weapons included, to the Saracens, an action counted as treachery of the most dangerous sort in a Christendom at that time engaged for two hundred years in the semipermanent state of war against Islam that constituted the Crusade.[79] It is also noteworthy that a letter of his to insist on legislation against usury, addressed to eight ordinaries in 1296, makes no mention of the Jews.[80] But, in addition to a letter on the legal status of Jews in County Venaissin,[81] lately acquired by the Holy See, there is a text on usurers there that specifies that many offenders were Christian foreigners and many were Jews. The rector of the county was instructed to expel all manifest usurers and to admit no others.[82]

The most important text of Boniface VIII on the Jews, however, is one of 1299 in response to a petition addressed to him by the Jewish community in Rome. Their plea was against a procedure of the Inquisition, for that tribunal protected its sources of damaging information by withholding the names of witnesses from the accused. Despite an instruction of the Pope that where there was no danger owing to the "power" of the accused, the names of accusers and of other witnesses ought to be made available to the defendant, Inquisitors continued to refuse the names of their accusers to Jews, presumably because Jews were considered to be men of power, and this, the letter of Boniface suggests, because of their wealth. Not so, held the Pope:

We, however, considering your weakness, and hence, even though you may abound in wealth, ascribing you to the number of those who are bereft of power, desire that the aforesaid Inquisitors, in the cases in which, thanks to this same authority, they may be able to press an inquiry in your regard, should make the aforesaid publication to you as to men who are without power. Nor ought they to pretend that they have the right to deny this, unless it be that the power of the man against whom inquiry is made be notorious.[83]

On this note—juridical, to be sure, but humane for all that—the record of papal concern with the Jews in the thirteenth century may be concluded. The capacity of those Popes to express in legal forms their zeal for the spread and defense of the Church could be tempered only by their consciences, and the very considerable amplitude of their power to put theory into practice. It is not without significance that Boniface VIII, the most imperial of popes, in the name of a justice that acknowledged the genuine weakness that underlay the apparent power of wealthy Jews, curbed the authority of the Inquisition itself in the very city of the Popes.

VIII

THE LAST TWO HUNDRED YEARS

From the days of Pope Boniface VIII until the end of the Middle Ages, papal legislation and correspondence concerning the Jews is repetitious; despite the high tragedy of the events that required the attention and the intervention of the popes in those years, no specifically new element appeared to modify Jewish-papal relations.

Pope Clement V

The Grand Master of the Knights of the Hospital of Saint John sent a detailed and extensive *aide-mémoire* on the subject of the Crusade to Pope Clement V (1305–1314), probably in 1305. Needless to say, the Jews received their meed of the Grand Master's reflections. He thought it particularly reasonable that the capture of Jerusalem be furthered by those who had rendered the city holy by there crucifying the Virgin's son, and that, consequently,

It would be good if the Lord Pope should arrange a certain tally and tax on all Jews living in Christian lands, up to a tenth of all their goods at least, although we believe it would not be excessive if one half of all their goods were seized.[1]

Whether the Pope accepted this renewal of the old suggestion of Peter the Venerable or not, in 1308 he was renewing the conventional provisions for excusing Crusaders from the usury they might owe to Jews.[2] In 1306 there was an expulsion of the Jews from France, together with the confiscation of all their goods, except what might be considered necessary for their going forth[3]; in the same year and, no doubt, as a result of this, the Pope received an inquiry from a feudal lord, who had unjustly acquired goods and money from Jews in his territory, as to how he might make suitable restitution. The Pope directed restitution to the poor.[4] In the year 1306, too, he gave Queen Marie of France clearance for restitution to the Crusade of funds exacted from Jews,[5] and in 1312 he decided that she might retain half the ten thousand pounds of Tours that she had confiscated from Jews in connection with their expulsion from the country.[6] In the Council of Vienne, two resolutions entered the canonical collection that has come down under Pope Clement's name. For one, kings and princes were besought not to grant Jews and Saracens the privilege of immunity to conviction in court cases through the testimony of Christians, a conciliar rule sanctioned by excommunication for the Christians involved and by the "judgment of the Jews" for infidels.[7] The other decision of the Council was to provide for the study of oriental languages, for the sake of the missions, at the peripatetic Roman Curia, and at the universities of Paris, Oxford, Bologna, and Salamanca.[8] Like many another pope, Clement V mitigated the harshness of the Inquisition—this to the distress of the Inquisitor Bernard Gui,[9] who was particularly zealous against Jews[10] and their books.[11]

Pope John XXII

Although he is reputed to have been seventy-two years of age when he was elected to the papacy in 1316,[12] John XXII was to rule the Church until 1334, and his longevity is by no means the only noteworthy trait of his reign. Entrusted as they are with a role more noble than that of theological technician, most popes have been content to leave the refinements of theology to professional theologians. Despite the fact that he had never taken a degree in theology,[13] John XXII was willing to deal with the controverted questions of the conception of Mary,[14] the poverty of Jesus and its implications for religious with a vow of poverty, and he has even burdened the history of dogma with some infelicitous speculation of his own on the state of the just before the Last Judgment. Still, he had the grace to withhold his papal authority from these personal pronouncements on the end of man; left to the judgment of the Church by a blanket submission on the very day before he died, the Pope's theses were promptly disavowed.[15] Last, it was John XXII who canonized the eminently orthodox Brother Thomas Aquinas.

This energetic old man, who was to remain active through so long a pontificate,[16] was to have much to contend with, and the Jews were not to be absent from his concerns.[17] In March, 1317, a plot against his life was uncovered. Investigation revealed that a Jew had made waxen images for the black magic with which the conspirators supplemented their poison.[18] Even though it is known that the Pope had no excessive fear of magic, and was not inclined to ward it off with equally superstitious devices,[19] the episode and the presence among the plotters of a Jew can hardly have failed to impress him.

In a more positive way, Pope John showed his interest in the foundation of chairs for the Hebrew, Arabic, and Chaldaean languages at the University of Paris by questioning the bishop there, and, in a letter of 1319, he undertook to provide for the support of a converted Jew, John Salvati, who was to translate Hebrew books and to teach either Hebrew or Chaldaean at Paris.[20]

The Rising of the Pastorelli

Most popes from the twelfth to the sixteenth century were tireless in urging Catholic sovereigns to Crusades against the common peril from Islam, and most kings, more sensitive to their own provincial concerns than to those of Christendom as a whole, resisted answering the papal summonses. John XXII, however, dissuaded Philip of France from attacking the Saracens; against the power of the Sultans, John argued, no single Christian prince could oppose adequate strength; until peace among the princes should permit a united effort, the Crusade must be postponed.[21]

Despite the Pope's success in preventing an inopportune official Crusade, chronicles for the year 1320 record a "shepherd's crusade," one of those obscurely inspired and disastrously mismanaged popular risings of swineherds and shepherds termed, in the Latin of the day, *pastorelli*.[22] This adventure was under the most suspect leadership: an unfrocked parish priest and a fugitive Benedictine monk[23]; we cannot help noting the familiar conjunction of personal religious tensions with a demonic burst of energy in rousing intemperate mass passions. Among the most tragic consequences of this pseudo crusade was the savagery it unleashed against the Jews. First mentioned as raging in the vicinity of Paris,[24] the movement seems to have attracted in its early stages the favor of many a priest and religious, as well as that of the King.[25] Daily swollen by new recruits, including some from as far as England,[26] the undisciplined mob proceeded across Aquitaine, pillaging as it went. There, if we can trust the judgment of one chronicler,

In order to gain favor with the populace, and in order that their own zeal might be apparent in some degree, they spread the word that they would kill all Jews who refused to be baptized by them, wherever these might be found, without the intervention of any other judge.[27]

As the *pastorelli* approached Carcassonne, there is confirmation of the view that the anti-Jewish prejudices of the population did play a role in the disasters about to ensue. The civil authorities tried to rally the countryside for the defense of the threatened Jews on the legal ground that, as serfs of the crown, Jews merited all the protection the king's subjects could provide, but "many rejoiced in the destruction of the Jews, and stated that they themselves ought not to oppose those who had the faith for the defense of those without faith."[28] However this may be, there can be no doubt as to the looting and massacre that marked the progress of the mob toward the French Mediterranean ports.

Seeking out, through cities and towns and villages, those Jews who refused baptism the mob slaughtered them without any legal process and, seizing their goods, used these for their own purposes. Great was the massacre of the Jews in the Kingdom of France, especially in the Province of Bordeaux, and in the regions of Saint Bazas, the Province of Toulouse, in the dioceses of Cahors and Albi. . . . Had not Providence and the power of the magnates opposed them, they would have advanced upon the Roman Curia at Avignon.[29]

At some unspecified point in their progress through Aquitaine, on the road to Carcassonne, the *pastorelli* provoked one of those suicidal resistances that recur in accounts of Jewish disasters, one more medieval counterpart to the unsavory incident in which Flavius Josephus saved his own life, and to the doomed gallantry of the garrison of Masaba. Given permission to take refuge in a fortification, five hundred Jews defended themselves until their supply of missiles, stones, and balks of timber, was exhausted. Then the Jews threw down their own children, chose one of their number to cut the throats of his companions, lest any fall alive into the hands of their tormentors. This unfortunate slit the throats of all but a few children, and with them surrendered to the *pastorelli,* from whom he requested baptism. He was torn apart by the savage "crusaders," and the children were baptized forcibly.[30]

Clerics and churches suffered from the depredations of the *pastorelli,* and, as they neared Avignon, the Pope's chamberlain ordered the religious to preach against them and all who might offer them aid.[31] Pope John intervened in person, and commanded Christian princes and nobles to defend the Jews against their savagery. On Ascension Day, the Pope put under censure any who did not leave the movement by a date he fixed, and he advised the Archbishop of Toulouse to call in representatives of the people from every village in his diocese to plan resistance. Last, he circularized the secular magistrates, accusing the *pastorelli* of stupidity and wickedness, including their cruelty toward the Jews.[32]

With a suddenness that impressed the annalists, this uncouth and incoherent tumult vanished; the marauders were dispersed, and so disappeared from history.[33]

Jews, Lepers, and Poisoned Wells

In the very next year, 1321, an aspect of the suffering in store for the Jews at the time of the Black Death was anticipated. The rumor arose in Aquitaine that lepers had poisoned the wells in order that all Christians might die or suffer infection with leprosy; when this word reached the King, all the lepers in the province are said to have gone to the stake. To compound the horror, the feudal lord of Parthenay sent to the King a confession by a leper who implicated a rich Jew as instigator of the alleged crime.[34] In many regions, according to one chronicler, Jews were then burned indiscriminately, whereas in Paris only the "guilty" suffered,[35] a distinction that presumably means judicial forms,

including the question under torture, were observed at Paris.
Another account assigned the initiative in the alleged well-
poisoning to the Saracens, held to have persuaded lepers and
Jews to carry out the plot in order to scatter the Crusaders,
who were gathering in the ports for an expedition under
Philip of France.[36] The Jews who escaped went into perpetual exile, but this fate was delayed for a few rich ones
who were charged with collecting funds to pay the debts of
all the rest, and thus 150,000 pounds accrued to the royal
treasury.[37] No indications seem to have survived concerning
the Pope's attitude toward this upheaval; although there is
no evidence that he protected the Jews against so improbable
an accusation, neither is there evidence that Pope John gave
the calumny any credence.[38]

Confiscation of Synagogues and Conversion

Pope John XXII, in his turn, ordered the observance of
the old rule established by the Third Lateran Council against
the expropriation of a convert's goods on the occasion of his
baptism:

Since to deprive Jews of the goods they formerly possessed,
and to expose them to beggary because, under the Lord's
inspiration, they have been converted to the Christian faith
(for they were wealthy men while they persisted in Jewish
disbelief) is absurd, contrary to law, and opposed to reason,
We are giving a strict command and order. Each and every
official of County Venaissin (acknowledged to belong of
full right to the Holy See), and those of all other Counties
and territories of that same See . . . must know that they
are not to distress or hamper them in this way, nor permit
those converts to be molested by anyone else, but rather
they are to favor them, protect them, and defend them from
injustice and violence.[39]

The Pope sent special preachers to the Jews in the papal
cities of southern France in the hope of mass conversions.
Because the Jews of Novarum and Carpentras refused baptism despite this, they were exiled and their synagogues were
razed. Chapels were built in their stead and dedicated to the
Virgin. At Bédarrides too, a chapel that housed three altars,
one to the Virgin, one to John the Baptist, and the third to
all holy virgins, replaced the old synagogue.[40] No text proves

that the Pope's sister, "Sancha" or "Sanguisa," denounced these congregations to her brother, and thus provoked their suppression. On the other hand, the evidence is incontrovertible that it was the Pope himself who supplied the funds for the churches that replaced the synagogues, and for the endowment of incomes for their pastors.[41]

Talmud Suppression

If John XXII was interested in fostering the study of Semitic languages by Christians for the sake of converting Jews to Christianity, he was also concerned to suppress the Talmud, long counted a Jewish offense against the Christian faith. He seems not to have initiated, but to have reinforced, the systematic campaign of the Inquisition against Jewish books, for this appeared first in a communication from Bernard Gui, the Inquisitor, to a subordinate official in 1309.[42] In August, 1320, the Pope ordered two Franciscans to examine Jewish books, and a five-week period of such examination at Avignon ended on October 2, 1320. On the fourth of September, 1320, the Pope renewed the anti-Talmud legislation of Eudes de Chateauroux, of Clement IV, and of Honorius IV; on the same day he wrote to the Archbishop of Toulouse and his suffragans to the same effect. On October 9, the same instructions were sent to the Bishop of Paris.[43] An undated order on the affair, addressed by the Pope to the Inquisition, survives in the *Practica Inquisitionis* of Bernard Gui.[44] As one chronicler put it, were not the sufferings of the Jews under the scourge of the *pastorelli* evidence of divine justice, exercised against the blasphemies of the Talmud and the fables it contains, designed as they are to mislead the simple? So it appeared to the source that has provided us with some of the most important documents on the affair.[45] Prohibitions already old in the days of Pope John XXII, to be sure, but, as the same chronicler remarked, "owing to Jewish mischief, the Talmudic impiety would spring up anew."[46]

The Black Death and Pope Clement VI

Without intending to imply that any other generation might have endured the terrors of the plague years with more equanimity than did the generation upon which they fell, we cannot fail to mention that those who experienced the Black Death were stupefied by the magnitude of the disaster. Unequipped with a medical science that would permit them to understand, and so cope with, the causes and transmission of the disease,[47] terrified by the suddenness with which it killed, the population responded in a fashion desperate and irrational. Vast numbers of pagans, for instance, like all others, fell victims to the infection and, ascribing the scourge to the ineffectiveness of their ancient religious cults, presented themselves for baptism. Discovering that as Christians they were no less vulnerable than they had been as pagans, they promptly relapsed into their accustomed ways.[48] Deplorable though their retrogression may be, its logic is unassailable; experience taught them that religion is not an insurance policy against disease. Indeed, the Pope of those days, Clement VI (1342–1352) used the same reasoning in his attempt to exonerate the Jews from responsibility for the plague. A disease that killed Jews, he pointed out, could hardly be the result of an anti-Christian Jewish plot,[49] for the classic calumny of well-poisoning by Jews had reappeared. In the words of a contemporary:

To this evil another was added; there arose some tale that devotees of witchcraft, Jews especially, were putting potions in the waters and fountains, and that this was the reason the aforesaid pestilence was spreading so. On this account many Christians as well as Jews, although innocent and blameless, were burned, slaughtered, and otherwise maltreated in their persons, whereas, in fact, this thing happened for no reason other than the conjunction of the stars, or the divine wrath.[50]

No doubt there were Christians among the victims of the mob, as this account claims, but there is overpowering evidence that Jews were the chief sufferers, and that Pope Clement VI was their principal defender. Two lives of Clement contain an identical line:

In the following year Jews were burned throughout all of Germany, for it was laid to their charge that they had poisoned fountains and wells, and some, having been tortured, confessed that this was true.[51]

Once again baptism offered safety to the tormented Jews; we can only presume that, in the eyes of the mob, to renounce the Synagogue and to join the Church carried with it a pardon from the alleged guilt of mass poisoning. The ambiguous conversions that followed from this led the Pope, on July 4, 1348, to reaffirm the rights of Jews to their religious freedom, to life, to property, and, finally, to baptism, should they seek it freely:

Let no Christian compel Jews to come to baptism by violence, these same unwilling or refusing. But, if one of them takes refuge among Christians spontaneously, and for the sake of the faith, let him be made Christian without calumny. For he, indeed, who is known to come to Christian baptism, not spontaneously but unwillingly, is not considered to possess authentic Christian faith. Too, let no Christian have the presumption to wound or to kill those same Jewish persons, nor to take their money from them, apart from the lawful sentence of the lord of the region, or city, or countryside which they inhabit.[52]

In a few months the Pope felt obliged to repeat this command, and on September 26 he added to the papal tradition of protecting the Jews some sobering reflections on the general disaster:

Lately there has come to Our hearing the fame, or more precisely the infamy, that certain Christians, seduced by that liar the devil, are imputing to poisonings by Jews the pestilence with which God is afflicting the Christian people. For He is outraged by the sins of this people who, acting on their own temerity, and taking no account of age or sex, have impiously annihilated some from among the Jews. These same Jews are prepared to submit to judgment before a competent judge on the false allegation of this sort of crime, but the violence of those Christians has not grown cool on this account; rather, their fury rages all the more against them; where they offer no resistance, their aberration is taken to be proved!
  Now, if the Jews were guilty, their conscience burdened by a crime so great, We would wish them struck by a penalty of suitable severity—although a sufficient one could hardly be conceived. Still, since this pestilence, all but universal everywhere, by a mysterious judgment of God has afflicted, and does now afflict, throughout the divers regions of the earth, both Jews and many other nations to whom life in common with Jews is unknown, that the Jews have provided the occasion or the cause for such a crime has no plausibility.[53]

The Pope concluded by commanding all ordinaries to announce to their people, as they gathered to celebrate the liturgy, that the Jews were not to be struck, not to be wounded, not to be killed, and that all those who did these things put themselves under the ban of the Church. Last, if any had quarrels with the Jews, there existed both a law and judges competent to hear their suits.[54]

Unfortunately, these papal efforts did not succeed; outside papal territory, the Jews continued to suffer persecution for witchcraft and poisoning. In the following year, one annalist claimed that twelve thousand Jews were put to death in Mayence alone, and once more there were mass suicides of Jews, rendered frantic by their enemies.[55]

Converts in Italy and Spain, 1388 and 1391

In the annals for the year 1388 it is remarked that an exceptionally large number of Jews came into Italy, announcing that they wished to enter the Church. This occasioned a letter of Pope Urban VI (1378–1389) on the phenomenon, and his words bear witness once more to the consistent papal concern to make the entrance of Jews into the Church easy, whereas lesser authorities in the hierarchy at times were reluctant to admit them. This letter is remarkable for its reference to the well-known prayer of the Church for the conversion of the Jews, for the Pope adverted to the fact that this intention is often the object of our prayer, and that in times past it had by no means remained fruitless. In his own day too, the Pope had seen evidence of its efficacy.[56] The text makes it clear that the converts were drawn from among Jews who had come to Italy from afar, and since the Pope pointed to their generosity in contributing to the expenses of the Crusade, we may infer that the local bishops needed just such evidence to persuade them of the sincerity of these converts. Urban contrasted this sign of the Church's vitality with her sorrows due to schism:

In testimony of their unfeigned, sincere conversion, they are offering freely, for the support of the Holy Land and of Holy Mother Church, in so many ways torn by schismatics, no small quantity of money from their resources toward the remission of sin . . . take care to baptize them and to confer on them the sacrament of confirmation.[57]

In contrast with the spontaneous conversion of Jews in Italy—perhaps because they here found a Christian attitude less harsh than in their homelands—the riots and the sacking of the Jewish quarters in Spanish cities in 1391 must be mentioned. True enough, those disorders and the mass baptisms under violence and the threat of violence are not directly connected to any papal policy, but from that tragic year there developed relentlessly the tensions between "new Christians" and "old Christians" that would end only with the great expulsion of 1492 in Spain and that of 1496 in Portugal. Popes, to be sure, would be obliged to deal with the problem, but it arose from the direct violation of consistent papal teaching: Jews are to be attracted to the Church by persuasion, not dragged to baptism by force.

Pope Martin V

Pope Martin V (1417–1431) is reputed to have exercised a certain severity in his dealings with the Jews of Avignon in 1418, when they were the object of three serious accusations: of sorcery, of proselytizing among simple Christians, and of demanding extremely onerous usury.[58] But against the memory of this can be cited a letter of his issued in 1419 to defend the Jews. In it he recounted the reflections that prompted him to listen with kindness to their requests, in accordance with the practice of earlier popes, that familiar list of those who had issued bulls and constitutions in their favor. Among those motives was the fact that the Jews "possess the image of God; that remnants of them will be saved; and that contact with them is surely useful, namely, in the services they offer to Christians."[59] Hence, within their synagogues, they were to be free from molestation, despite any contrary law or custom. On the other hand, the Jews ought not to abuse the freedom that had been granted them for the sake of the good life, and not in order that they might feel free to make light of the Christian faith. Forced baptism was forbidden and, although the lawful rights of the Jews must be respected, they in their turn must refrain from work in public on the Lord's Day. While no one ought to force upon them any sign of their Jewishness other than that prescribed by the customs of the regions in which they lived, they, in turn, ought to be loyal in observing whatever obligations those customs did impose. Finally, the Pope guaranteed their right to engage in trade, but ended with a restatement of the principle that it was his intention to offer protection only to those Jews who were not inclined to plot against the Christian faith.[60]

In 1422, the same pope found it necessary to issue yet another statement of this attitude, and the occasion seems to have been preaching unfriendly to the Jews. Pope Martin referred, for instance, to the assertion by some preachers that Jews ought to have no contacts with Christians; he forbade strictly that this, or anything like it, be proclaimed in the future. His wish, on the contrary, was that "every Christian treat the Jews with a humane kindness," and he acknowledged that mutual advantages might be expected to result from such relations between Jews and Christians.[61] Still, he ended this noteworthy expression of papal confidence in the possibility of harmony between the two communities with his customary reservation: his intention was not to protect Jews who might presume to conspire against his faith.

Pope Eugene IV

On precisely the ground that Pope Martin V contemplated when he added his concluding reservation, his immediate successor, Eugene IV (1431–1447), was moved to reinstate every restriction that had formerly affected the Jews and Saracens of Spain. Hence, although historians are inclined to see the two popes as opposed in policy, their dissent is on the plane of fact rather than on the plane of principle. Temperament, to be sure, must enter into the evaluation of every factual situation, but the severity of Pope Eugene IV was, so to speak, already foreseen and admitted in principle by Pope Martin, and that in the very document in which the latter expressed his hope for improved relations with the Jews. Pope Eugene did not take issue with his predecessor's theoretical solution, but claimed that papal indults and concessions had been abused by non-Christians, to the scandal of the Church. His solution was to rescind all particular provisions for Jews and Moslems in the kingdoms of Castile and Leon, as well as in the personal holdings of John, king of those two kingdoms; only the provisions of general law remained in force with respect to the Jews and Moslems of those jurisdictions. Pope Eugene was undisturbed by the fact that he was rescinding what had been established by documents drawn up "for the perpetual memory of the affair," and proceeded to qualify his own decree as "forever valid, and irrefragibly to be observed." Under this imposing rubric the Pope then itemized the disabilities which his conception of his pastoral responsibilities required him to impose on Spanish Jews and Saracens. These are both detailed and onerous:

Christians were not to eat and drink with Jews or Moslems, not to admit them to their own entertainments, not to live with them, nor to bathe with them, not to accept the services of their physicians. An exhaustive list of occupations was closed to Jews and Saracens, all pertaining to fiscal or matrimonial affairs, including the roles of marriage broker and obstetrician. They could exercise no function in a Christion household, nor have any office, society, administration, art, or production in common with Christians, nor could a Christian bequeath anything to a Jew or a Moslem in his will. Jews were to be permitted no new synagogues, and in the repair of old ones were not to render them larger or more precious than they had been before. On the days of ritual lamentation and commemoration of the Passion of Jesus, Jews and Saracens were not only forbidden the streets, but were not so much as to open their doors and windows. They were held to tithes on all their business dealings and on all their possessions. Christians could testify against them in any and all cases, but the testimony of a Jew against a Christian was invalid. All court cases concerning Jews or Saracens were to be heard by the ordinary Christian judges, never before judges deputed especially for that purpose; still less were such cases to be held before the elders of the Jewish or Saracen communities.

Christians, on the other hand, could not be engaged by Jews to light their fires on the Sabbath, or on feast days, could not prepare food for them, or do anything else to enhance their worship. Secular judges were to impose fines, or other penalties, on Jews who blasphemed God or the Virgin Mary; Jews and Moslems, of both sexes and of all ages, were to wear distinctive garb and easily identifiable badges; they must live in segregated areas. Future usury from Christians was forbidden Jews and Moslems; past usury was to be restored without resistance.

The Pope appealed to all authorities, both ecclesiastical and secular, to enforce this complex decree, and he struck with excommunication any Christian, of whatever dignity in the Church or in the civil administration, who might fail to conform, in whole or in part, within thirty days. A Jew or Saracen who resisted was subject to total confiscation of his goods in favor of the "fabric" of the local cathedral—that is, the funds to maintain it, or any other church that local conditions might suggest to the bishop of the place as a more worthy beneficiary.[62]

This revival, and minute restatement, of the hostile elements in the Spanish tradition of dealing with Judaism and Islam, after the friendly legislation of Pope Martin V, marks the establishment of a policy that was to proceed without interruption toward the events of 1492 and 1496.

Pope Nicholas V

Among the aspects of Jewish-Christian relations that attracted the attention of Pope Nicholas V (1447–1455) was the status in the Christian Spanish kingdoms of the "new Christians," converts from Judaism especially, but also from Islam, and even from paganism. The tenor of this pope's decree regarding them is to confirm an existing civil law of King Henry, lately supported by his successor, John, King of Castile and Leon, to the effect that discrimination ought not to be made between "old" and "new" Christians; indeed, the Pope went so far as to name King Henry and King John in the same line as Saint Paul himself, who had announced that there is no distinction in the Lord between Jew and Greek (Rom. 10 : 12). In order to attract converts, but also for the sake of the Church, to which they had so much to offer, "new" Christians were to be received with charity and honor; every dignity, ecclesiastical or secular, was to be open to them.[63]

At the same time, this pope renewed the legal disabilities imposed upon unconverted Jews and Saracens in Spain by his predecessor, Eugene IV, adding as he did so a slight modification, intended to guarantee that Christian officials should run no risk of incurring excommunication when they enforced those disabilities.[64] His renewal also made specific mention of the policy, traditional since *Turbato corde* in the thirteenth century, of using the Inquisition and the secular arm against crypto-Jews and crypto-Moslems among the converts in Castile and Leon.[65]

Almost in passing it may be mentioned that Pope Pius II (1458–1464) can be quoted as one in the long line of popes whose concern to attract converts to the Church inspired them to recommend tact and courtesy on the part of Christian spokesmen. Pope Pius sent a letter to a Franciscan vicar general, north of the Alps, with respect to the preachers under his control:

When mention is made of Jews, Moors, neophytes, or Praguers, or of others like them, even when these men are present, why, the preachers customarily soar off in a fervor of the Spirit and in a zeal for God, with all too little ballast. They irritate these men with their curses and reproaches, rather than attacking and refuting their errors, in conformity to the precept of your glorious Father and Master in the Rule transmitted to you, namely, that you ought to warn them prudently, and attract them, so that they might regain wisdom and, having had a change of heart, might accept the Truth![66]

We cannot help remarking that Saint Francis of Assisi, here cited to his sons by the Pope, is the saint who, in a crusading century, thought it right to seek an interview with Saladin.

Reconquest and Expulsion

As the Christian kingdoms of Spain approached the moment when their long warfare against the Moors would end in victory, and thus make possible a unified and secure Christian society, they increased their pressures against the Jews as well as against the Saracens within their frontiers. There can be no doubt that this reflects the conviction of Spanish Christians that Jewish populations constituted a threat to their military and political security; in our own time, minority groups held to be unreliable in time of war have suffered comparable repression. Various episodes during the concluding years of the Crusade in Spain attracted papal notice.

Pope Sixtus IV

When Ferdinand of Aragon was reported to the Sultan as having persecuted Saracens within his territories, the Sultan directed his complaints to Pope Sixtus IV (1471–1484). His reply illustrates the more general problem of religious minorities in societies of religious orientation during the last decades of the fifteenth century, and thus bears citation in full:

Great and Powerful Lord:
When your letter concerning the demolition of mosques, which, you claim, has come to pass by the agency of Our most beloved son in Christ, Ferdinand of Aragon, within his Kingdom, We wrote to him promptly in order that, if what you had written to Us were true, We might forbid it with suitable remedies. We have discovered that all these things were reported to you in a false rumor, for neither have any mosques been demolished, nor have any of your people, the Saracens, who live in those regions in peace and quiet, been injured by anything lawless or harmful.

True, when they constructed on those mosques certain very lofty towers and pinnacles, which they call "tresses," in excess of the ancient usage, and when they invoked Mohammed from their highest peaks by means of the human voice, it was by no lawless act that this religious King prohibited what went beyond custom, and which was not without scandal for the Christian population. He thus commanded that "tresses" of this sort be brought down to the level of the mosques, and that the aforesaid invocation be made only by the sound of the trumpet, in accord with the ancient arrangement. Now if these are just provisions, you ought not to be disturbed by them, since you prohibit in the same way both bell towers and the ringing of bells in those churches of ours that are in your dominions.

We exhort you to bear with equanimity what has been done without contempt and without disadvantage to your people. Repel the lies of evil men, and especially of those who desire discord and rivalry to prevail with you over reason, equity, and your own moderation! Warmly do We commend to you all those Christians of Ours, religious men, who tarry within your lands; whatever favor and courtesy you show to them will be held in gratitude.[67]

During those years, the Spanish kings came to believe that the unreliability of the "new" Christians—the "Marranos," as the offensive popular usage termed them—had been demonstrated. The kings' first response to this religious and political, even military, crisis was to charge the ecclesiastical authorities with admonishing the converts, both publicly and in private, in order to confirm them in their adopted faith. Convinced that this device had borne small fruit, they then proceeded with an appeal to Rome for the appointment of Inquisitors to deal with what was considered a new heresy. It was hoped that the Inquisitors might first receive the submission of those who would repent, and, second, administer the harsh antiheresy laws with effect against the rest.

The first phase is said to have brought approximately seventeen thousand to repentance, all of them given punishments short of death, whereas those who withheld their submission were arrested, on the information of witnesses the court considered reliable, and tortured. Some confessed; some resisted, and even called upon the name of Moses; those in both categories went to the stake, but those who had confessed, a chronicler pointed out, "had bought life at the price of death." Still others, by their repentance, escaped the stake, but were condemned to perpetual imprisonment, or declared infamous. These last were deprived of all offices, forbidden to wear gold or silk, and doomed to wear flame-colored crosses sewn to their outer garments. The dead were exhumed, if their guilt was considered proved, their bones burned, their heirs deprived of offices and honors, their goods confiscated. Under this regime, vast numbers took refuge outside the country; many, ill-advised, went into Portugal, many to Navarre, others to Italy, or to France. Their possessions were expropriated to support the war of the Catholic princes against the Moors "and other barbarians"; in one province alone, it is said that five thousand houses stood empty. Last, all unconverted Jews were expelled, and reduced to penury by a prohibition against selling their houses or taking their money with them.[68]

Word spread inevitably that the motives behind this appalling policy were not necessarily the highest, and Elizabeth, Queen of Castile, was so distressed that nothing short of a papal letter of confidence could console her. Pope Sixtus IV sent her a message assuring her that he did not share the doubts entertained by others; "there never was a suspicion of this with Us."[69]

The same pope thought it necessary to take action against the Talmud in Sicily, for he had heard the time-honored reports of blasphemies against Jesus and His mother to which that work was said to induce Jewish readers. Hence he ordered prelates, abbots, priors, and local wardens to cooperate with the Inquisitor in the suppression of what he counted an expression of Jewish ingratitude in the face of the hospitality extended to them in Christian lands.[70]

Pope Innocent VIII

In 1485, Pope Innocent VIII (1484–1492) was moved by the plight of certain Marranos in high places, who found the normal judicial process of reinstatement into the Church, after a temporary relapse into Judaism, exceptionally onerous because of their eminence in Spanish society. He consequently wrote to provide the Inquisitors with an easier, but effective, procedure for such persons: They might make their abjuration of error privately, so far as the general public was concerned, but, for the sake of the future security of the realm, in the presence of the King and Queen of Castile, Leon, and Aragon. This mitigation of the customary severity was accompanied by the provision that a future relapse would be subject to the usual punishment, without possibility of escape.[71]

There are other indications of some scruples with respect to the harshness of the anti-Marrano Inquisition. The fact that the names of the accusers were not produced was termed a violation of Aragonese liberty, and, in Aragon too, it was suggested that the punishment of confiscation be abrogated. But the suspicion was abroad that this suggestion originated with a Marrano plot, intended to retain in Marrano control funds sufficient to bribe the officials of king and pope, and to serve as the first step toward undermining antiheresy legislation in general. In any case, support for the version of the Inquisition established in Spain was not universal; many magnates professed the fear that the harshness of the tribunals was leading to the enslavement of the nation, and to the destruction of her traditions of civil freedom.[72]

It was against this background that the Inquisitor Peter Arbues was stabbed to death at his prayers in the cathedral of Saragossa. The populace was deterred from a massacre of the "new" Christians only by the timely intervention of Archbishop Alphonsus, who rode through the streets to disperse the mob that was forming. But courts were convened immediately, and the assassins punished.[73] Meanwhile, owing to the fear inspired by King Ferdinand, many Marranos left Spain; these became numerous at Rome where they proceeded to accumulate wealth and offices in the Church. The Pope appointed two cardinals to act as inquisitors in their regard, but these Roman inquisitors did not impress every observer; one historian felt they were responsible for a certain papal laxity with respect to Marranos: "The Pope proceeded against them, but not with the ardor that the case required." The charges against the Marrano higher clergy are identical with those commonly pressed against the Roman Curia of that day, and, despite the reservations modern critics register against him, Volterranus can be adduced as an echo of contemporary opinion on the genesis of the Marrano crisis:

Under pressure from Vincent [Ferrer] of the Order of Preachers, who later was numbered among the Saints, John [King of Castile] ordered all Jews to leave Spain, and to abandon their property, unless they wished to become Christians. A good part, therefore, out of fear of losing their possessions, were washed in the sacred font, but secretly they guarded their ancestral laws, and became that worst of the races of men, those whom the vulgar today term "Marranos."[74]

Thus did the hostility that dated from Visigothic times, infinitely compounded, first, by the threat of Islamic invasion and then by its all but total success—the onslaught welcomed, so it seemed to Spanish Christians, by a disgruntled and treacherous Jewish minority—grow rather than diminish as victory in the Crusade came into sight. In the fateful year 1492, the Christian armies of Spain completed the dislodgment of the Moors, and Rodrigo de Borja ascended the papal throne as Alexander VI. The victorious Spanish crown, now master of all Spain, lost no time in expelling from the realm all its Jews.[75] The victims of this edict, promulgated in March, were given the choice of exile or baptism, and this time those who left were allowed four months in which to sell their goods or to arrange to take them away. But this mitigation of the harshness that had characterized former expulsions was reduced to a dead letter—at least to the point that his orders were obeyed—by the Inquisitor, Tomás de Torquemada; he forbade the faithful any dealings with the Jews for the disposal of their property, and forbade them to assist the fugitives by supplying them with food or with any other necessities. Hence, a multitude of impoverished Jews left Spain and went into Portugal, to the Moslem countries of the East or Africa, and to Italy, thus constituting "Sephardic" Jewry, distinguished permanently by an attachment to the Spanish tongue. Many accepted baptism rather than renounce Spain, and of these, it was reported, some were sincere in their conversion whereas others were not. Many were sold into slavery; many others perished, victims to hardship or the plague.[76]

Pope Alexander VI

From the point of view of the Church, which he ruled as though it were his personal fief, Alexander VI (1492–1503) is an improbable hero. Still, despite some ambiguities, his relationship with Jews, and especially with Marranos, makes fewer demands on his defenders than do most of his policies. This is the more worthy of note in that he was a Spanish grandee whose sense of family and class solidarity was particularly, not to say excessively, well developed, and who thus might have been expected to reflect more faithfully the millennium of distrust and bitterness that marked the Jewish-Christian encounter in Spain.

No less qualified a judge than the triumphant King Ferdinand himself was to find it strange that the Pope should be willing to open the states of the Church to Marranos, whom the King had thought it right to expel from Spain as a threat to the security of a Christian nation. Ferdinand did not fail to exhort the Pope to follow Spanish precedent in the matter, the more so since, as rumor had it, the exiled Jews brought the plague with them, and not a few baptized Jews had managed to establish themselves in administrative posts of the Roman Curia.[77]

No doubt Ferdinand's influence played some role in Alexander's judicial proceedings against certain Marranos, notably against Peter d'Aranda, Bishop of Calahorra, and against that worthy's natural son, who rejoiced in the office of Protonotary Apostolic. Both drew life sentences; they were imprisoned in the Castle sant'Angelo, and the chronicle of their fall includes a summary statement of the "Marrano heresy" with which they had been charged.[78] Proceedings against a group of forty less eminent crypto-Jews ended with nothing more burdensome for the convicted than public penance; the Church then received them back, as a contemporary account put it, "with her accustomed clemency."[79] But these were normal judicial proceedings against a handful from among the multitudes who arrived, first from Spain in 1492, then, in 1496, from Portugal; in the latter kingdom, negotiations for a royal marriage with a Spanish princess made the expulsion of the Jews a condition of the contract.[80]

That Alexander VI was not totally exempt from the very general distrust of the Iberian converts is visible in his prohibition against the reception of Marrano candidates into the Order of Preachers,[81] but the most significant episode in his relations with the Jews shows another side of his policy. According to an anecdote transmitted through Jewish sources, the Roman congregation of Jews is said to have refused to admit the refugees from Spain and even to have offered Alexander a bribe of a thousand ducats to enlist his support for their refusal. But the Pope, in his turn, threatened to exile the inhospitable Roman Jews, demanded two thousand ducats as a fine, or a bribe, and forced the Jews of the City to take in the refugees despite everything.[82]

It may be that the imposition of a tax on the Jews to help finance a Crusade against the Turks in 1500 ought to count as an unfriendly act, but there are reasons to think that this was not the Pope's own view. Alexander VI had few scruples against imposing taxes in any circumstances, and on this occasion he could claim that "if We burden all ecclesiastics" with a tax for the war "the Jews ought not to be immune from it." As the Pope saw the Crusade, it was waged for the common good of all who lived in Christian lands, whether Christians or Jews:

If this agony falls upon the Christians—which may God in his mercy avert!—the Jews themselves would share in the disasters; it would be a question of their peril as much as of our own.[83]

Chancery style is not always convincing, but it is difficult to believe that Alexander would have appealed to the advantages enjoyed by Jews who resided among Christians had there been a notable discrepancy between his claims and the facts. It would have been simple enough simply to impose the tax, and to deny his numerous detractors one more theme for satiric comment. Jews, he remarked,

are permitted to lead their life, free from interference from Christians, to continue in their own rites, to gain wealth, and to enjoy many other privileges; and finally, they obviously support themselves, and nourish their families owing to the favor of Christians.[84]

Last, the tax for the Crusade levied on the clergy was a tenth of their income, whereas that imposed on the Jews was only a twentieth. But it was to be calculated from all sources, including, perhaps especially, that derived "through the wickedness of usury."[85]

One attraction of the rowdy celebration of the Roman Carnival was a footrace by Jews,[86] and it is remembered to his discredit that Alexander VI extended the course in order to prolong the spectacle and his own enjoyment of it. Modern authors have seen in this annual event an undignified and humiliating exhibition, as indeed it may have been, but is it certain that it seemed so to the Jews of Renaissance Rome?

If Alexander was not above patronizing the clownish amusements of the Carnival, even at the price of Jewish embarrassment, he was ready to reward more respectable contributions that Jews might make, chief among them the notorious expertise of Jews in the practise of medicine. Continuing a long-standing papal tradition that implies self-interest, to be sure, but also an important relaxation of the legal restrictions on Jewish freedom, Alexander made a place at his court for Jewish physicians.[87] One eminent Jew who held such a post was variously styled Maestro Boneto, Bonet de Lattes, Bonet Provenzali. Expelled from Provence in 1493, he had taken refuge in the papal city of Carpentras, in order to profit by the friendly reception generally to be expected by Jews in towns under the control of the popes. Since this rabbi possessed, in addition to his medical knowledge, a remarkable competence in astronomy as well, it was possible for him to give striking evidence of his gratitude to the Pope. This he did by dedicating to him a work called *The Astronomical Ring,* in which he explained the use of a convenient astrolabe of his own invention, to be worn on the finger as a ring. By 1499, Maestro Boneto had become the rabbi of the Jewish congregation in Rome and personal physician to Pope Alexander VI, an office he would retain under Leo X. Owing to his influence with Pope Leo, Maestro Boneto was in a position to assist Reuchlin in defending the Talmud against the attacks of Pfefferkorn and Hoogstraten. He seems also to have had some part in moving Pope Leo to send a letter that shows sympathetic understanding of the Talmud, and of Jewish literature in general, to the Bishops of Speyer and Worms.[88]

Thus the medieval confrontation of Jew and Christian ended with a short-lived wave of sympathetic Christian, and above all papal, interest in Judaism and in Jews, in the Hebrew Bible and in the Kabbala, an interest to be associated, no doubt, with the general movement of humanism. But the unfriendly legislation was still on the statute books, and it would be easy for those who thought the popes of the day lacking in zeal against the Jews to join that accusation to well-founded criticism of Renaissance Rome. Alexander VI and his immediate successors are located in the historical no-man's-land that links, or separates, the Middle Ages from modern times. Medieval popes end on a note of friendship and sympathy with Jews, but they were harbingers of a doomed spring, hardly to survive Reform and Counter-Reform. The papacy, besieged by disenchanted Christians, would think it necessary to enforce against dissent on every plane what we can only term "martial Law."

IX

REFLECTIONS

At this point it may be permissible to take inventory of the more significant points at which popes and Jews made contact in the Middle Ages. On some of these, our texts afford a certitude that excludes all reasonable doubt. Most pervasive and most certain of all, beneath the particular determinations of law and theory is the massive fact that medieval popes and Jews knew themselves to be in opposition on matters each considered of primary importance. A day would come when Jews, and not a few Christians, would find assimilation to the world around them the most seductive of temptations. The world of the Jews who have been our concern was medieval Christendom; for them, assimilation meant baptism. Some, indeed most, resisted to death or to exile every pressure for conversion; some, in order to escape persecution, accepted baptism, but reluctantly and without inner assent; still others requested baptism with an air of sincerity we can scarcely impugn, since it satisfied the popes who were the converts' contemporaries.

Neither Jews nor Christians argued that baptism does not matter; neither adopted the stance of theological indifference in the presence of Judaism and Christianity; neither held that one is as true, or as false, as the other. Aware of a widespread thirst for peace, ecumenical leaders today feel bound to disavow a superficially attractive unity such as would mask rather than reconcile our profound divergencies. Medieval spokesmen for Judaism and for the papacy—Ibn Pakuda, for instance, and Martin V—revealed their theological preeminence in another fashion; they discerned the reality and the relevance of those all but submerged possibilities of friend-

ship, invisible to less percipient believers. Hardly less fundamental is the Christian conviction that among all the
religious groupings of men the Jews occupy a unique position,
and this by an option of Providence.

Theological Perspectives

The singularity of the Jews was interpreted by the popes
as a consequence, in the first instance, of Jewish origins. For
does not the Church count the Hebrew patriarchs as her own
fathers, listen with joy to the promises and with compunction
to the strictures of the Hebrew prophets? Does she not
cherish, as did Peter himself (2 Pet. 1 : 16–18), the memory
of Jesus on the mountain of the transfiguration, flanked by
Moses and Elijah, by the prophet of Commandments and
by the prophet of charismatic zeal? Hebrew Scriptures, the
popes well knew, constitute an indispensable portion of the
"archives" of Christian faith. More than once, medieval popes
invoked this inheritance as a Jewish claim to esteem on the
plane of faith itself and as a glory that demands a specifically
Christian recognition.

In the second place, how often popes would appeal to
the end of the Jews' affair—the conversion of their remnant—
as another title to reverence by Christians. Christianity must
ever be seen as ineluctably oriented to "last things." Not only
the concluding book of the Christian's Bible—heavily symbolic revelations of things hidden—but also crucial sayings of
the Lord preserved in the Gospel[1] and tantalizingly cryptic
remarks of Saint Paul[2] justify our calling the word of the
Church to the world of men a "discourse on the last things";
in a theologian's technical Greek, Christian doctrine is, above
all, an "eschatology." Hardly a detail in the awesome
prophecies, obscurely freighted with terrors and with glory,
is as categorically stated as is the destiny announced for the
Jews; their remnant will be saved. The Jew we encounter,
sufficiently venerable as the remote posterity of prophet and
patriarch, has thus another claim on the respect of the
Church; in his turn, the contemporary Jew is the ancestor of
saints. Medieval popes did not evade their duty to remind
Christians that this knowledge must temper the cruder of
their evangelistic exploits.

But between the Jewish past that is sacred history, and

the Jewish future that will be an eternal victory, between
the heroic era of the Hebrew fathers and the time when
Jewish holiness will triumph over all resistance, the popes
were bewildered by the disconcerting traits of the Jews'
"middle portion," their *medietas*.[3] The enigma was only
deepened by the consciousness of Christians that they had
come to believe in the Law and the Prophets through the
Gospel, for the Master had been concerned lest any smallest
fragment of the Covenant be destroyed (Matt. 5 : 17–20);
how could those same Christians find plausible the persuasion of Jews, who had come to the same Covenant from
its farther side, and who, as Christians saw it, refused to
advance with the progressive current of God's confidences to
men into the ripening fulfillment of the Jewish Promise?
Hence, blindness and disbelief are the most common of the
complaints that medieval popes urged against the Jews they
knew.

　If the criticism by the popes that Hebrews read Hebrew
books with less insight than did the sons of pagans is a paradoxical one, medieval Christians were confident that they
knew how to diagnose the causes of what seemed to them
the Jewish failure. A multifaceted problematic of sign and
reality, everywhere present in medieval theorizing on meaning and communication, provided the Christian apologist
with a neat, not to say facile, explanation. Jewish devotees of
the Law and of its external rituals doomed themselves to
remain slaves of the "letter"; inhibited by the "literal" sense
of their own polyvalent Scriptures, they were blind to the
more profound implications of those texts in their materiality.
In short, the Jews seemed to make ultimate reality of what
is in truth but its sign. Christians, on the contrary, rejoicing,
as they believed, in the liberty proper to sons by adoption,
breathed the freer air of the Spirit who proclaims beneath
and through the letter a truth no material text can constrain
within its own narrow limits.

　Needless to say, in making their own interpretation of
Torah, medieval rabbis were little affected by the unsolicited
assistance of gentile exegetes, whereas Christians were not
inclined to extend much confidence to Jewish allegorizing.
Biblical believers, Jews and Christians alike, have always
been ready to concede that the sacred text is never exhausted
by our understanding of it. We can suggest without arrogance

that medieval rabbis and scholastics not only were far from plumbing the depths of Scripture, but were also almost totally incapable of understanding each other. Indeed, the popes did not hesitate to prolong into their own experience with contemporary Jewish exegesis the polemic of Jesus against scribe and Pharisee. Rightly or wrongly, the popes considered the rabbinical Judaism of the Jews they knew to be in doctrinal continuity with that of the enemies of Jesus. When thirteenth-century popes—Gregory IX,[4] Innocent IV,[5] Clement IV,[6] and Honorius IV[7]—wrote to arraign the Judaism they knew as a distortion of the Mosaic Law and of the Hebrew prophets, the chancery style of their texts does not conceal their conviction that they were echoing their Master's disclaimers against a tradition that had perdured without substantial change from the time of Jesus.

Scriptural Warrants

Despite the pervasively biblical air within which popes and Jews made and make their disparate options, the texts explicitly cited by medieval popes to ground their decisions concerning the Jews are not very numerous, and it is only when the verses to which the popes made appeal are collected in one place that their extreme paucity is visible. For the defense of Jewish lives, precisely because the Jews are the chosen of the Lord, there is Psalm 58 (59) : 12, and the mark of Cain (Genesis 4 : 15) was taken to be a figure of the divine protection and accusation of the Jews in general; like Cain, they were held to be at once guilty and sacrosanct. For the defense of their right to freedom in choosing to accept or to reject baptism, Psalm 53 (54) : 8 and Psalm 58 (59) : 8, and Psalm 27 (28) : 7 were invoked. For the final conversion of the Jews, Isaiah 4 : 2–3; 24 : 13–14; 65 : 8; 66 : 22; Jeremiah 23 : 5–6; and Romans 4 : 1–13; 9 : 3–24; all seemed to proclaim the entrance of the Jews into the Church in her penultimate days. Association of Jews and Gentiles in the Church—occasion of the first internal crisis she had suffered (Acts 15 : 1–31)—seemed to medieval popes one "spiritual" sense of the two walls of Ephesians 2 : 14, of the ox and the ass that tradition (not without a free use of Isaiah 1 : 3) delighted to see at the manger of Jesus, and of the Magi whom Matthew (2 : 1–11) put there

without mentioning the shepherds noted by Luke (2 : 8–12).
Mary Magdalene, Peter, and John at the empty tomb were
taken to be figures of the entrance of Gentiles into the Church
before the Jews, and in the same context popes saw, well
outside the letter, incidental references to the stone tablets
of the Law, to the splitting of stones on the death of Jesus
as a revelation that the Mosaic Law of the stone tablets had
been superseded by a new Covenant. Social segregation of
Jews seemed commanded, or at least justified, by 2 Corin-
thians 5 : 9–13; 6 : 14–15, and the popes who thought so
may well have been influenced by Matthew 7 : 6. The illness
of Peter's mother-in-law, contrasted with her daughter's
health, served to represent the roots of the Church in the
Synagogue as well as the Church as sole hope of the Synagogue; thus salvation was understood as truly "from the
Jews" and Jesus as truly the promised Messiah (John 4 : 22–
30). Last, the indignation of Christians over those Jews who
returned to the practices of Judaism after baptism invited
them to apply the biblical image of a dog and his vomit
(Proverbs 26 : 11). Not a biblical text, nor the saying of a
pope, Saint Bernard's aphorism nevertheless merits inclusion:
that the Jews themselves are a kind of Scripture in whom,
as in the flourishes of a scribe, a divine message can be read
by perspicacious Christians. The popes of his time and of
succeeding generations all read Bernard, and this conceit is
typical of medieval Christian speculation.

　　The list is brief enough, but to count verses is too superficial a norm for gauging the biblical quality of the understanding of Jews and Judaism contrived by the popes of the
Middle Ages. Their theology of Israel remains totally biblical
and invokes their understanding of the Bible in its totality.
Thus, for instance, the scriptural notion of the communal
consequences that can flow from the guilt of a single man
provided Christians with an ambiguous conception of corporate responsibility that is basic to their attitude toward
Jews. The Bible insists upon the incommunicable responsibility of each man for his own actions, but on another plane
Scripture insists upon the societal dimension of sin and virtue.
Abraham's fidelity, and the incredulity of Achaz were as little
private as we should expect in descendants of Adam, whose
very name is simply "man," and of Eve, rightly named as
she is, "the mother of all the living" (Gen. 3 : 20). Jews and

popes did not differ in accepting the notion that sin and its consequences go far beyond the individual and his personal guilt; it was owing to "our sins," wrote Salomo bar Simeon, that their enemies triumphed over the Rhineland Jews in 1096,[8] and Pope Innocent III was insistent, with Saint Peter, that it was "our sins" that Jesus bore in His body on the cross.[9] No rigid and univocal conceptions of "sin," "guilt," and "punishment" can bear the weight that Jews and Christians alike put upon them.

Hence, the summary identification of Jews born in the fourteenth, or in the sixth, century with that fraction of the Jerusalem population who cried out for the crucifixion of Jesus is by no means condoned when we remark that, for all its deficiency and theological primitivism, this mode of thought was inevitable in medieval readers of the Bible. Besides, Jews too made the same identification at times; it ought not to be overlooked that no less a rabbi than the great Moses Ben Maimon was eager to associate himself and his contemporaries with the decision of the Sanhedrin to condemn Jesus as a pseudo-Messiah.[10] In any case, papal defense of the Jews against persecution was nearly always in terms of a biblical view of Jewish origins and destiny, precisely as papal repression of the Jews was, without exception, in terms of their opposition to that new and spiritual Israel, that Israel of God which is the Church, daughter of the Synagogue, if the popes were right, and inheritor of her promises.[11]

The only hint that the personal attitude of contemporary Jews, as distinguished from the communal destiny of the whole People, carried weight with medieval popes as a motive for protecting them was in papal recognition that the Jews of Christendom were not warlike, or even rebellious against feudal arrangements. Everywhere willing to do feudal service, Jews were admittedly a world removed from the militaristic and powerful Saracens.[12] Here too, however, not the innocence and harmlessness of the individual Jew, but the common attitude of the community is what counted. True enough, an individual Jew might well find favor with a given pope;[13] the protection of a Jew in such circumstances has almost no significance beyond itself, unless it be that even one exception must invalidate a universal. That the popes who befriended individual Jews held no anti-Jewish universals sacrosanct is an inescapable inference from these instances. In a matter where the popes saw their duty as one of governing a community, they were perforce content with procedures that promised to meet the requirements of most cases; when human law undertakes the awesome task of securing divine interests it remains human and cannot be held to do more than function "for more cases" than not, to reach its goals *pro pluribus*.[14]

Legal Precedents

Between the Church and the Roman Law of the Christian emperors, the causal nexus is obscure. To what point did the Church cause the enactment of the laws? To what point did the precedents of civil law result in the canons of pope or council? Since Roman civil law acknowledged the competence of bishops on all questions of religion,[15] it is incontrovertible that the Church has some degree of responsibility for the general status of the Jews under the imperial statutes. On the other hand, bishop and pope, like the emperors themselves, were born into an empire that had made few contributions as effective as its law and, to that extent, the Church underwent a formative influence from the law, mediated by her most sophisticated administrators. It was a law that did not shrink from brutality in order to guarantee efficiency, to be sure, and no faith that lays claim to a prophetic role can take refuge in an appeal to the ways of the world as a device to palliate the sins of the just. Still, the glacially slow advance of the Christian social conscience is not the less sincerely deplored when an obstacle to its development as formidable as was the Christianized Empire is acknowledged to have had its effect.

What cannot be gainsaid is that from centuries of pagan juridical tradition Christian emperors inherited the policy that qualified Judaism as a licit religion, but one outside the official cult of the gods. When the emperors became Christian, they had only to reverse the positions of the formerly illicit Church and of the formerly established paganism. Judaism retained in principle its old position, for the favor that might still be traced to the history of the diplomatic and military alliance between Rome and the Maccabees, more than damaged as it was by conquest and rebellion, could then be matched by the theological prestige of the Chosen People. The most fundamental provision of the new religious settlement was the acceptance, with few hesitations, of the Roman tradition that supreme religious authority and supreme political power in some way ought to coincide. Although the Supreme Pontiff was no longer the same man as the Emperor, the Church never ceased to press her claim that the sanctions of the secular arm ought to support her decisions and policies. The wisdom and the expediency, even the justice, of this may well be scrutinized, but until the end of the Middle Ages, and in "Catholic" states into modern times, the fact cannot be contested.

With Roman legal sanctions went Roman punishments and torture. That under torture the strong will confess nothing whereas the weak will confess anything is a fragment of Aristotle's wisdom to which, alas, our fathers gave no heed. Hence a twofold tragedy: first, that of the tortured Jews who, in some instances, confessed to crimes as implausible as well-poisoning to spread pestilence, and, second, the tragedy of their tormentors, whose stupid brutality[16] has made their memory a reproach to the Church they professed to serve. Roman Law bears its indirect witness to Jewish proselytizing in pagan times, and the maintenance by the popes of legal inhibitions against seeking converts to Judaism at the expense of the Church makes it certain that the Jews of the Middle Ages were as aggressive as their fathers had been in striving to extend the Covenant. It is incredible that the persistent reappearance in papal documents of the complaint that Jews were inducing Christians, not all of them "Marranos," to apostasize is a smoke without fire. Christian Roman Law provided only limited precedents for excluding Jews from designated occupations; the Councils of Toledo extended this discrimination to every office from which a Jew might lord it over Christians. In Spain, no doubt, this must be seen in the context of the military and political threat against Catholics by Visigoth and Moslem, but from the time of Gregory the Great, popes were ready to generalize the policy on theological grounds, much as they transferred to the theological plane the problem of Jewish masters and Christian slaves. Last, the readiness of a Christian emperor to legislate on the sacred books of the Jews was more than matched by the popes, who so often spoke with respect of the Law and the Prophets, but with such disdain of their interpretation at the hands of talmudic masters.

Because the world needs redemption, the Church must speak to the world both in an idiom the world can understand and in clear opposition to the world's corruption. The world of the first verses of Genesis, exceedingly good in all its parts, is not quite the world in which Cain slew Abel, not identical with the world destined for the cleansing waters of the Flood, for the scourge of Egypt and Assyria. Indeed there is a world so corrupt that Jesus refused to pray for it (John 17 : 14–21). Hence the Church cannot forgo the perilous duty of denouncing the corruptions of the world, although she must so play the prophet as to leave intact the human values that are worth redemption. Exactly to the point that the Church is faithful to the Word of God, she will respect the values which the Word has formed in the world; exactly to the point that her sons succumb to sin, they will suffer contamination from the techniques and aspirations of the world. Roman Law was a value that Christian Romans could scarcely have been expected to jettison, but history must forgive us for regretting that they did not exorcise the law more thoroughly in the course of its baptism.

Absent Motives

Like the negative fact that Rome never conquered Ireland, the consequences of which are with us still, so certain classic motives for anti-Semitism are absent from papal documents and the significance of this hiatus ought not to be overlooked. Not one word suggests that any "racial" theory played a part in forming the policy of popes. In Spain, medieval Christians spoke of "pure blood," and acted on that dubious conception, but the King of the great expulsion in 1492 expressed his dismay that the Pope ignored that ideal: Marranos, expelled from Spain, found a haven in the Roman Curia. Medieval popes could not but recognize that communities of families constituted the Jewish "race," the *gens,* or the *natio Judaeorum,* and thus a biologically compact grouping of men who also practiced the Mosaic religion. But for all its inescapable biological connotation, the Latin word *gens* as applied to the Jews by the popes is free from all biological determinism. It was used on the plane of fact rather than of theory, in the order of existence rather than in the order of essential nature. For the popes consistently defended the propriety of receiving the sincere Jewish convert into the Church, and, indeed, the first Pope we have had occasion to cite, Gelasius I, adverted to the fact that the primitive Church had been a church of Jews.[17] Although the Church of the last days will not be totally Jewish, all the Jews then remaining will be welcomed, the popes believed, within that Church in her moment of victory. In the measure that to be a Jew was counted a disadvantage by medieval popes, it was a theological option, a point of faith and not of blood or race. The only "anti-Semitism" to be discerned in the popes is but the obverse of their faith in Jesus as Messiah. Hence the popes held consistently that a Jew who sought baptism must be received "without calumny" and—using a technical term from Roman Law, without *praejudicium,* "prior judgment," as connoting pejorative consequences—they thus excluded the notion of unalterable Jewish wickedness grounded, as so many Christians have alleged, in that fateful "prior judgment" by which Jerusalem's officialdom rejected Jesus.

Humanity and Equity

Although less important in the estimate of medieval believers than are theological grounds for respecting and protecting Jews, considerations of natural equity, based upon our common human nature, were nonetheless present to the minds of the popes. Comparable reasons recommended reciprocal friendship with the Moslems, for whom theological and scriptural indications were wanting. If motives of this order held the last place with medieval men, they hold the first place with our own contemporaries. This is not necessarily because our society is so thoroughly secularized; perhaps our harsh experience has taught us to prize more highly those foundations of civic peace that are the more humble precisely because they are the more basic. With full recognition, therefore, that medieval men ordered their motives according to another scale, we have every reason to take stock of those papal pronouncements from the Middle Ages that are most easily intelligible to the men of our time. To admit that our perspective has shifted is but to concede that we are no longer living in the Middle Ages; to recognize that medieval popes were not blind to the foundations on which we still struggle to found social justice is no more than to recognize that, consciously or not, we remain the sons of our fathers. True enough, we have been overwhelmed with evidence that medieval popes, from beginning to end, tried to encourage conversions from Judaism with devices that only the closest kind of reasoning can discriminate from bribery, but it would falsify reality should evidence for the popes' sense of human equity be submerged.

Thus, Saint Gregory the Great thought that coveting another's property—so often, alas, a motive in the pogroms—is "unworthy of a civilized man."[18] Despite reservations that may have been only too well founded, Innocent III besought a sultan for Moslem treatment of Christians as benign as that of Moslems by Christians,[19] and nearly three centuries later, Sixtus IV would urge the same reciprocity[20] as had Innocent's immediate successor, Honorius III, specifying that mutual religious tolerance is justified by the "equal, humane, solace" it affords.[21] Gregory IX conceded that, while the Crusade ought not to suffer because of regulations made for Christian Florentine moneylenders, neither ought justice to suffer,[22] and in the repression of Jewish crimes, he held, new crimes must be avoided.[23] Gregory IX is also the author of that golden principle for the guidance of Christians who might legislate on the Jews: they ought to show Jews the kindness Christians desire at the hands of pagans.[24] Least elevated of all is the remark of Martin V that contact with Jews is "useful" to Christians because of the services they render;[25] but we must remember that the Pope prefaced this with biblical reasons that are totally disinterested.

Incertitudes

Not every aspect of the medieval encounter between popes and Jews is as certain as are the foregoing. Further publication of original sources—another pope's "Register" or another medieval Jewish chronicle—may bring unexpected disclosures. Then too, although it is inconceivable that popes and Jews should not constitute valid and significant categories in any examination of medieval society, both groups are but fragments of a more extensive whole, apart from which

neither is intelligible; new historic perspectives may be developed in which our certitudes may remain certain but will
receive interpretations we cannot now anticipate. Third, if
instances of incontrovertible heroism or chicanery or stupidity
be excluded, value judgments on the historic past cannot
attain the certitude accessible in straight narrative, and still
less one akin to that of classical geometry.

That a yet to be discovered text might one day prove
that popes never protected Jews from persecution is not a
serious possibility, but whether the motives of what was certainly a policy of protection were in whole or in part open
to reproach, and on what grounds, we cannot hope to see
settled to the satisfaction of every observer. The vicissitudes
of the public reputation of Pope Pius XII as a defender of
the Jews offers historians sobering reflections. A man of our
own time, whose life was lived out in the glare of contemporary publicity, a Pope whose personal use of our means
of communication was unparalleled, Pius XII died in an
atmosphere of public acclaim to which his unostentatious
endeavors to save a remnant of Israel from Nazi fury certainly
contributed. To call this monumental reputation into doubt,
nothing more than a play has been necessary; how much
more fragile the reputations of his medieval predecessors!

If solutions are not possible, to calendar problems raised
by this aspect of our medieval experience is not useless.
Before all others, there is the enigma—less a problem than
the ultimate ground of our communal tensions—generated by
the confluence in human existence of the temporal and the
eternal. The City of God and the Earthly City, Augustine was
wise enough to see, are realities too rich to terminate at the
neat frontiers of definition. With full recognition of the limitations of medieval polity and of the futility of attempting its
resurrection in any of its details, we cannot fail to honor the
effort of medieval Jews to remain faithful to the Law as they
understood it, and that of medieval popes to secure Jewish
rights. For the papal effort was in defense not only of the
Jews' human rights but of their religious ones as well, and
it was carried out under the popes' concern to proclaim and
to defend the Christian faith. Popes and Jews alike wished
to embody their respective creeds in their laws and customs,
and so to make the Earthly City into a true City of God. To
the extent that their creeds differ, friction was inevitable, and

limited agreement in posing the theological question could only render their dissent in the social and political order the more acute.

Heralds or Proselytizers?

For as long as men dissent on faith, theologians and statesmen must contend, in ever shifting circumstances, with the conscientious imperative of the believer to act on his belief and the right of the dissenter to his ultimate autonomy, for the first easily trespasses on the second. The consistent defense of the Jews against forced baptism is not the only instance of this tension that history provides, but none is more instructive. The issue of forced baptism brought others in its train: Where does legitimate persuasion end and illicit force begin? What is just and what is expedient in demanding that a free commitment, made for life, be fulfilled? Is it too much to require that men act as if they are capable of irrevocable choices, or must we, sometimes at least, vindicate the right of an adult to withdraw his most solemn expressions of fidelity? Does the Preacher, *Koheleth*, set too high a standard when he demands that, if we vow, we honor the vows we make? (Eccles. 5 : 3–4)

Impossible, perhaps, to speak with assurance on the point; still, it would seem that papal tolerance of means short of insuperable physical force to bring Jews to baptism, was incompatible with their allegiance to the principle that only in the confluence of grace and freedom can authentic faith come to fruition. The ever-present social pressure, the sporadic outbreak of mob violence, and forced attendance at conversionist sermons are incompatible with a realistic estimate of human freedom. The theologian is invited by this side of the papal-Jewish encounter to clarify the believer's conviction that he must proclaim his faith to others, lest silence mask insincerity and disregard for his brother. A simplistic solution that would suppress the right of the believer to announce his belief in order to avoid awkward reactions is surely an assault on the believer's natural impulse to communicate what he considers his most precious insights. Still, it cannot be denied that, as a medieval Pope could recognize, "zeal" can lead to what is less an exposition of conviction than an offensive personal attack.[26] Needless to say, the religious complexity of our time and the immemorial roots of our very diverse theological and ecclesiological traditions, surviving in the presence of a political dispensation that remains consciously neutral in matters of faith, make an understanding of this problematic more pressing for us than it was for the Middle Ages. At the very least, the personal dignity of the believer and of his hearer, to say nothing of the faith itself, precludes techniques that might be tolerable in a salesman or a recruiting sergeant and much the more bribery or terrorism; the medieval experience has shown, in an infinitely less exacting atmosphere, how fragile a faith is induced by measures redolent of compulsion.

Excommunication

With the mention of our religious fragmentation, it seems right to advert to the device of excommunication that played so notable a role in medieval legislation on the Jews. The conception that a community has the right and duty to exclude from its membership those who persistently and seriously impugn the congregation's consensus on the faith is common to Jews and to Christians because the latter learned it from the former. In one form or another, excommunication is the obverse of admission into any intelligibly structured society, and it is inconceivable that a community, united precisely by its shared faith, should not maintain the self-discipline that censures the distortion of its creed and extrudes the recalcitrant communicant. Whatever the views of religious formations united on grounds less susceptible to communication and formulation, neither the medieval synagogue nor the church of the popes ever questioned the communal judgment of dogma and of the believer. The Jew who would give credit to an idol, or the Christian who would deny resurrection, is in some way already excluded from his religious fellowship; in such cases, formal excommunication does little but render formal what the excommunicate has himself chosen.

Quite apart from evident abuses of this device, there are souls for whom it is repulsive; Simone Weil, for instance, deplored the formula in which Church councils, borrowing terminology as well as inspiration from the Hebrew Scriptures, proscribe the man deficient in the faith: "If anyone should say . . . let him be anathema"; no longer an observant Jew, she had not become a Catholic. Her human sympathy for the errant believer and his plight retains full value, even though it must be remarked that the Middle Ages, Jewish or Christian, would have found her scruples incomprehensible. No doubt medieval theologians often went well beyond the evidence in their virile confidence in their science, and thus they have been excessive in speaking of heresy and of excommunication, above all in a society that added civil penalties to condemnation for failures against the faith. But both excommunication and the faith it was invoked to protect proceed in principle from positive allegiance to the Word of God, and not from a thirst for violence and vengeance. To see excommunication as a response to what was conceived to be a culpable betrayal of the faith is far from defending every use that has been made of this canonical penalty, but to envision it in any other way is to render the conception unintelligible because false.

Usury

Like excommunication, usury provoked legislation during the Middle Ages that is now a stone of stumbling to the men of our day. By an equivocation on the term "nature," difficult to qualify as guileless, it is claimed that, since medieval theory on the nature of charges for the use of money, that complex human artefact, is held to apply no longer in the modern fiscal world, medieval convictions as to the nature of man must be equally reformable. However this may be, papal texts on usury give the impression that they fall within the general contemporary consensus that the practice of charging interest for the use of money was a suspicious one, easily subject to abuse, but not always to be denied tolerance. It should be remarked, too, that the practice was not confined to Jewish moneylenders. Unlike other aspects of Christian legislation concerned with Jews, that on usury is not a title on which the decisive word was spoken by popes. The most common concern of the popes with usury was to establish a kind of bounty to encourage enlistment in the Crusade. To grant exemptions and advantages in the name of the total community to those who risk their lives in its defense is, of course, not confined to the Middle Ages; the most striking parallels can be cited in our own recurrent wars.

Other papal decrees on usury and usurers are those issued for papal territories, and these tell us less of what popes thought of Jews than of what all medieval rulers thought of interest charges on borrowed money. In our own more sophisticated economy, the protection of the unwary and the desperate still demands laws to control interest rates, and the efforts of medieval theologians and canonists, reflected in papal decrees, bear the marks of pioneer work. Medieval doctrine on the morality of usury was the work of scholars, of the *viri scholastici*; its triumphs and failures are not those of the popes.

The Mystery of Israel

The most obscure of all elements in the chronicle of the Jews is the intervention of what we can only call the demonic, sinister counter-theme of the Providence that has so often rescued Jewish survivors when all human hope seemed lost. Can the tragic history of the Jews be understood apart from a senseless malice, only the more evil because so often cloaked in the trappings of religious zeal? Salomo bar Simeon thought it right to introduce episodes of the 1096 massacres in the Rhineland and the French persecutions of 1104 with a phrase from the Book of Job (2 : 1): "Satan came."[27] The pretended zeal of Count Emicho and his ruffians made of those wretches classic human collaborators with the father of lies and ape of God.

Medieval Christians were often puzzled by the tenacity and courage of Jewish resistance, for the persecuted communities often enough fought back against the most overpowering odds: "Each of the men of Israel girded himself with his weapon," wrote Salomo bar Simeon, and we have seen him ascribe their unsuccess to their own sins: "But our sins were the reason that the enemy triumphed, and took the tower."[28] Diabolic hatred and offenses against the Divine Law seemed to him the last explanation of Jewish disasters; our Christian faith assures us that the mighty deeds of God with respect to Israel will not cease until time and history have reached their term.

Obscurities, historical and theological, are not the only reason for abstaining from an anticipation of the Last Judgment by registering personal evaluations of the popes who dealt with the Jews in the Middle Ages. Whether it was a benign or a tyrannical dispensation that put popes in a position to exercise politically supported power over the Jews is a part of the infinitely broader question of the two Cities men construct for time and for eternity. The vestiges of the Jewish-papal encounter must be taken into account if the larger question is to be weighed, but it is not to be hoped that the whole might be discovered within this part. Without presuming to sit in judgment on the conscientious successes and failures of medieval popes, we must insist that they and their public policies be taken in the context of their own times. Thus, the popes of any generation can be compared justifiably with their contemporaries; as Pius XII might be juxtaposed with Churchill, Einstein, and Stalin for a rough evaluation of his career and its human value, so Innocent III is better understood when we remember that his world was that of Frederick II, Saint Francis of Assisi, and John Lackland; Gelasius I is illumined by comparison with Clovis, Theodoric, and Boethius.

On this norm, it is undeniable that the file of Roman pontiffs has been an eminent succession. Men of our race, the popes have needed redemption and the divine mercy that the prophets have taught us to implore; small profit in our taking the role of devil's advocate to inquire into the sins of our fathers. Their humanity is sufficiently obvious, and no Jew will misunderstand my option to emulate Sem and Japheth, to leave to others the ignoble amusement of Cham.

NOTES

Chapter I

1. H. H. Graetz, *History of the Jews* (Philadelphia, The Jewish Publication Society of America, 1945; first English trans. of this influential work, 1891), I, 33–34.
2. V. Petra, *Commentaria ad constitutiones apostolicas seu bullas singulas summorum pontificum* (Venice, Typographia Balleoniana 1741), III, 256, number 6: Verum posse Judaeos, sicut et alios Infideles, cogi ad audiendam Praedicationem Evangelii, docent communiter Canonistae, et Theologi.
3. Graetz, *op. cit.*, III, 25; cf. the more temperate remarks of S. Grayzel, *The Church and the Jews in the XIIIth Century* (Philadelphia, Dropsie College, 1933), p. 81.
4. G. Gordon, *Medium Aevum and the Middle Age* (Oxford, The Clarendon Press, 1925), for an indispensable discussion of this term, including the usage of Augustine.
5. J. R. Marcus, *The Jew in the Mediaeval World* (Cincinnati, Sinai Press, 1938), p. 3.
6. Graetz, *op. cit.*, I, 33; Grayzel, *op. cit.*, p. 81; S. Baron, *A Social and Religious History of the Jews* (New York, Columbia University Press, 1957–1960), IV, 7; E. Rodocanachi, *Le saint-siège et les juifs* (Paris, Firmin-Didot, 1891), p. 5.
7. See his *Introduction aux devoirs des coeurs*, trans. A. Chouraqui (Paris, n.d.), pp. 78, 106–107, and the notes of the editor given there.
8. *Hebräische Berichte über die Judenverfolgungen während der Kreuzzüge*, herausgegeben von A. Neubauer und M. Stern, in Deutsche übersetzt von S. Baer (Berlin, Verlag von L. Simion, 1892), pp. xxviii–xxix (remarks of H. Bresslau).
9. I. S. Révah, "Les Marranes," *Revue des études juives*, 3e série, 1959–1960, I (CXVIII), pp. 29–77, esp. pp. 30–31.
10. *Tractatus de erroribus Abaelardi*, J. P. Migne, *Patrologiae cursus completus, series latina* (henceforth abbreviated *PL*, Paris: Garnier-Migne, 1844 ff), 182, 1055 A–1061 B.

11. *Epistola* 28, *PL*, 189, 113 A.
12. *Cartulaire général de l'ordre des Hospitaliers de Saint Jean de Jérusalem*, J. Delaville le Roulx (Paris, E. Leroux, 1894), I, 85, number 95.
13. *Veterum scriptorum et monumentorum . . . amplissima collectio*, E. Martene et U. Durand (Paris, Montalant, 1724), I, 1235–1236.

Chapter II

1. *Theodosiani libri xvi cum constitutionibus Sirmondianis et leges novellae ad Theodosianum pertinentes*, eds. Th. Mommsen et Paulus M. Meyer, 2 vols. (Berlin, Weidmann, 1905).
2. *Corpus iuris civilis*, Vol. I: *Iustiniani institutiones*, ed. Paulus Krueger, et *Iustiniani digesta*, eds. Th. Mommsen et Paulus Krueger (Berlin, Weidmann, 1922), Vol. II: *Codex Iustinianus*, ed. Paulus Krueger (Berlin, Weidmann, 1915), Vol. III: *Novellae*, eds. Rudolfus Schoell et Guilelmus Kroll (Berlin, Weidmann, 1895).
3. For anti-pagan legislation, see *Theodosiani* 16, 10, 1–25, I, 897–905; temples escaped demolition for a time as cultural monuments, 16, 10, 3, decree of A.D. 342, but later (A.D. 435) were condemned to destruction, 16, 10, 25; idols were preserved thanks to their artistic value, but all pagan worship was proscribed, 16, 10, 1 ff.; the sole legal protection afforded pagans was defense against Christian zealots, a defense in which the Jews also shared and which was limited to those cases in which Jew or pagan had not contravened the law, 16, 10, 24.
4. *Theodosiani* 16, 11, 1, I, 905: Quotiens de religione agitur, episcopos convenit agitare; ceteras vero causas, quae ad ordinarios cognitores vel ad usum publici iuris pertinent, legibus oportet audiri (20 August 399).
5. Saint Ambrose, to be sure, succeeded in wringing consent from the Emperor Theodosius I to his view that Christians who had burned a synagogue at Kallinicum in A.D. 388 ought not to be compelled to rebuild it, but he barely succeeded, and the contrast between the attitudes of Saint Ambrose and Saint Gregory the Great provoked interesting, if not very convincing, attempts at reconciliation; for the apposite texts and for such an attempt to reconcile them, see *Annales ecclesiastici Caesaris Baronii*, cura Od. Raynaldi et Jacobi Laderchii, et ad nostra usque tempora perducti ab Augustino

Theiner . . . (Barri-Ducis: L. Guerin, Parisiis: H. Lagny 1864–1883), sub anno 388, VI, 20–23, numbers 82–92.

6. *Theodosiani* 16, 8, 9, I, 889: Iudaeorum sectam nulla lege prohibitam satis constat. Unde graviter commovemur interdictos quibusdam locis eorum fuisse conventus. Sublimis igitur magnitudo tua hac iussione suscepta nimietatem eorum, qui sub Christianae religionis nomine inlicita quaeque praesumunt et destruere synagogas adque expoliare conantur, congrua severitate cohibebit. Cf. *ibid.*, statutes 21, 25.

7. An instance of the mitigation of the severity of pagan law on Christian principles is visible in the restriction of torture and of corporal punishment during Lent: *Theodosiani* 9, 35, 4 and 5; Isaurian brigands were denied this grace on somewhat questionable theological reasoning: *ibid.*, 7, I, 491: Provinciarum iudices moneantur, ut in Isaurorum latronum quaestionibus nullum quadragensimae nec venerabilem pascharum diem existiment excipiendum, ne differatur sceleratorum proditio consiliorum quae per latronum tormenta quaerenda est, cum facillime in hoc summi numinis speretur venia, per quod multorum salus et incolumitas procuratur; crucifixion, it should be noted, still had its place in a decree of Constantine himself, *ibid.*, 9, 5, 1, I, 443–444, Ad legem Iuliam maiestatis.

8. *Codex Iustinianus* 1, 9, 8, II, 61: Iudaei Romano communi iure viventes in his causis, quae tam ad superstitionem eorum quam ad forum et leges ac iura pertinent, adeant sollemni more iudicia omnesque Romanis legibus conferant et excipiant actiones. Si qui vero ex his communi pactione ad similitudinem arbitrorum apud Iudaeos in civili dumtaxat negotio putaverint litigandum, sortiri eorum iudicium iure publico non vetentur. Eorum etiam sententias iudices exsequantur, tamquam ex sententia cognitoris arbitri fuerint attributi.

9. *Ibid.* 1, 9, 17, II, 62: Iudaeorum primates, qui in utriusque Palestinae synedriis nominantur vel in aliis provinciis degunt, periculo suo anniversarium canonem de synagogis omnibus palatinis compellantibus exigant ad eam formam, quam patriarchae quondam coronarii auri nomine postulabant: et hoc, quod de occidentalibus partibus patriarchis conferri consueverat, nostris largitionibus inferatur.

10. *Theodosiani* 16, 8, 2, I, 887: Qui devotione tota synagogis Iudaeorum, patriarchis vel presbyteris se dederunt et in memorata secta degentis legi ipsi praesident, immunes ab omnibus tam personalibus quam civilibus, muneribus perseverent, ita ut illi, qui iam forsitan decuriones sunt, nequaquam ad prosecutiones aliquas destinentur, cum oporteat istiusmodi homines a locis in quibus sunt nulla conpelli ratione discedere. Hi autem, qui minime curiales sunt, per-

petua decurionatus immunitate potiantur. Cf. *ibid.* 16, 8, 4, I,
887: Hiereos et archisynagogos et patres synagogorum et
caeteros, qui synagogis deserviunt, ab omni corporali munere
liberos esse praecipimus.

11. *Ibid.* 16, 8, 11, I, 889: Si quis audeat inlustrium patriarcharum contumeliosam per publicum facere mentionem, ultionis
sententia subiugetur.

12. *Ibid.* 16, 8, 13, I, 890: Iudaei sint obstricti caerimonis suis:
nos interea in conservandis eorum privilegiis veteres imitemur,
quorum sanctionibus definitum est, ut privilegia his, qui
inlustrium patriarcharum dicioni subiecti sunt, archisynagogis
patriarchisque ac presbyteris ceterisque, qui in eius religionis
sacramento versantur, nutu nostri numinis perseverent ea,
quae venerandae Christianae legis primis clericis sanctimonia
deferuntur. Id enim et divi principes, Constantinus et Constantius, Valentinianus et Valens divino arbitrio decreverunt.
Sint igitur etiam a curialibus muneribus alieni pareantque
legibus suis.

13. *Ibid.* 12, 1, 99, I, 687: Iussio, qua sibi Iudaeae legis homines
blandiuntur, per quam eis curalium munerum datur im-
munitas, rescindatur, cum ne clericis quidem liberum sit
prius se divinis ministeriis mancipare, quam patriae debita
universa persolvant. Quisquis igitur vero deo dicatus est,
alium instructum facultatibus suis ad munera pro se complenda constituat; for the same decree in briefer form, see
Codex Iustinianus 1, 9, 5, II, 61; the revocation of the privilege of Christian clerics to which reference is made:
Theodosiani 16, 2, 21, I, 841–842: Ii, qui ecclesiae iuge
obsequium deputarunt, curiis habeantur immunes, si tamen
eas ante ortum imperii nostri ad cultum se legis nostrae
contulisse constiterit: ceteri revocentur, qui se post id tempus
ecclesiasticis congregarunt.

14. *Codex Iustinianus* 1, 9, 13, II, 61–62: Die sabbato ac reliquis
sub tempore, quo Iudaei cultus sui reverentiam servant,
neminem aut facere aliquid aut ulla ex parte conveniri debere
praecipimus (ita tamen, ut nec illis detur licentia eodem die
Christianos orthodoxos convenire, ne Christiani forte ex inter-
pellatione Iudaeorum ab officialibus praefatis diebus aliquam
sustineant molestiam), cum fiscalibus commodis et litigiis
privatorum constat reliquos dies posse sufficere.

15. *Theodosiani* 16, 8, 27, I, 894: Quae nuper de Iudaeis et
synagogis eorum statuimus, firma permaneant: scilicet ut nec
novas umquam synagogas permittantur extruere nec aufer-
endas sibi veteres pertimescant. Cetera vero vetita in
posterum sciant esse servanda, quemadmodum nuper constitutionis latae forma declarat. . . .

16. *Ibid.* 16, 8, 25, I, 893–894: Placet in posterum nullas omnino

synagogas Iudaeorum vel auferri passim vel flammis exuri et si quae sunt post legem recenti molimine vel ereptae synagogae vel ecclesiis vindicatae aut certe venerandis mysteriis consecratae, pro his loca eis, in quibus possint extruere, ad mensuram videlicet sublatarum, praeberi. Sed et donaria si qua sunt sublata, eisdem, si necdum sacris mysteriis sunt dedicata, reddantur, sin redhibitionem consecratio veneranda non sinit, pro his eiusdem quantitatis pretium tribuatur. Synagogae de cetero nullae protinus extruantur, veteres in sua forma permaneant.

17. *Ibid.* 16, 8, 19, I, 891–892: Coelicolarum nomen inauditum quodammodo novum crimen superstitionis vindicavit. Ii nisi intra anni terminos ad dei cultum venerationemque Christianam conversi fuerint, his legibus, quibus praecepimus haereticos adstringi, se quoque noverint adtinendos. Certum est enim, quicquid a fide Christianorum discrepat, legi Christianae esse contrarium. Quam quidam adhuc, vitae suae etiam et iuris immemores, adtrectare ita audent, ut de Christianis quosdam foedum cogant taetrumque Iudaeorum nomen induere. Et quamvis qui haec admiserint, priscorum principum legibus iure damnati sint, non tamen paenitet saepius admonere, ne mysteriis Christianis inbuti perversitatem Iudaicam et alienam Romano imperio post Christianitatem cogantur arripere. Ac si quisquam id crediderit esse temptandum, auctores facti cum consciis ad poenam praeteritis legibus cautam praecipimus constringi, quippe cum gravius morte sit et inmitius caede, si quis ex Christiana fide incredulitate Iudaica polluatur. Et idcirco iubemus, ne ecclesiis quisquam nocens vel cuiusquam abducere fideli ac devota deo praeceptione sancimus, sub hac videlicet definitione, ut, si quisquam contra hanc legem venire temptaverit, sciat, se ad maiestatis crimen esse retinendum.

18. *Codex Iustinianus* 1, 9, 3, II, 61: Iudaeis et maioribus eorum et patriarchis volumus intimari, quod, si quis post hanc legem aliquem, qui eorum feralem fugerit sectam et ad dei cultum respexerit, saxis aut alio furoris genere, quod nunc fieri cognovimus, ausus fuerit attemptare, mox flammis dedendus est et cum omnibus suis participibus concremandus.

19. The text of this decree is given in a more extensive form in the collection of Theodosius (16, 8, 1, I, 887) and adds to the foregoing this sentence: Si quis vero ex populo ad eorum nefariam sectam accesserit et conciliabulis eorum se adplicaverit, cum ipsis poenas meritas sustinebit.

20. *Theodosiani* 16, 8, 5, I, 888: Eum, qui ex Iudaeo Christianus factus est, inquietare Iudaeos non liceat vel aliqua pulsare iniuria, pro qualitate commissi istiusmodi contumelia punienda.

21. *Ibid.* 16, 8, 28, I, 894–895: Si Iudaei vel Samaritae filius filiave seu nepos, unus aut plures, ad Christianae religionis lucem de tenebris propriae superstitionis consilio meliore migraverint, non liceat eorum parentibus, id est patri vel matri, avo vel aviae, exheredare vel in testamento silentio praeterire, vel minus aliquid eis relinquere, quam poterant, si ab intestato vocarentur, adipisci. . . .

22. *Ibid.* 16, 8, 7, I, 888: Si quis lege venerabili constituta ex Christiano Iudaeus effectus sacrilegis coetibus adgregetur, cum accusatio fuerit conprobata, facultates eius dominio fisci iussimus vindicari.

23. *Ibid.* 16, 8, 23, I, 893: Et veteribus et nostris sanctionibus constitutum est, cum propter evitationem criminum et pro diversis necessitatibus Iudaicae religionis homines obligatos ecclesiae se consortio sociare voluisse didicerimus, non id devotione fidei, sed obreptione simulandum fieri. Unde provinciarum iudices, in quibus talia commissa perhibentur, ita nostris famulatum statutis deferendum esse cognoscant, ut hos, quos neque constantia religiosae confessionis in hoc eodem cultu inhaerere perspexerint neque venerabilis baptismatis fide et mysteriis inbutos esse, ad legem propriam, quia magis Christianitati consulitur, liceat remeare.

24. *Ibid.* 16, 8, 18, I, 891: Iudaeos quodam festivitatis suae sollemni Aman ad poenae quondam recordationem incendere et sanctae crucis adsimulatam speciem in contemptum Christianae fidei sacrilega mente exurere provinciarum rectores prohibeant, ne iocis suis fidei nostrae signum inmisceant, sed ritus suos citra contemptum Christianae legis retineant, amissuri sine dubio permissa hactenus, nisi ab inlicitis temperaverint.

25. *Ibid.* 16, 8, 6, I, 888: Quod ad mulieres pertinet, quas Iudaei in turpitudinis suae duxere consortium in gynaeceo nostro ante versatas, placet easdem restitui gynaeceo idque in reliquum observari, ne Christianas mulieres suis iungant flagitiis vel, si hoc fecerint, capitali periculo subiugentur.

26. *Ibid.* 9, 7, 5, I, 448: Ne quis Christianam mulierem in matrimonio Iudaeus accipiat neque Iudaeae Christianus coniungium sortiatur. Nam si quis aliquid huiusmodi admiserit, adulterii vicem commissi huius crimen optinebat, libertate in accusandum publicis quoque vocibus relaxata. Cf. *ibid.* 3, 7, 2, I, 142.

27. *Codex Iustinianus* 1, 9, 7, II, 61: Nemo Iudaeorum morem suum in coniunctionibus retinebit nec iuxta legem suam nuptias sortiatur nec in diversa sub uno tempore coniugia conveniat.

28. *Theodosiani* 16, 9, 3, I, 896: Absque calumnia praecipimus Iudaeis dominis habere servos Christianos hac dumtaxat condicione permissa, ut propriam religionem eos servare permit-

tant. Ideoque iudices provinciarum fide publicationis inspecta
eorum insolentia noverint reprimendam, qui tempestivis
precibus insimulandos esse duxerint, omnesque subreptionis
fraudulenter elicitas vel eliciendas vacuandas esse censemus.
Si quis contra fecerit, velut in sacrilegum ultio proferatur.

29. *Ibid.* 16, 9, 4, I, 896–897, decree of A.D. 417, reinforced by
that of A.D. 423, *ibid.* 16, 9, 5, I, 897: Christiana mancipia
Iudaeorum nemo audeat comparare. Nefas enim aestimamus
religiosissimos famulos impiissimorum emptorum inquinari
dominio. Quod si quis hoc fecerit, statutae poenae absque
omni erit dilatione obnoxius.

30. *Ibid.* 3, 1, 5, I, 128: Ne quis omnino Iudaeorum Christianum
conparet servum neue ex Christiano Iudaicis sacramentis
adtaminet. Quod si factum publica indago conpererit, et servi
abstrahi debent et tales domini congruae atque aptae facinori
poenae subiaceant, addito eo, ut, si qui apud Iudaeos vel
adhuc Christiani servi vel ex Christianis Iudaei repperti
fuerint, soluto per Christianos conpetenti pretio ab indigna
servitute redimantur.

31. *Digesta* 48, 8, 11, I, 853: Circumcidere Iudaeis filios suos
tantum rescripto divi Pii permittitur: in non eiusdem religionis qui hoc fecerit, castrantis poena irrogatur . . . (Ad
legem Corneliam de sicariis et veneficiis).

32. *The Babylonian Talmud,* Translated by I. Epstein (London:
Soncino Press, 1935–52), Seder Nashim, Yebamoth II, 70*b*,
477: Might [it not be said:] As the [non]circumcision of one's
male children and slaves debars one from the eating of the
Paschal lamb . . . . Seder Mo'ed, Shabbath 135*b*, II, 681–
682: There is [a slave] born in his [master's] house who is
circumcised on the first [day], and there is one born in his
[master's] house who is circumcised on the eighth [day];
there is [a slave] bought with money who is circumcised on
the first [day] and there is [a slave] bought with money who
is circumcised on the eighth day . . . .

33. *Ibid.,* Giṭṭin 43*b*, 188: Our rabbis have taught: If a man
sells his slave to a heathen he gains his freedom, but he
[still] requires a deed of emancipation from his first master.
[NOTE: The deed required in the contingency that the ex-slave
wished to marry an Israelitish woman.]

34. *Ibid.,* Yebamoth I, 48*b*, 320: For it was taught: If one bought
a slave from an idolater, and the slave refused to be circumcised, he bears with him for twelve months. [If by that time]
he has not been circumcised, he resells him to idolaters.

35. *Theodosiani* 16, 9, 1, I, 895: Si quis Iudaeorum Christianum
manicipium vel cuiuslibet alterius sectae mercatus circumciderit, minime in servitute retineat circumcisum, sed libertatis
privilegiis, qui hoc sustinuerit, potiatur.

36. *Ibid.* 16, 9, 2, I, 896: Si aliquis Iudaeorum mancipium sectae alterius seu nationis crediderit conparandum, mancipium fisco protinus vindicetur: si vero emptum circumciderit, non solum mancipii damno multetur, verum etiam capitali sententia puniatur. Quod si venerandae fidei conscia mancipia Iudaeus mercari non dubitet, omnia, quae aput eum repperiuntur, protinus auferantur nec interponatur quicquam morae, quin eorum hominum qui Christiani sunt possessione careant.

37. *Codex Iustinianus* 1, 10, 2, II, 62.

38. *Ibid.* 1, 9, 16, II, 62: Iudaei et bonorum proscriptione et perpetuo exilio damnabuntur, si nostrae fidei hominem circumcidisse eos vel circumcidendum mandasse constiterit.

39. *Ibid.* 1, 9, 18 (19), II, 62: Hac victura in omne aevum lege sancimus neminem Iudaeorum quibus omnes administrationes et dignitates interdictae sunt, nec defensoris civitatis fungi saltem officio nec patris honorem adripere concedimus, ne adquisiti sibi officii auctoritate muniti adversus Christianos et ipsos plerumque sacrae religionis antistites velut insultantes fidei nostrae iudicandi vel pronuntiandi quamlibet habeant potestatem. Illud etiam pari consideratione rationis arguentes praecipimus, ne qua Iudaica synagoga in novam fabricam surgat, fulciendi veteres permissa licentia, quae ruinam minatur. Quisquis igitur vel infulas ceperit, quaesitis dignitatibus non potiatur, vel si ad officia vetita subrepserit, his penitus repelletur, vel si synagogam extruxerit, compendio catholicae ecclesiae noverit se laborasse: et quid ad honores et dignitates inrepserit, habeatur, ut antea, condicionis extremae, etsi honorariam illicite promeruerit dignitatem: et qui synagogae fabricam ceperit non studio reparandi, cum damno auri quinquaginta librarum fraudetur ausibus suis. Cernat praeterea bona sua proscripta, mox poenae sanguinis destinandus, qui fidem alterius expugnavit perversa doctrina.

40. *Ibid.* 1, 9, 15, II, 62: Si qua inter Christianos et Iudaeos sit contentio, non a senioribus Iudaeorum, sed ab ordinariis iudicibus dirimatur.

41. *Theodosiani* 16, 8, 16, I, 890: Iudaeos et Samaritanos, qui sibi agentum in rebus privilegio blandiuntur, omni militia privandos esse censemus.

42. *Ibid.* 16, 8, 24, I, 893: In Iudaica superstitione viventibus adtemptandae de cetero militiae aditus obstruatur. Quicumque igitur vel inter agentes in rebus vel inter palatinos militiae sacramenta sortiti sunt, percurrendae eius et legitimis stipendiis terminandae remittimus facultatem, ignoscentes facto potius quam faventes, in posterum vero non liceat quod in praesenti paucis volumus relaxari. Illos autem, qui gentis huius perversitate devincti armatam probantur adpetisse militiam, absolvi cingulo sine ambiguitate decernimus, nullo

veterum meritorum patrocinante suffragio. Sane Iudaeis liberalibus studiis institutis exercendae advocationis non intercludimus libertatem et uti eos curalium munerum honore permittimus, quem praerogativa natalium et splendore familiae sortiuntur. Quibus cum debeant ista sufficere, interdictam militiam pro nota non debent aestimare.

43. *Novellae* 146, 1, III, 715: Sancimus igitur licentiam esse volentibus Hebraeis et synagogas suas, in quem Hebraei omnino locum sunt, per Graecam vocem sacros libros legere convenientibus et patria forte lingua (hac dicimus) et aliis simpliciter, locis translatis lingua et per ipsius lectionis, per quam clara sunt quae dicuntur convenientibus omnibus deinceps, et secundum haec vivere et conversari; et non fiduciam esse his qui apud eos sunt expositoribus solam Hebraicam tradentibus malignari hanc, quemadmodum voluerint, multorum ignorantia suam eis abscondentes malam consuetudinem. Verumtamen hi qui per Graecam legunt septuaginta utantur traditione, quae omnibus certior et ab aliis melior iudicata, praecipue propter quod interpretatione contigit, quia et per multos divisos et per diversa interpretantes loca tamen unam omnes tradiderunt compositionem. . . . *Ibid.* 716: Non tamen tamquam eis residuas excludere sanxerimus interpretationes, licentiam damus et Aquilae uti, vel si alienae tribus ille et non competentem in aliquibus sermonibus habet a septuaginta interpretatione dissonantiam. Eam vero quae ab eis dicitur secunda editio interdicimus, utpote sacris non coniunctam libris neque desuper traditam de prophetis, sed inventionem constitutam virorum, ex sola loquentibus terra et divinum in ipsis habentibus nihil.

44. *Novellae* 3, II, 7–11.

45. *Codex Iustinianus* 1, 9, 14, II, 62: Nullus tamquam Iudaeus, cum sit innocens, obteratur nec expositum cum ad contumeliam religio qualiscumque perficiat: non passim eorum synagogae vel habitacula concrementur vel perperam sine ulla ratione laedantur, cum alioquin, etiam si sit aliquis sceleribus implicitus, idcirco tamen iudiciorum vigor iurisque publici tutela videtur in medio constituta, ne quisquam sibi ipse permittere valeat ultionem. Sed ut hoc Iudaeorum personis volumus esse provisum, ita illud quoque monendum esse censemus, ne Iudaei forsitan insolescant elatique sui securitate quicquam praeceps in Christianae reverentiam cultionis admittant.

46. *Theodosiani* 16, 5, 46, I, 870: Ne Donatistae vel caeterorum vanitas haereticorum aliorumque eorum, quibus catholicae communionis cultus non potest persuaderi, Iudaei adque gentiles, quos vulgo paganos appellant, arbitrentur legum ante adversum se datarum constituta tepuisse, noverint iudices

universi praeceptis earum fideli devotione parendum et inter praecipua curarum quidquid adversus eos decrevimus non ambigant exequendum. . . .

Chapter III

1. *Epistola VIII* ad Anastasium imperatorem, *PL* 59, 42 A–B: Duo quippe sunt, imperator Auguste, quibus principaliter mundus hic regitur: auctoritas sacra pontificum, et regalis potestas. In quibus tanto gravius est pondus sacerdotum, quanto etiam pro ipsis regibus Domino in divino reddituri sunt examine rationem.

2. See Gerd Tellenbach, *Church, State and Christian Society at the Time of the Investiture Contest*, trans. R. F. Bennett (Oxford, B. Blackwell, 1940), pp. 12, 13, on the conception of *auctoritas* and *potestas* in juridical and patristic thought.

3. *PL* 59, 131 D–132 A: . . . ut Judas apostolus qui praevaricando, quod est appellatus amisit, sicut idem èt discipulus dictus est, cum quidem nec Christi discipulus esset, sed potius diaboli, sicut de eo dictum est: *Unus ex vobis diabolus est* [John 6 : 71], quod diaboli esset operarius . . . ex parte totum saepius nuncupatur: sicut et tunc homo Juda cum totam gentem procul dubio nominaret.

4. *PL, 59*, 107 C: . . . sic etiam de gente Judaeorum a Deo etiam per Isaiam prophetam peremptorie veluti pronuntiatum est: *Claude oculos tuos . . . ne umquam convertantur, et sanem illos* [Isa. 6 : 10]. Hic etiam correctio et emendatio interdicta monstratur, et resipiscendi quoque spes prorsus abscinditur. De quo tamen populo apostolos et Ecclesiam primitivam novimus processisse, et mille hominum una die baptismate fuisse salvata [Acts 2 : 41].

5. *PL* 59, 120 C: Ne tamen usquequaque propositum fidele demergat; ac ne forsitan, ut solent quidam vanis opinionibus arbitrari, quod haec B[eatus] apostolus Paulus sub alterius nescio cujus persona pronuntiet, quam de seipso fateatur; quamvis nihil illic tale valeat prorsus ostendi, tamen cum ait: *Miser ego homo, quis me liberabit de corpore mortis hujus? Gratia Dei per Jesum Christum* [Rom. 7 : 24], tam gentilis, quam Judaei remota probetur esse persona. . . .

6. *PL* 59, 103 A–B: . . . Sanctus Petrus primus apostolorum, sic existimans Novi Testamenti gratiam praedicandam, ut a legis veteris non recederet institutis, quaedam per simulationem legitur inter Judaeos gentilesque gessisse. Numquid ideo aut

illa ejus sequenda sunt, quae merito et coapostolus ejus facta redarguit, postea consequenter ipsa vitavit, pariterque assumenda sunt cum his quae (ut pote primus apostolus) salubria praedicavit?

7. Gelasius Quinigesio Episcopo, *Ut Judaei conversi honorentur, PL* 59, 146 C: Vir clarissimus Telesinus, quamvis Judaicae credulitatis videatur, talem se nobis approbare contendit, ut merito nostrum appellare debeamus; qui pro Antonio parente suo specialiter postulavit ut eum dilectioni tuae commendare debeamus; et ideo fratrem supradictum voluntatis nostrae mandatorumque respectu ita te habere convenit ut non solum in nullo penitus opprimatur, verum etiam in quo ei opus fuerit tuae se gaudeat dilectione adjutum.

8. H. Voegelstein, *Rome*, trans. M. Hadas (Philadelphia, 1940), III; see also S. Baron, *op. cit.*, III, 27.

9. *PL* 59, 146 D–147 A: Judas, qui Judaicae professionis exstitit mancipium, juris sui quod ante paucos annos se asserit comparasse, nunc ad ecclesiam Venefranam confugisse suggessit, sicut petitorii tenor annexus ostendit, eo quod dicat sibi ab infantia Christiano nuper a praefato domino signaculum circumcisionis infixum. Quapropter diligenter vestra inter utrumque sollicitudo rerum fideliter examinet veritatem, quatenus nec religio temerata videatur, nec servus hac obsectione mentitus competentis jura domini declinare contendat.

10. See above, Chap. II, nn. 31–38.

11. This has been done: S. Katz, "Pope Gregory the Great and the Jews," *The Jewish Quarterly Review*, XXIV (1933–1934), 113–136.

12. The letters of Pope Gregory I are cited according to book and number, as collected in the *Monumenta Germaniae Historica, Epistolarum*, Vols. I and II (henceforth abbreviated *MGH*); this line is from IX, 195, vol. II, p. 183: quia hoc maxime tempore, quando de hoste formido est, divisum habere populum non debetis.

13. *Ibid.*, VIII, 23, vol. II, p. 24: . . . quia et temporis qualitas propter eam quae saevit cladem impellit . . . .

14. *Ibid.*, XIII, 3, vol. II, p. 368, is a representative instance of the usage.

15. As is well known, the terms *perfidia* and *perfidus* as applied to Judaism and to Jews have long been discussed, owing especially to their presence in the Good Friday liturgy until removed by Pope John XXIII; although this is not the place to prolong the debate on their significance, their frequent incidence in papal documents forbids us to ignore the problem. The following bibliographical references will assist the reader in acquainting himself with modern views on the

meaning of these terms, and some instances of their use with respect to groups other than Jews are added: Erik Peterson, *Le mystère des juifs et de gentiles dans l'église* (Paris, 1935); John M. Oesterreicher, "Pro Perfidis Judaeis," *Theological Studies*, VIII (March, 1947), 80–96; B. Blumenkranz, "Perfidia," *Archivum latinitatis medii aevi*, XXII (1951–1952), 156–170; Kathryn Sullivan, "Pro Perfidis Judaeis," *The Bridge*, II (1956–1957), 212–223; St. Ambrose applied the terminology to Arians, *Expositio in ps. 118*, 22, 10, *Corpus scriptorum ecclesiasticorum Latinorum* (Vienna, Prague: F. Tempsky, Leipzig: G. Freytag, 1913), 42, 493; Pope Hadrian I, *PL* 96, 1215, to the Longobard nation; Innocent III, Mansi *Sacrorum conciliorum nova et amplissima collectio* (Florence: A. Zatta, 1759–1798), XXII, 957, to the Saracens; B. Guidonis, *Practica Inquisitionis* (Paris: Picard, 1886), 3, 33, p. 132, to the heretics, styled *boni homines* and *boni christiani*; see Blumenkranz, *op. cit.*, p. 156, on distinction between the "sens strictement moral ou civil" (i.e., treachery) and the "sens religieux" (i.e., disbelief). My only comment is that in the texts that follow the second sense predominates, but the first cannot have been far from the mind of Latin speakers; furthermore, since both Judaism and Christianity are religions of covenant, any deficiency in religious faith is in some way a violation of trust as well as a failure to assent to dogmatic propositions.

16. *MGH*, I, 45, vol. I, p. 72; I, 69, vol. I, p. 89.
17. In Roman civil law "superstitio" is the technical term for Judaism as well as for other religions outside the official cult, v.g., *Codex Iustinianus* 1, 9, 8, II, 61; see above, Chap. II, n. 8.
18. *MGH*, III, 37, vol. I, p. 195: . . . ne quod absit Christiana religio Iudaeis subdita polluatur; . . . sacrilega seductione deceperit . . .
19. *Ibid.*, IV, 31, vol. I, p. 267.
20. *Dialogorum* III, 7, *PL* 77, 229 B–232 C.
21. *XL Homiliarum in ev.* II, 22, *PL* 76, 1176 D: Postquam intravit Petrus, ingressus est et Joannes. Posterior intravit qui prior venerat. Notandum, fratres, est quod in fine mundi ad Redemptoris fidem etiam Judaea colligetur, Paulo attestante . . . .
22. *Moralium* XXIX, in cap. 38 B. Job, *PL* 76, 481 C–D: Judaea igitur, circa veritatis notitiam, etiam cum servire videretur, sicut vestimentum stetit, quia per exteriora mandata servire se Domino ostendit, sed adhaerere ei per charitatis intelligentiam noluit . . . .
23. *Moralium* XVIII, in cap. 28 B. Job, XXIX, 38, XXXIII, 40, XXVII, 37, *PL* 76, 62 C, 505 D, 673 B, 428 B.

24. *Moralium* XXXV, 42, *PL* 76, 772 A–C: Agnoscamus ergo in ovibus fideles atque innocentes ex Judaea populos, legis dudum pascuis satiatos. Agnoscamus in camelis ad fidem simplices ex gentilitate venientes, qui prius sub ritu sacrilego, quasi quadam de formitate membrorum, valde turpes ostensi sunt, videlicet foeditate vitiorum . . . possunt rursum in bobus Israelitae accipi, quasi jugo legis attriti; asinis vero, ut dictum est, gentiles populi designari, qui dum se colendis lapidibus inclinabant, non reluctante mente, quasi dorso stulte supposito, quibuslibet idolis bruto sensu serviebant.

25. *MGH*, XIII, 3, vol. II, p. 368: . . . in order to recall the exterior rite of the Law . . . (. . . ut exteriorem ritum legis revocet . . .).

26. See 1 Cor. 7 : 21–24; Gal. 3 : 28, 4 : 7; Eph. 6 : 5–9; Col. 3 : 11; and, in a more concrete sense, Philemon.

27. *Regula pastoralis* 3, 5, *PL* 77, 56 C: Aliter admonendi sunt servi, atque aliter domini. Servi scilicet, ut in se semper humilitatem conditionis aspiciant; domini vero, ut naturae suae qua aequaliter sunt cum servis conditi, memoriam non amittant; we ought to remark on Gregory's juxtaposition of the two senses of *condere-conditio,* the human and temporal arrangements of society and the creative gift of nature, equally dispensed to all men.

28. Gal. 3 : 23–29.

29. *MGH*, III, 37, vol. I, p. 195: . . . Fertur siquidem quod Nasas, quidam sceleratissimus Iudeorum, sub nomine beati Heliae altare punienda temeritate contruxerit multosque illic Christianorum ad adorandum sacrilega seductione deceperit. Sed et Christiana ut dicitur mancipia comparavit et suis ea obsequiis ac utilitatibus deputavit. Dum igitur severissime in eum pro tantis facinoribus debuisset ulcisci, gloriosus Iustinus, medicamento avaritiae ut nobis scriptum est delinitus, Dei distulit iniuriam vindicare. Gloria autem vestra haec omnia districta examinatione perquirat . . . .

30. *Ibid.,* IV, 21, vol. I, pp. 255–256: . . . Oportebat quippe te respectu loci tui atque christianae religionis intuitu nullam relinquere occasionem, ut superstitioni Iudaicae simplices animae, non tam suasionibus, quam potestatis iure, quodammodo deservirent. Quamobrem hortamur fraternitatem tuam, ut secundum piissimarum legum tramitem, nulli Iudaeo liceat Christianum mancipium in suo retinere dominio . . . .

31. *Ibid.,* IX, 213, vol. II, p. 200: . . . Quid enim sunt Christiani omnes nisi membra Christi? Quorum videlicet membrorum caput cuncti novimus, quia fideliter honoratis. Sed quam diversum sit, excellentia vestra perpendat, caput honorare et membra ipsius hostibus calcanda permittere. Atque ideo petimus, ut excellentiae vestrae constitutio de regno suo

huius pravitatis mala removeat, ut in hoc vos amplius dignas cultrices omnipotentis Domini demonstretis, quod fideles illius ab inimicis eius absolvitis.

32. *Ibid.*, IX, 215, vol. II, pp. 201–203.

33. *Ibid.*, IX, 228, vol. II, pp. 221–225.

34. *Ibid.*, VI, 30, vol. I, p. 408: Res ad nos omnino detestabilis et legibus inimica pervenit, quae, si vera est, fraternitatem tuam vehementer accusat, quia eam de minori sollicitudine probat esse culpabilem. Comperimus autem, quod Samaraei degentes Catanae pagana mancipia emerint atque ea circumcidere ausu temerario praesumpserint . . . si ita reppereris, mancipia ipsa sine mora in libertatem modis omnibus vindica et ecclesiasticam eis tuitionem impende nec quicquam dominos eorum de pretio quolibet modo recipere patiaris: qui non solum hoc damno multandi, sed etiam alia erant poena de legibus feriendi.

35. *Ibid.*, VIII, 21, vol. II, pp. 22–23; the text of the phrase quoted is: nec ratio legis nec reverentia religionis admittat.

36. *Ibid.*, VII, 21, vol. I, p. 464; the text quoted is: omnino grave execrandumque est Christianos esse in servitio Iudaeorum.

37. *Ibid.*, VI, 29, vol. I, pp. 407–408.

38. *Ibid.*, IV, 9, vol. I, pp. 241–242: . . . Pervenit etiam ad nos, servos ancillasque Iudaeorum fidei causa ad ecclesiam refugientes aut infidelibus restitui dominis, aut eorum ne restituantur pretium dari. Hortamus igitur, ut nullatenus tam pravam consuetudinem manere permittas. Sed quilibet Iudaeorum servus ad venerabilia loca fidei causa confugerit, nullatenus eum patiamini praeiudicium sustinere. Sed sive olim Christianus, sive nunc fuerit baptizatus, sine ullo pauperum damno religioso ecclesiasticae pietatis patrocinio in libertatem modis omnibus defendatur.

39. *Ibid.*, IX, 104, vol. II, pp. 111–112.

40. *Ibid.*, IX, 195, vol. II, pp. 182–184; the lines quoted are: . . . sicut legalis definitio Iudaeos novas non patitur erigere synagogas, ita quoque eos sine inquietudine veteres habere permittit. Ne ergo suprascriptus Petrus vel alii qui ei in hac indisciplinationis pravitate praebuere solacium sive consensum hoc zelo fidei se fecisse respondeant, ut per hoc quasi eis necessitas fieret convertendi, ammonendi sunt atque scire debent, quia haec circa eos temperantia magis utenda est, ut trahatur ab eis velle, non ut ducantur inviti, quia scriptum est: "Voluntarie sacrificabo tibi"; item: "Et ex voluntate mea confitebor illi." . . .

41. This is not the opinion of the editors of the *MGH*, who postulate a "lost letter" to which they believe the second extant letter refers, arguing that the first letter does not deal with the Jews' psalmody (vol. I, p. 105, n. 1); a third letter

would make the interpretation of the two we possess easier, but these are coherent and history is seldom as tidy as historians may be pardoned for wishing it to be.

42. *Ibid.*, I, 34, vol. I, p. 48: . . . Sed si ita est, volumus, tua fraternitas ab huiusmodi se querela suspendat et ad locum, quem, sicut praediximus, cum tua conscientia quo congregentur adepti sunt, eos sicut mos fuit ibidem liceat convenire. Hos enim, qui a christiana religione discordant, mansuetudine, benignitate, admonendo, suadendo ad unitatem fidei necesse est congregare, ne quos dulcedo praedicationis et praeventus futuri iudicis terror ad credendum invitare poterat, minis et terroribus repellantur. Oportet ergo magis, ut ad audiendum de vobis verbum Dei benigne conveniant, quam austeritate quae supra modum extenditur, expavescant.

43. *Ibid.*, II, 6, vol. I, p. 105: . . . Praedictos vero Hebraeos gravari vel affligi contra rationis ordinem prohibemus. Sed sicut Romanis vivere legibus permittuntur, annuente iustitia actosque suos ut norunt nullo inpediente disponant.

44. *Ibid.*, VIII, 25, vol. II, p. 27: Sicut Iudaeos non debet esse licentia quicquam in synagogis suis ultra quam permissum est lege praesumere, ita in his quae eis concessa sunt nullum debent praeiudicium sustinere . . . . Cf. *Ibid.*, IX, 38, vol. II, p. 67: . . . sicut illis quicquam in synagogis suis facere et, ut ipsi prius scripsimus, ultra, quam lege decretum est, non debet esse licentia, ita eis contra iustitiam et aequitatis ordinem nec praeiudicium nec aliquod debet inferri dispendium.

45. *Ibid.*, IX, 38, vol. II, p. 67: . . . fratrem nostrum incongrue aliquid egisse . . . eas esse inconsulte ac temere consecratas . . . quod semel consecratum est Iudaeis non valet ultro restitui . . . .

46. *Ibid.*, I, 66, vol. I, 86–87: . . . Opilionem diaconem, sed et Servum-dei et Crescentium clericos Benafranae ecclesiae, oblitos timorem futuri iudicii, ministeria antefatae ecclesiae Hebreo cuidam quod dici nefas est vendidisse . . . memoratum Hebreum, qui oblitus vigorem legum . . . . Suprascriptos autem diaconem vel clericos, qui tantum nefas commiserunt, in poenitentia religare non differas, ut tale tantumque delictum suis lacrimis possint diluere.

47. *Ibid.*, I, 63, vol. I, p. 84: Sicut res ad ius ecclesiae pertinentes amittere non debemus, ita alienas appetere incivile esse nihilominus iudicamus.

48. *Ibid.*, IX, 40, vol. II, p. 68.

49. *Ibid.*, XIII, 15, vol. II, p. 383: see Appendix I for full text of this important letter, which became a part of medieval canon law: Gratian, *Decret.*, pars I, distinctio 45, canon 3, *Corpus iuris canonici*, eds. A. L. Richterus et A. Friedberg (Leipzig, 1879), vol. I, col. 160.

50. *MGH,* I, 69, vol. I, p. 89.
51. *Ibid.,* VII, 41, vol. I, p. 489: . . . quod dici nefas est, iniquitate maleficiorum eam laedere moliatur . . . .
52. *Ibid.,* II, 38, vol. I, pp. 133–139.
53. *Ibid.,* V, 7, vol. I, pp. 288–289: . . . Pervenit vero ad me esse Hebraeos in possessionibus nostris qui converti ad Deum nullatenus volunt. Sed videtur mihi, ut per omnes posses- siones, in quibus ipsi Hebraei esse noscuntur, epistolas trans- mittere debeas eis ex me specialiter promittens, quod quicumque ad verum Deum et Dominum nostrum Iesum Christum ex eis conversus fuerit, onus possessionis eius ex aliqua parte inminuetur . . . debet relaxatio fieri . . . ut et ei qui convertitur onus relevetur et ecclesiastica utilitas non gravi dispendio prematur. Nec hoc inutiliter facimus, si pro levandis pensionis oneribus eos ad Christi gratiam perduca- mus, quia, etsi ipsi minus fideliter veniunt, hi tamen qui de eis nati fuerint iam fidelius baptizantur. Aut seipsos ergo aut eorum filios lucramur . . . .
54. *IV Sent.,* d. 4, q. 9, number 1 (Vivès ed., vol. 16, p. 488*a*): Ergo maxime debet Princeps zelare pro dominio servando supremi Domini, scilicet Dei, et per consequens non solum licet, sed debet Princeps auferre parvulos a dominio parentum volentium eos educere contra cultum Dei, qui est supremus et honestissimus dominus, et debet eos applicare cultui divino . . . ; number 2 (*ibid.* p. 489*a*): Imo quod plus est, crederem religiose fieri si ipsi parentes cogerentur minis et terroribus ad suscipiendam Baptismum, et ad conservandum postea susceptum . . . .
55. See above, n. 38.
56. *MGH,* IV, 31, vol. I, pp. 266–267: Eis quos de Iudaica perditione Redemptor noster ad se dignatur convertere ration- abili nos oportet moderatione concurrere, ne victus quod absit inopiam patiantur. Ideoque tibi huius praecepti auctoritate mandamus, quatenus filiis Iustae Ex-Hebreis, id est Iulianae, Redempto et Fortunae, a tertia decima succedenti indictione annis singulis . . . solidos dare non differas, quos tuis noveris modis omnibus rationibus inputandos.
57. *Ibid.,* VIII, 23, vol. II, pp. 24–25: . . . Quibus tamen si longum vel triste videtur sollemnitatem sustinere paschalem et eos nunc ad baptisma festinare cognoscis, ne, quod absit, longa dilatio eorum retro possit animos revocare . . . aut die dominico aut, si celeberrima festivitas fortassis occurrerit, eos omnipotentis Dei misericordia protegente baptizet, quia et temporis qualitas propter eam quae saevit cladem impellit, ut desideria eorum nulla debeant dilatione differri. Quos- cumque vero ex eis pauperes et ad vestem sibi emendam non sufficere posse cognoscis, te eis vestem quam ad baptisma

habeant, comparare volumus ac praebere; in quibus pretium
quod dederis tuis noveris rationibus imputandum . . . .
58. *Ibid.*, I, 45, vol. I, p. 71–72: . . . multos consistentium in
illis partibus Iudaeorum vi magis ad fontem baptismatis quam
praedicatione perductos. Nam intentum quidem huiuscemodi
et laude dignum censeo et de Domini nostri descendere dilectione profiteor. Sed hanc eandum intentionem, nisi competens
scripturae sacrae comitetur effectus, timeo, ne aut mercedis
opus exinde non proveniat, aut iuxta aliquid animarum quas
eripi volumus quod absit dispendia subsequantur. Dum enim
quispiam ad baptismatis fontem non praedicationis suavitate,
sed necessitate pervenerit, ad pristinam superstitionem re-
means inde deterius moritur, unde renatus esse videbatur . . . .
Adhibendus ergo illis est sermo . . . et eorum quantos Deus
donaverit ac regenerationem novae vitae perducat.
59. *Ibid.*, III, 52, vol. I, pp. 208–209: Quid autem de episcopis,
qui verberibus timeri volunt, canones dicant, bene fraternitas
vestra novit. Pastores etenim facti sumus, non persecutores.
Et egregius Praedicator dicit: "Arguite, obsecra, increpa, cum
omni patientia et doctrina." Nova vero atque inaudita est
ista praedicatio, quae verberibus exigit fidem. See Gratian,
Decret., pars I, distinctio 45, canon 1, ed. cit., vol. I, col. 160.
60. *Ibid.*, XIII, 3, vol. II, pp. 367–368.

Chapter IV

1. Mansi, *op. cit.* . . . , vol. XII, col. 94 B–D: Pro nefandis
denique Judaeis infra fines regni nostri degentibus . . . hos
in transmarinis partibus Hebraeos alios consuluisse, ut
unanimiter contra genus Christianum agerent . . . ; col.
101 D–E: . . . plebs Judaeorum . . . qui per sua scelera
non solum statum ecclesiae perturbare maluerunt, verum
ausu tyrannico inferre conati sunt ruinam patriae ac populo
universo . . . .
2. *España Sagrada*, (Madrid: J. Rodriguez, 1879), vol. 10,
p. 578: Mauri Barcinoniam Judaeis prodentibus capiunt,
interfectisque pene omnibus Christianis, et urbe vastata impune redeunt . . . .
3. See *Koran* II, 105–113; III, 64–67; IV, 153–171; V, 5–19,
51–53, 65–76.
4. *Ibid.* V, 57.
5. *Ibid.* V, 82.
6. For an English translation of this text, see J. R. Marcus,

op. cit., pp. 13–15; for remarks on the significance of the Covenant, see James Kritzeck, "Jews, Christians, and Moslems," *The Bridge,* III (1958), 102, 109, n. 85.

7. V. Petra, *op. cit.,* vol. III, p. 249: Imo etsi Judaei cogi non possint ad suscipiendum Baptismum, tamen si de facto coacti illum suscipiant, adhuc sub poenis haereticorum resilire non possunt, nam licet coactus id fecerit, coactus tamen voluit; voluntas enim coacta, voluntas est . . . dummodo tamen coactio non fuerit absoluta, se praecisa, et omnimoda . . . . Si enim quis per vim non conditionatam, sed absolutam, Baptismum suscipiat, Christianus dici non potest, et consequenter uti talis ad Fidem servandam cogi nequit . . . .

8. See below, n. 12.

9. *Isidori Historia Gothorum, MGH,* AA, vol. XI, p. 291: . . . Sisebutus post Gundemarum regali fastigio evocatur, regnans annis VIII mensibus VI, qui in initio regni Judaeos ad fidem Christianam permovens aemulationem quidem habuit, sed non secundum scientiam: potestate enim conpulit, quos provocare fidei ratione oportuit.

10. *Epistola* 21, Sancti Braulionis, *PL* 80, 669 C: . . . Nam et ad nos perlatum est (quod tamen incredibile nobis, nec omnino creditum est) oraculis venerabilis Romani principis permissum esse Judaeis baptizatis reverti ad superstitionis suae religionis; quod quam falsum sit sanctimonia vestra melius novit.

11. Mansi, *op. cit.,* vol. XIII, cols. 428–429: Quoniam errantes hi qui ex Hebraeorum superstitione consistunt, subsannare se Christum Deum existimant, simulantes Christianizare, ipsum autem negant, clam et latenter sabbatizantes, et alia Judaeorum more facientes: definimus hos neque in communionem, neque in orationem, neque in ecclesiam suscipi; sed manifeste sint secundum religionem suam Hebraei: neque pueros eorum baptizari, neque servum emi vel acquiri. Si vero ex sincero corde ac fide converterit se quis eorum, et confessus fuerit ex toto corde, divulgans mores eorum et res, ut alii etiam arguantur et corrigantur, hunc suscipi et baptizari, et pueros ejus: quin et observari eos, ut recedant ab Hebraicis adinvenionibus, definimus: alias autem nullatenus admittendos.

12. Gratian, *Decretum,* pars I, distinctio 45, canon 5, Friedberg ed., vol. I, cols. 161–162; for this text of Gregory IV, see Appendix II.

13. *Epistola* 71, *PL* 98, 345 A–B: . . . multi dicentes catholicos se communem vitam gerentes cum Judaeis et non baptizatis paganis tam in escis quamque in potu, seu in diversis erroribus, nihil polluisse inquiunt; et illud quod inhibitum est, ut nulli liceat jugem ducere cum infidelibus . . . .

14. *Responsa Nicolai ad consulta Bulgarorum* [sic], *PL* 119,

1014 D: . . . A quodam Judaeo, nescitis utrum Christiano, an
pagano, multos in patria vestra baptizaros asseritis, et quid
de his sit agendum consulitis . . . .

15. *Epistola* 14, Ad Friduricum Moguntinum Archiepiscopum,
PL 132, 1084 D–1085 A: De Judaeis autem unde vestra
fraternitas nostram conquaesivit auctoritatem, utrum melius
sit eos sacrae subjugare religioni, an de civitatibus vestris
expellere: hoc vobis praeceptum mandamus ut fidem sanctae
Trinitatis, mysterium Dominicae incarnationis cum omni
sagacitate et prudenti consilio Dei cum reverentia illis
praedicare non desistatis, et si credere et baptizari toto corde
voluerint, immensis laudibus omnipotenti Domino referimus
gratias; si autem credere noluerint, de civitatibus vestris cum
nostra auctoritate illos expellite, qui non debemus cum
inimicis Domini societatem habere, dicente Apostolo: Quae
enim communicatio luci ad tenebras, aut quae pars fideli cum
infideli? Per virtutem autem et sine illorum voluntate atque
petitione nolite eos baptizare, quia scriptum est: *Nolite
sanctum dare canibus, et nolite margaritas vestras ante porcos,
ne forte conculcent eas pedibus suis* [Matt. 7 : 6] . . . .

16. Mansi, *op. cit.*, vol. II, col. 384 C: Si quis Christianus filiam
suam Judaeo in conjugio copulare praesumpserit, nisi per-
fecte crediderit Christo, et baptizatus fuerit; vel servum aut
ancillam eidem Judaeo Christianus venumdare praesumpserit,
et si vidua Christiana Judaeum duxerit virum, vel consent-
ientibus ei, anathema sit.

17. *Acta synodi Romanae, MGH*, Epist. Merowingici et Karolini
Aevi I (Berolini, 1892), p. 318: . . . hereticus, qui dicitur
Clemens . . . Iudaismum inducens, iustum esse iudicet
christiano, ut, si voluerit, viduam fratris defuncti accipiat
uxorem . . . .

18. See Appendix X, the bull *Turbato corde* of Clement IV.

19. See above, Chap. III, nn. 29, 30.

20. *Epistola* 1, Ad episcopos et presbyteros Scotiae, *PL* 80, 601:
. . . reperimus quosdam provinciae vestrae contra orthodoxam
fidem novam ex veteri haeresim renovare conantes, Pascha
nostrum in quo immolatus est Christus nebulosa caligine
refutantes, et quarta decima luna cum Hebraeis celebrare
nitentes. Quo epistolae principio manifeste declaratur, et
nuperrime temporibus illis hanc apud eos haeresim exortam,
et non totam eorum gentem sed quosdam ex eis hac fuisse
implicitos . . . .

21. *PL* 129, 857: . . . sumus dolore tacti, usque ad mortem
anxiati, cum cognovissemus per teipsum, quod plebs Judaica
Deo semper rebellis, et nostris derogans caeremoniis infra
fines et territoria Christianorum allodia haereditatum in villis
et suburbanis, quasi incolae Christianorum, possideant per

quaedam regum Francorum praecepta: quia ipsi inimici Domini . . . sunt, ei periculose mercati sunt: et quod vineas et agros illorum Christiani homines excolant: et infra civitates et extra, masculi et feminae Christianorum cum eisdem praevaricatoribus habitantes, die noctuque verbis blasphemiae maculantur, et cuncta obsequia quae dici aut excogitari possunt, miseri miseraeve praenotatis canibus indesinenter exhibeant . . . ab ipso Domino jurata et tradita istis incredulis . . . pro ultione crucifixi Salvatoris merito sint ablata . . . .

22. *Expositio super Jeremiam,* lib. XI, cap. XXX, *PL* 111, 1024 B–C: Hic locus Jeremiae prophetae repromissiones mysticas continebit, quas Judaei putant et nostri Judaizantes in consummationem mundi esse complendas. Necdum enim sub Zorobabel possunt expletas convincere: nos autem sequentes auctoritatem apostolorum et evangelistarum, et maxime apostoli Pauli, quidquid populo Israel carnaliter repromittitur, nobis spiritualiter completum esse monstramus, hodieque impleri: nec inter Judaeos et Christianos ullum aliud esse certamen, nisi hoc ut cum illi nosque credamus Christum Dei Filium repromissum, et ea quae sunt futura sub Christo a nobis impleta, ab illis explenda dicantur.

23. *Prudentii Trecensis Annales,* anno 839, *MGH,* SS I, 433, lines 4–20.

24. Rhabanus in libro adversus Iudaeos, cap. 42, *ibid.*

25. *Anales Bertinianos,* anno 847, *España Sagrada,* vol. 10, p. 578: Bodo, qui ante annos aliquot Christiana veritate derelicta ad Judaeorum perfidiam concesserat, in tantum mali profecit, ut in omnes Christianos Hispaniae degentes, tam Regis quam gentis Sarracenorum animos concitare statuerit, quatenus aut relicta Christianae fidei Religione ad Judaeorum insaniam, Sarracenorum dementiam se converterent, aut certe omnes interficerentur . . .

26. *Epistolarum,* IX, 2, E. Caspar, *Das Register Gregors VII,* *MGH,* Epist. select., vol. 2, fasc. 2, p. 571: . . . ex debito inhibere compellimur, dilectionem tuam monemus, ut in terra tua Iudaeos christianis dominari vel supra eos potestatem exercere ulterius nullatenus sinas. Quid enim est Iudaeis christianis supponere atque hoc illorum iudicio subicere nisi ecclesiam Dei opprimere et sathanae synagogam exaltare et, dum inimicis Christi velis placere, ipsum Christum contemnere?

27. *Epistolarum,* VII, 21, *ibid.,* p. 498: . . . Prohibendum videtur, quod de gente vestra nobis innotuit, scilicet vos intemperiem temporum corruptiones aeris quascunque molestias corporum ad sacerdotum culpam transferre. Quod quam grave peccatum sit, ex eo liquido potestis advertere quod Iudaeis etiam

sacerdotibus ipse Salvator noster lepra curatos eis mittendo honorem exhibuerit . . . cum profecto vestri, qualescunque habeantur, tamen illis longe sint meliores.

28. *Epistolarum,* II, 49, *ibid.,* p. 189: . . . Eos autem, inter quos habito, Romanos videlicet Longobardos et Normannos, sicut saepe illis dico, Iudeis et paganis quodammodo peiores esse redarguo.

Chapter V

1. See *Histoire littéraire de la France,* (Paris: Imprimerie Nationale, Hachette, 1839 ff), vol. 7, p. 616.
2. Baronius, *op. cit.,* vol. 16, pp. 432 ff., collates accounts of Ademar and Glaber, the second to be found in *PL* 142, 657 C ff.: . . . ecclesia, quae apud Hierosolymam sepulchrum continebat Domini ac Salvatoris nostri, eversa est funditus jussu principis Babylonis . . . occasio . . . diabolus per assuetam sibi Judaeorum gentem verae fidei cultoribus venenum suae nequitiae propinare . . . hujus generis apud Aurelianensem Galliarum regiam urbem non modica multitudo . . . corruperunt quemdam data pecunia, videlicet girovagum sub peregrino habitu, nomine Robertum, fugitivum utique servum beatae Mariae Melerensis coenobii . . . ad principem Babylonis cum Hebraicis characteribus, scriptis epistolis . . . .
3. Glaber goes on from the mention of the destruction of the Church to Christian reprisals; Ademar to an account of the persecution of Christians in the Caliph's domains: Tunc Nabuchodonosor Babyloniae, quem vocant Admiratum, concitatus suasu paganorum in iram, afflictione non parvam in Christianos exercuit, deditque legem, ut quicumque de sua potestate nollent fieri Saraceni, aut confiscarentur, aut interficerentur. Unde factum est, ut innumerabiles Christianorum converterentur ad legem Saracenorum; et nemo pro Christo morte dignus fuit praeter Patriarcham Hierosolymorum, qui variis suppliciis occisus est, et duos adolescentes germanos in Egypto, qui decollati sunt et multis claruerunt miraculis (Baronius, *ibid.,* p. 434).
4. Glaber, *ibid.,* pp. 432 ff., *PL* 142, 658 B ff.; . . . Everso igitur, ut diximus, templo, post paululum manifeste claruit quoniam Judaeorum nequitia tantum nefas sit patratum; ut et divulgatum est per orbem universum, communi omnium Christianorum consensu decretum est, ut omnes Judaei ab

illorum terris vel civitatibus funditus pellerentur. Sicque universi odio habiti, expulsi de civitatibus, alii gladiis trucidati, alii fluminibus necati, diversisque mortium generibus interempti, nonnulli etiam sese diversa caede interemerunt. Ita scilicet, ut digna de eis ulcione peracta vix pauci illorum in orbe reperirentur Romano. Tunc quoque decretum est ab episcopis atque interdictum, ut nullus Christianorum illis se in quocumque sociaret negotio . . . quicumque illorum [baptizatorum] sese tales mentiendo fieri poposcerant, paulo post ad morem pristinum sunt impudenter reversi . . . [Robertus] comprehensus, acribusque agitatus verberibus, propriae delationis confitetur crimen. Moxque a ministris regis in conspectu totius plebis extra civitatem igni est traditus atque consumptus . . . .

5. *Ibid.*: Judaei tamen profugi ac vagabundi, qui in locis abditis delitescentes praedictae superfuerant cladi, post quinquennium eversionis templi coeperunt in urbibus apparere perpauci. Et quoniam oportet, quamvis ad illorum confusionem, ut ex illis aliqui in futurum supersint, vel ad confirmandum proprium nefas, seu ad testimonium fusi sanguinis Christi . . . .

6. S. Loewenfeld, *Epistolae pontificum romanorum ineditae* (Leipzig: Veit, 1885), pp. 43–44: Omnes leges tam ecclesiastice quam seculares effusionem humani sanguinis dampnant, nisi forte conmissa crimina aliquem iudicio puniant, vel forte, ut de Sarracenis, hostilis exacerbatio incumbat. Consulte igitur et laudabiliter fecisti quia Iudeos sine causa adgravari non adquievistis. Monemus etiam, ut dehinc, si opus fuerit, simili modo faciatis.

7. *Epistola* 102, *PL* 146, 1387 B: Noverit prudentia vestra nobis placuisse quod Judaeos qui sub vestra potestate habitant tutati estis ne occiderentur. Non enim gaudet Deus effusione sanguinis, neque laetatur in perditione malorum.

8. S. Loewenfeld, *ibid.*, p. 52: Licet ex devotionis studio non dubitamus procedere, quod nobilitas tua Iudeos ad christianitatis cultum disponit adducere, tamen quia id inordinato videris studio agere, necessarium duximus, admonendo tibi literas nostras dirigere. Dominus enim noster Iesus Christus nullum legitur ad sui servitium violenter coegisse, sed humili exhortacione, reservata unicuique proprii arbitrii libertate, quoscumque ad vitam praedestinavit aeternam non iudicando, sed proprium sanguinem fundendo ab errore revocasse. Item. Beatus Gregorius, ne eadem gens ad fidem violentia trahatur, in quadam sua epistola interdicit.

9. See Appendix III.

10. *Historia rerum transmarinarum* I, 29, *PL* 201, 248 D–249 A: . . . factum est, ut cum in timore Domini iter debuissent inceptum peragere, et divinorum memores mandatorum, ob-

servata evangelica disciplina, pro Christo peregrinari, con-
verterunt se ad insanias et Judaeorum populum in civitatibus
et oppidis per quae erat eis transitus, nil tale sibi verentem,
et se habentem incautius, crudeliter obtruncabant . . . .

11. Ekkehard of Aura, *Chronicon universale, MGH,* SS, vol. VI,
p. 208: Qui et ipsi nefandissimas Iudaeorum reliquias, ut
vere intestinos hostes aecclesiae [sic] per civitates quas
transibant aut omnino delebant aut ad baptismatis refugium
compellebant, quorum tamen plurimi, sicut canes ad vomitum,
postea retro rediebant . . . .

12. *Quellen zur Geschichte der Juden in Deutschland,* II Band:
*Hebräische Berichte über die Judenverfolgungen während der
Kreuzzüge* (henceforth abbreviated *Hebräische Berichte*),
herausgegeben von A. Neubauer und M. Stern; in Deutsche
übersetzt von S. Baer (Berlin, 1892), p. 123: Im Jahre 900
habe ich Salomo bar Simon diese Begebenheit abgeschrieben
in Mainz. Dort habe ich von den Alten das Ereigniss erfragt
und nach ihren Ausagen jede Sache gehörig geordnet; sie
haben mir diese Heiligung erzählt.

13. *Ibid.,* p. 190: Auch ich, der unbedeutende Schreiber, befand
mich damals als dreizehnjähriger Knabe in dieser Festung
Wolkenburg bei meinen Verwandten, die grössentheils zur
Familie meiner Mutter—sie ruhe im Paradiese—gehorten.

14. *Ibid.,* p. 166.

15. *Ibid.,* pp. 82–83: Sehet, wir siehen den weiten Weg, um die
Grabstätte* aufzusuchen und uns an den Ishmaeliten zu
rächen, und siehe, hier wohnen unter uns die Juden, deren
Väter ihn unverschuldet umgebracht und gekreuzigt haben!
So lasset zuerst an ihnen uns Rache nehmen und sie austilgen
unter den Völkern, dass der Name Israel nicht mehr erwähnt
werde; oder sie sollen unseresgleichen werden und zu unserem
Glauben* sich bekennen. A word marked with an asterisk
is one that the translator has bowdlerized: see Chapter I, the
section headed "Hard Sayings."

16. Ekkehard, *ed. cit.,* p. 215: Surrexit etiam diebus ipsis quidam
vir militaris, comes tamen partium illarum quae circa Renum
sunt, Emicho nomine, dudum tyrannica conversatione nimis
infamis, tunc vero velut alter Saulus revelationibus, ut fate-
batur, divinis in huiusmodi religionem advocatus, fere 12,000
signatorum sibimet usurpans ducatum; qui nimirum per
civitates Reni, Moeni quoque atque Danubii deducti, execrabilem Iudeorum quacumque repertam plebem, zelo christianitatis etiam in hoc deservientes, aut omnino delere aut etiam
intra aecclesiae satagebant compellere sinum.

17. *Hebräische Berichte,* pp. 83–84: Am Sabbath, den 8 Jjar,
überfielen die Feinde die Gemeinde Speyer und erschlugen
eilf heilige Personen. Diese waren die Ersten, die an dem

heiligen Sabbathtage ihren Schöpfer heiligten, da sie sich nicht taufen lassen wollten. Darunter befand sich auch eine angesehene, fromme Frau, die sich zur Heiligung des göttlichen Names selbst schlachtete. Sie war die Erste von denen aller Gemeinden, die sich selbst schlachteten oder geschlachtet wurden. Die Uebrigen worden, ohne ihren Glauben wechseln zu mussen,* von dem Bischof gerettet, wie dies alles oben beschrieben ist.

18. Bernoldi *Chronicon, MGH,* SS, vol. V, pp. 464–465: Hoc anno [1096] in quibusdam civitatibus Iudei magna cede trucidati sunt ab his qui Hierosolimam petierunt; ita dico, ut apud Spiram fugientes in palacium regis et episcopi, etiam repugnando vix se defenderent, eodem episcopo Iohanne illis auxiliante. Qui etiam postea ob hoc ira commotus, et pecunia Iudeorum conductus, quosdam fecit obtruncari christianos.

19. *Hebräische Berichte,* p. 84.

20. Bernoldi *Chronicon, ed. cit.,* p. 465: Item apud Wormaciam Iudei persequentes fugiendo christianos, ad episcopum properabant. Qui cum non aliter illis salutem, nisi baptizarentur, promitteret, inducias colloquii rogaverunt. Et eadem hora episcopi cubiculum intrantes, nostris foras expectantibus quid responsuri essent, diabolo et propria duricia persuadente, se ipsos interfecerunt.

21. *Hebräische Berichte,* p. 163: "Horet mich, ihr Juden! Anfangs habe ich euch versprochen, euch zu schirmen und zu schützen, so lange noch ein Jude in der Welt lebt. Dies Versprechen habe ich euch gegeben und auch so gehandelt und gehalten. Von nun aber an kann ich nichts mehr thun zu eurer Rettung vor all diesen Völkern. Sehet daher zu, was ihr thun wollt! Ihr wisset wohl, dass wenn ihr nicht so und so thuet, die Stadt eingerissen wird. Es ist also besser für mich, euch ihrer Gewalt zu überliefern, als dass sie mit Belagerung über mich kommen und die Burg nieder reissen." Darauf antworteten sie Alle von Klein bis Gross: "Wir sind bereit, unsern Hals hinzustrecken zum Tode für den Glauben an unsern Schöpfer und an die Einheit seines Namens."

22. *Ibid.,* pp. 116–131, 144–152.

23. Ottonis Frisingensis, *Gesta Friderici imperatoris, MGH,* SS, XX, 372.

24. *Ibid.,* 372–374: At praefatus Clarevallensis abbas huiusmodi doctrinam praecavendam docens, ad Galliae Germaniaeque populos nuncios seu litteras destinavit, in quibus ex auctoritate sacrae paginae luculenter ostendit Iudaeos ob scelerum suorum ex[c]essus non occidendos sed dispergendos fore . . . . Maguntiam quoque veniens, Radolfum in maximo favore populi morantem invenit. Quo accersito praemonitoque, ne contra monachorum regulam per orbem vagando propria

auctoritate verbum praedicationis assumeret, tandem ad hoc eum, ut sibi promissa obedientia in coenobium suum transiret, induxit, populo graviter indignante et, nisi ipsius sanctitatis consideratione revocaretur, etiam seditionem movere volente.

25. *Hebräische Berichte*, p. 188: Es ist schön von euch, dass ihr gegen die Ismaeliten ziehen wollt; jedoch wer einen Juden anrührt, um sich an dessen Leben zu vergreifen, das ist so sündlich, als rühre er Jesum selbst an; mein Schuler Rudolf, der gegen sie gesprochen hat, um sie zu vertilgen, hat nur Unrichtiges gepredigt; denn es stehet über sie im Psalmenbuche geschrieben: "Totet sie nicht, damit mein Volk nicht vergessen werde!"

26. *Epistola* 363, Ad Orientalis Franciae clerum et populum, *PL* 182, 567 A–B: Audivimus et gaudemus, ut in vobis ferveat zelus Dei; sed oportet omnino temperamentum scientiae non deesse. Non sunt persequendi Judaei, non sunt trucidandi, sed nec effugandi quidem. Interrogate eas divinas paginas. Novi quid in Psalmo legitur prophetatum de Judaeis: Deus ostendit mihi, inquit Ecclesia, super inimicos meos ne occidas eos, nequando obliviscantur populi mei.

27. Baronius-Raynaldus, *op. cit.*, XVIII, 648, anno 1146: Sed et quod stylo diserto eos exagitavit Petrus abbas Cluniacensis, crevit magis (in Judaeos odium), adeo ut de omnibus Judaeis necandis data fuerit ea occasio proclamandi, quam nuper vidimus per S. Bernardum esse repressam.

28. *Epistola* 36, Ludovico . . . regi Francorum, *PL* 189, 367 A: Quid proderit inimicos Christianae spei, in exteris aut remotis finibus insequi, ac persequi, si nequam, blasphemi, longeque Sarracenis deteriores Judaei, non longe a nobis, sed in medio nostri, tam libere, tam audacter, Christum cunctaque Christiana sacramenta impune blasphemaverint, conculcaverint, deturpaverint?

29. *Ibid.* 367 D–368 D: Non, inquam, ut occidantur admoneo, sed ut congruenter nequitiae suae modo puniantur exhortor . . . . Quod loquor omnibus notum est, non enim de simplici agri cultura, non de legali militia, non de quolibet honesto et utili officio horrea sua fragibus, cellaria vino, marsupia nummis, orcas auro sive argento cumulant, quantum de his quae ut dixi Christicolis dolose subtrahunt . . . . Auferatur ergo, vel ex maxima parte imminuatur Judaicarum divitiarum male parte pinguedo, et Christianus exercitus, qui ut Sarracenos expugnet, pecuniis vel terris propriis, Christi Domini sui amore non parcit, Judaeorum thesauris tam pessime acquisitis non parcat. Reservetur eis vita, auferatur pecunia, ut per dextras Christianorum, adjutas pecuniis blasphemantium Judaeorum, expugnetur infidelium audacia Sarracenorum.

30. *PL* 180, 1065 C–D: Quicumque vero aere premuntur alieno, et tam sanctum iter puro corde incoeperint, de praeterito usuras non solvant; et si ipsi, vel alii pro eis occasione usurarum adstricti sunt, sacramento vel fide Apostolica eos auctoritate absolvimus; this important text is also to be found in Baronius-Raynaldus, *op. cit.*, XVIII, 635, no. 32, *MGH*, SS, XX, 372, and Mansi, *op. cit.*, XX, 626.

31. *Hebräische Berichte*, p. 196: Denn der König von Frankreich hatte einen Befehl ergehen lassen, dass einen Jeden, der sich zum Kreuzzüge nach Jerusalem entschliesse, seine Schulden, die er den Juden schuldig sei, erlassen sein sollten. Die miesten Darlehen der französischen Juden aber geschahen auf blossen Credit; dadurch verloren sie ihr Vermögen.

32. *De consideratione* III, 1, 3, *PL* 182, 759 D: Esto, de Judaeis excusat te tempus: habent terminum suum qui praeveniri non poterit. Plenitudinem gentium praeire oportet . . . .

33. *Sermo* 60, *PL* 183, 1068 A: Nimium me fortasse queratur in sui suggillatione Judaeus, qui intellectum illius dico bovinum. Sed legat in Isaia, et plus quam bovinum audiet. *Cognovit,* inquit, *bos possessorem suum et asinus praesepe domini sui: Israel non cognovit me*; populus meus non intellexit. Vides me Judaee, mitiorem tibi propheta tuo. Ego te comparavi jumentis, ille subjicit.

34. *Sermo* 75, *PL* 183, 1149: Habet mundus iste noctes suas, et non paucas. Quid dico, quia noctes habet mundus, cum pene totus ipse sit nox, et totus semper versetur in tenebris? Nox est Judaica perfidia, nox ignorantia paganorum, nox haeretica pravitas, nox etiam Catholicorum carnalis, animalisve conversatio.

35. *Epistola* 363, *PL* 182, 567 C.

36. *Ibid.* 567 A–B: Vivi quidam apices nobis sunt, repraesentantes Dominicam passionem . . . . Propter hoc dispersi sunt . . . duram sustinent captivitatem sub principibus christianis.

37. *Epistola* 365, *PL* 182, 571: Nonne copiosius triumphat Ecclesia de Judaeis per singulos dies vel convincens, vel convertens eos, quam si semel et simul consumeret eos in ore gladii? Numquid incassum constituta est illa universalis oratio Ecclesiae quae offertur pro perfidis Judaeis?

38. *Epistola* 139, *PL* 182, 294: Ut enim constat Judaicam sobolem sedem Petri in Christi occupasse injuriam; sit procul dubio omnis qui in Sicilia regem se facit, contradicit Caesari.

39. Baronius-Raynaldus, *op. cit.*, XVIII, 454, anno 1131: [Innocent II celebrates Easter at Paris] nec etiam ipsa Judaeorum Parisiensium excaecata defuit synagoga, quae legis litteram, rotulam scilicet et velatam offerens: ab ore ejus Pontificis scilicet, hanc misericordiae et pietatis obtinet supplicationem: Auferat Deus omnipotens velamen a cordibus vestris. For a

modern study of this ceremony, see F. Wasner, "The Popes' Veneration of the Torah," *The Bridge,* IV (1962), 278 ff.

40. See *The Itinerary of Rabbi Benjamin of Tudela,* trans. and ed. A. Asher (New York, Hakesheth n.d.), II, 18.
41. *Epistola* 185, Martene et Durand, *op. cit.,* II, 786 E–787 B.
42. Mansi, *op. cit.,* XXII, 355–357; also, *ibid.,* col. 231, for a prohibition of the practice of expropriating the goods of a convert Jew or Moslem on the occasion of his baptism.
43. See Appendix VI.

Chapter VI

1. It has been argued, for example, that Innocent III played a more effective role than did Gregory VII in laying the foundation for a "second age of theocracy" under Innocent IV, an age to which Boniface VIII would add nothing essential: thus, Marcel Pacaut, "L'autorité pontificale selon Innocent IV," *Le Moyen Age,* LXVI (4ᵉ série, XV), 85–119.
2. *Epistola* 30, *PL* 216, 824 A: . . . Illius ergo testimonium invocamus qui testis est in coelo fidelis quod inter omnia desiderabilia cordis nostri duo in hoc saeculo principaliter affectamus, ut ad recuperationem videlicet terrae sanctae ac reformationem universalis Ecclesiae valeamus intendere cum effectu . . . . A modern historian has assigned two other goals to Innocent III: "It is well known that Innocent's activities as pope were largely concerned with the two problems of reviving and propagating the orthodox faith and firmly establishing the political power of the papacy." G. Kisch, *The Yellow Badge in History* (New York, 1942), p. 14.
3. *Epistola* 37, *PL* 216, 832 A: . . . ita quod apud te non sit deterior conditio gentis nostrae quam apud nos est conditio gentis tuae . . . .
4. *Epistola* 36, *PL* 216, 830 D: . . . Licet autem dura Saracenorum perfidia non consuevit humilibus Christianis precibus emolliri . . . (831 A) . . . Soldanum Damasci et Babyloniae, qui haereditatem Christi detinet occupatam apostolicis providimus litteris humiliter praemonendum . . . . Nam et dispositionibus nostris auditis, quae utinam cum possent omnino latere, fortassis omnipotens Deus suum in eum terrorem immittet, et benigne rogatus ostendet facere se spontaneum quod dure compulsus facturum se putaret invitum . . . .
5. *Epistola* 30, *PL* 216, 824 B: . . . providimus faciendum, ut quia haec [see above, n. 2: two goals, crusade and reform]

universorum fidelium communem statum respiciunt, generale concilium juxta priscam sanctorum Patrum consuetudinem convocemus . . . .

6. See E. Amann, "Innocent III," *Dictionnaire de théologie catholique* (Paris: Letouzey et Ané, 1923 ff), vol. VII, part 2, col. 1962, with respect to his theological writing: Heureusement la mort de Celestin III vient arracher Lothaire [to be elected as Innocent III] à ces occupations littéraires qui risqueraient de nous donner de son génie une idée plutôt fâcheuse; *ibid.*, col. 1974, on his exegesis of John 20 : 3: On voit par ce seul exemple en quel imbroglio s'embarrassait parfois la théologie d'Innocent III; en fait, sa thèse de la superiorité de l'Eglise romaine valait beaucoup mieux que les preuves qu'il en prétendait administrer; we shall have the experience of examining some of this reasoning.

7. *Sermo 22, PL 217*, 556 C–D: Roma, quae primatum et principatum super universum saeculum obtinebat et obtinet; quam in tantum divina dignatio voluit exaltare, ut cum tempore paganitatis sola dominium super omnes gentiles, habuerit, Christianitatis tempore sola magisterium super fideles habeat universos . . . . Ecce liquido patet, quantum Deus urbem istam dilexerit, ut eadem esset sacerdotalis et regia, imperialis et apostolica, obtinens et exercens non solum dominium super corpora, verum etiam magisterium super animas. This improvement in the role of Rome was ascribed explicitly to Peter: see *Sermo 21, PL 217*, 556 A–B: Per eum enim facta est veritatis magistra, quae fuerat caput erroris: et longe nunc excellentior est in apostolico magisterio quam olim fuerat in imperiali principatu . . . .

8. *Regestum de negotio romani imperii XXIX, PL 216*, 1025 A: Interest apostolicae sedis diligenter et prudenter de imperii Romani provisione tractare, cum imperium noscatur ad eam principaliter et finaliter pertinere: principaliter, cum per ipsam et propter ipsam de Graecia sit translatum, per ipsam translationis actricem, propter ipsam melius defendendam; finaliter quoniam imperator a summo pontifice finalem sive ultimam manus impositionem promotionis proprie accipit, dum ab eo benedicitur, coronatur, et de imperio investitur.

9. *Sermo II in consecratione pontificis maximi, PL 217*, 658 A: . . . Jam ergo videtis quis iste servus, qui super familiam constituitur, profecto vicarius Jesu Christi, successor Petri, Christus Domini, Deus Pharaonis: inter Deum et hominem medius constitutus, citra Deum, sed ultra hominem: minor Deo, sed major homine: qui de omnibus judicat, et a nemine judicatur: Apostoli voce pronuntians, "qui me judicat, Dominus est."

10. *PL 215*, 180 C: . . . juxta commonitionem praedicti abbatis,

vel nostram potius immo Dei, cum praedicto rege vel solidam pacem reformes, vel treugas ineas competentes . . . ut abbas praedictus, cum venerabili fratre nostro . . . . Bituricensi archiepiscopo, super hoc de plano cognoscat, non ratione feudi, cujus ad te spectat judicium, sed occasione peccati, cujus ad nos pertinet sine dubitatione censura . . . .

11. Michele Maccarone, *Vicarius Christi; storia del titolo papale* (Romae, 1952); Walter Ullman, *The Growth of Papal Government in the Middle Ages* (London, Methuen, 1955), p. 428, n. 4; E. Amann, DTC, *art. cit.*, col. 1972.

12. *PL* 217, 484 B: . . . Illius vere vicarius, de quo dicit Apostolus, "Deus erat in Christo mundum reconcilians sibi . . . Deo" mediatores enim sunt sacerdotes inter Deum et hominem, et ideo tales debent existere, ut et Deo sint grati, et hominibus accepti . . . .

13. *PL* 217, 697 B: . . . Vicarius meus papa, quem ego constitui loco meo in terris judicem tuum . . . .

14. *PL* 217, 821 B: Caeterum subdiaconus vel diaconus non manus, sed pedes Romani pontificis osculatur, ut summo pontifici summam exhibeat reverentiam, et eum illius ostendat vicarium esse, cujus pedes osculabatur mulier illa quae fuerat in civitate peccatrix.

15. *PL* 217, 911: Hujus rei causam, non allegoricam, sed historicam a nonnullis audivi, quam quia numquam in authentico scripto potui reperire, melius reticendam censui quam temere asserendam. Et licet non omnium, quae a majoribus introducta sunt, ratio reddi possit, reor, tamen quod in his profunda lateant sacramenta. Romanus pontifex ideo non communicat ubi frangit, sed ad altare frangit et ad sedem communicat. Quia Christus in Emmaus coram duobus discipulis fregit; in Hierusalem coram undecim apostolis manducavit [Luke 24 : 30–43].

16. *PL* 217, 779 B: . . . et cum omnes apostoli fugam arriperent, solus Petrus educens gladium, percussit servum pontificis, et dexteram ejus abscidit auriculam.

17. Heinrich Graetz, *op. cit.*, vol. 3, pp. 494, 496.

18. *PL* 217, 332 A: . . . Veniens autem "pax nostra qui fecit utraque unum, et medium parietem inimicitiae solvens," abstulit caeremoniam a Judaeis, et idolatriam a gentibus, "ut duos condat in semetipso" parietes in "lapide angulari," "in uno novo homine faciens pacem."

19. *PL* 217, 509 A–C: Judaeus namque caeremonias excolebat, gentilis idolatriam exercebat, utriusque ritus alterius displicebat. Sed veniens "pax nostra fecit utraque unum," destruxit macerias inimicitiarum, et concurrentes parietes in se angulari copulavit, ut de caetero esset "unum ovile et unus pastor" . . . nascitur in praesepe bovis et asini, quia pax est

inter homines et homines reparata. Per bovem enim judaicus, per asinum gentilis populus praefiguratur, secundum illud: "Non arabis in bove et asino" (Deut. 22 : 10).

20. *PL* 217, 811 B: Inter duo candelabra in altari crux collocatur media, quoniam inter duos populos Christus in Ecclesia mediator existit, lapis angularis, qui fecit utraque unum: ad quem pastores a Judaea, et magi ab Oriente venerunt.

21. *PL* 217, 527 B: . . . Illa quaestio facta est populo Judaeorum, ut nostra fieret populo Christianorum . . . bonum an malum? veritatem an vanitatem? iniquitatem an aequitatem? . . .

22. *PL* 217, 537 D–538 B: . . . Gravia quidem sunt ista, sed diligentibus levia reputantur . . . .

23. *PL* 217, 392 B–C: . . . quales sunt carnales Judaei, qui sensibilia tantum appetunt et corporeis solummodo sensibus delectantur.

24. *Ibid.*: . . . duodecim prophetarum, qui non carnaliter, sed spiritualiter sunt locuti.

25. *PL* 217, 463 D: Hic autem *puer* vocatur *Deus* substantive, secundum naturam. Ut autem confundatur haereticus, et erubescat Judaeus, producantur in medium testimonia, tam de Veteri, quam de Novo Testamento, ut rota contineantur in rota, et basis sit incolumna . . . [see Ezech. 1 : 16].

26. *PL* 217, 325 D: . . . Judas, qui nox fuit, obscurus et tenebrosus scientiam Dei, hoc est Filium Dei, tradidit nocti Judaeorum . . . .

27. *PL* 217, 336 D: . . . Judaei vero usque hodie scandalizantur, cum audiunt quod Deus sit flagellatus, crucifixus, et mortuus, dedignantes audire quod Deus indigna pertulerit . . . .

28. *PL* 217, 335 A: Erubescat ergo Judaeus qui mentitur Messiam nondum in mundum venisse, et nec esse Deum . . . .

29. *PL* 217, 561 D: Herodes diabolus, Judaei daemones; ille rex Judaeorum, iste rex daemonum . . . .

30. *PL* 217, 385 B–386 C: . . . infideles deseruit, et ad fideles accessit. Synagogam propter perfidiam reprobavit et Ecclesiam propter obedientiam praeelegit. . . . Quam prius dixerat Synagogam, modo Simonis socrum appellat. Socrus enim est mater uxoris. Mater autem Ecclesiae, quae uxor est Simonis, sacramentaliter sibi conjugio copulata, intelligitur Synagoga . . . nam de Synagoga nati sunt primum fideles, de qua secundum carnem et ipse Christus traxit originem. Propter quod et ipse dicebat: "Quia salus est ex Judaeis" [John 4 : 22] . . . . Synagoga quippe duabus praecipue febribus detinetur, erroris videlicet et invidiae . . . . Hiems erroris et infidelitatis et ignorantiae [John 10 : 22].

31. *Ibid.*: 386 C–387 B: O quam gravi torquetur invidia Synagoga, quando videt Ecclesiam habere regnum et sacerdotium, templum et altare, legem et prophetiam! . . . Tam grandi

tamen detinetur errore, ut nec sic intelligat veritatem . . . sed
qui sunt in domo fideles, orant pro ipsa, petentes, ut Deus
auferat velamen de cordibus ejus, ut Jesum Christum, qui
est veritas, agnoscat . . . "totum hominem sanum fecit in
Sabbato" [John 7 : 23]. Hoc autem implebitur, "quando
plenitudo gentium intrabit ad fidem, et tunc omnis Israel
salvus fiet" [Rom. 4 : 1–13]. Quoniam "in diebus illis salvabitur Juda" [Jer. 33 : 6–26] "et reliquiae Israel salvae fient"
[Rom. 9 : 3–24].

32. *PL* 217, 467 C: . . . ut peritissimi asserunt Hebraeorum . . . .
470 B: Et nota quod sicut apud Hebraeos illud ineffabile
nomen alio modo describitur, et alio modo profertur; scribitur
enim his quatuor litteris, I, E, V, E, et profertur *Adonai*: sic
apud Latinos illud excellentissimum nomen alio modo
scribitur, et alio modo profertur. Profertur Jesus, scribitur
IHS; cf. to this discussion *PL* 217, 519 C, where he gives
the four Hebrew characters as Joth, He, Vau, Heth; so also
782 C and 786 A.

33. *PL* 217, 330 A: . . . quatuor theologicos intellectus, histori-
cum, allegoricum, tropologicum, et anagogicum; cf. 396 A–B,
411 D–412 A, 541 A, 605 C.

34. *PL* 217, 561 C: Quia plane videmus historiam, pleno investi-
gemus allegoriam: sub littera spiritum, quasi sub cortice
nucleum requirentes . . . . Sicut enim in imagine non tam
intendimus tabulam quam picturam, sic in expositione non
tam debemus historiam quam figuram; quia tabulae historiae
non semper aeque respondent picturae, allegoriae est significatum quandoque sit malum et significatum bonum et
econverso.

35. *PL* 215, 456 C: Sane, per Mariam Magdalenam intelligitur
Synagoga, per monumentum vero vetus accipitur testamentum; per lapidem monumenti legis littera designatur, quae
fuit in tabulis lapideis exarata. Maria igitur, videlicet Synagoga, mane, id est, tempore primitivo, cum adhuc tenebrae
essent, tempus videlicet caecitatis et ignorantiae, antequam
lex per Moysen data fuisset . . . venit ad monumentum, id
est Vetus Testamentum accepit . . . .

36. *Ibid.* 456 D–457 A: . . . petrae scissae, ac monumenta legun-
tur aperta, vidit in primitivis fidelibus, qui ex circumcisione
fuerunt; nam salus ex Judaeis est, lapidem amotum ab ostio
monumenti, videlicet intelligentiam litterae a Veteri Testamento discretam quia legem non tam litteraliter quam spiritualiter intelligendum esse cognovit per doctores evangelicae
veritatis . . . .

37. *Ibid.* 458 CD: Quid est autem, quod Judaeorum populus
electus est prius ad culturam unius Dei, duo vero circa fines
saeculorum assumpti, nisi quod una est in Trinitate persona,

quae a nullo mittitur, quoniam est a nullo, duae vero, quae ab uno sunt, et ab uno mittuntur. Quod si populus Judaicus, qui est electus in Patribus, typum gerit illius a quo omnis potestas in caelo et in terra nominatur, cujus typus gerit Latinus cui datus est Christi vicarius, nisi ipsius Filii, qui traditur occurrisse beato Petro, et tam ipsi, quam pro ipso dixisse: Venio Romam iterum crucifigi? Quia vero Graecorum populo datus est beatus Joannes, a quo et incepit perfectorum religio monachorum, bene typum gerit illius Spiritus, qui quaerit et diligit spiritales . . . .

38. *Ibid.* 458 D–460 A: Caeterum, si est ita, quid est, quod Graeci nondum acceperunt posse credere, procedere Spiritum sanctum a Filio, sicut a Patre, nisi quod humiliter quidem acceperunt doctrinam a populo Judaico, qui gerit mysterium Dei Patris, sed hactenus sprevit humiliter recipere a Latino, qui habet in hac parte similitudinem Dei Filii, ut quomodo idem Spiritus accipere dicitur a Filio, quod annuntiet, ita Graecorum populus, qui doctrinam accepit aliquando ab Hebraeo accipiat tandem similiter a Latino? . . . quia nesciebat adhuc Scripturam Joannes quod videlicet oporteret Christum a mortuis resurgere, non est mirum, si Graeci adhuc nesciunt mortuam esse litteram. . . . Populo quippe Graecorum intrante, Synagoga Judaeorum stat foris, quia exteriorem litterae corticem intuetur necdum ad interiorem veritatis medullam attingunt.

39. *PL* 215, 694 B: Etsi Judaeos . . . quos etiam, propter eorum perfidiam, Saraceni, qui fidem Catholicam persequuntur, nec credunt in crucifixum ab illis, sustinere non possunt, sed potius a suis finibus expulerunt . . . .

40. These texts are to be found in *PL* 215, 501 C ff. and 1291 B ff.; owing to their length and importance, they are given in Appendix IV and Appendix V.

41. For a survey of recent and inadequate scriptural exegesis, as well as for the best current view on the crucial texts, see F. Festorazzi, "Populus Israel: Estne maledictus et repudiatus a deo?" *Verbum domini,* 39 (1961), 255–271.

42. Pars XX, Mansi, *op. cit.,* vol. XXII, p. 259.

43. *PL* 215, 694 C: Accepimus autem, quod Judaei . . . adeo sunt insolentes, ut illos committant excessus in contumeliam fidei Christianae, quos non tantum dicere, sed etiam nefandum cogitare. Faciunt enim Christianas filiorum suorum nutrices, cum in die Resurrectionis Dominicae illas recipere corpus et sanguinem Jesu Christi contingit, per triduum antequam eos lactent, lac effundere in latrinam . . . .

44. Titulus XXVI, Mansi, *op. cit.,* vol. 22, p. 231.

45. See above, Chap. III, n. 43.

46. See above, Chap. III, n. 44.
47. See Appendix VI, Licet perfidia Judaeorum.
48. See above, n. 2.
49. *PL* 216, 159 D, *Layettes du trésor des chartes,* ed. Alexandre Teulet (Paris, H. Plon, 1863), I, 340 ff., *passim.*
50. *PL* 214, 311 D–312 A: . . . Si qui vero proficiscentium illuc ad praestandas usuras juramento tenentur astricti, vos fratres archiepiscopi et episcopi, per vestras dioceses creditores eorum, sublato appellationis obstaculo, eadem districtione cogatis ut eos a sacramento penitus absolventes, ab usurarum ulterius exactione desistant. Quod si quisquam creditorum eos ad solutionem coegerit usurarum, eum ad restitutionem earum sublato appellationis obstaculo districtione simili compellatis. Judaeos vero ad remittendas ipsis usuras per vos, filii principes, et saecularem compelli praecepimus potestatem; et donec eas remiserint, ab universis Christi fidelibus, tam in mercimoniis, quam aliis, per excommunicationis sententiam eis jubemus communionem omnimodam denegari; cf. *ibid.* 828–832 and 832–835.
51. *PL* 215, 1470–1471.
52. *PL* 215, 1348 C–D.
53. Potthast, *Regesta pontificum romanorum* (Berlin: R. de Decker, 1874–75), number 5257: (frag.) Archiepiscopis et episcopis, per regnum Franciae constitutis mandatur ut inhibeant universis Christianis, maxime crucesignatis, ne Judaeos seu eorum familias molestent.
54. *PL* 216, 885 A–886 B; cf. Potthast, *Regesta,* number 4749.
55. *PL* 214, 475 B–C: . . . De infidelibus ad fidem conversis nos consulere voluistis, utrum si ante conversionem suam, secundum legis veteris instituta vel traditiones suas, citra gradus consanguinitatis a canone denotatos conjuncti fuerint, separari debeant post baptisma. Super hoc igitur devotioni vestrae duximus respondendum quod matrimonium sic ante conversionem contractum, non est post baptismi lavacrum separandum; cum a Judaeis Dominus requisitus, si licet uxorem ex qualicunque causa relinquere, ipsis responderit: Quod Deus conjunxit, homo non separet [Matt. 19 : 6], per hoc innuens esse matrimonium inter eos.
56. *PL* 215, 514 C–D: . . . Jesus inquit ad Simonem: Noli timere, quoniam ex hoc jam homines eris capiens [Luke 5 : 10], quasi dicat: Pro certo confide, quia, postquam ceperis pisces, id est postquam reduxeris Christianos, extunc homines capies, id est Judaeos et paganos convertes. Pisces enim, qui vivunt in aqua, Christianos designant, qui ex aqua et spiritu renascuntur; homines autem, qui vivunt in terra Judaeos et paganos significant, qui terrenis inhiant et inhaerent. Sed postquam

ad obedientiam apostolicae sedis omnes omnino reversi
fuerint Christiani, tunc multitudo gentium intrabit ad fidem,
et sic omnis Israel salvus fiet . . . [Rom. 4 : 1–13].

57. *PL* 215, 507 B: . . . quos a gratia libertatis in servitutis
opprobrium redigere nititur Judaismus.

58. *PL* 215, 616 C–617 D.

59. *PL* 214, 791 B: . . . Posthaec vero dimissis domo et omnibus
quae habebat, in domo cujusdam Judaei per tres, in ecclesia
vero Sanctae Mariae de Veiga per sex, latuit septimanas . . .

60. *PL* 215, 978 B–C: . . . quamplures Saraceni, concurrentes ad
ipsum cum instantia postulant baptizari, quorum domini, tam
Judaei quam et Christiani, timentes admittere commodum
temporale, eos prohibere praesumunt . . . mandamus, quatenus nemini petenti sacramentum fidei denegetis, sed tam
Judaeos quam Saracenos illud humiliter postulantes, . . .
baptizetis. . . .

61. *PL* 216, 630 B–631 A: . . . qualiter contra Judaeum procedere
debeas qui manus injecit in quemdam presbyterum violen-
tas . . . poena pecuniaria vel alia . . . temporali. . . .
Alioquin dominum ejus moneas . . . si . . . neglexerit . . .
Christianis per censuram ecclesiasticam interdicas ne cum
ipso Judaeo . . . commercia.

62. *PL* 214, 610 D–615 B: . . . quia cum clerici laicis spiritualia
ministrare non possent, laici clericis temporalia subtrahebant,
oblationes, primitias et decimas detinentes; unde cum clerici
ex his pro majori parte in partibus illis consueverint sus-
tentari, eis subtractis non solum mendicare sed fodere et
servire Judaeis in Ecclesiae et totius Christianitatis opprobrium cogebantur.

Chapter VII

1. Helene Tillmann, *Papst Innocenz III* (Bonn, L. Röhrscheid,
1954), 163 ff.

2. See Appendix VII.

3. *Ibid.*

4. See above, Chap. IV, n. 6.

5. J. Marcus, *op. cit.*, 193–197 for Jewish sumptuary and police
regulations.

6. For the first hint of friction of this sort, see above, Chap.
II, n. 24; Alexander III (Jaffé, *Regesta pontificum romanorum*
(Leipzig: Veit, 1885–88), number 9040) gave this legisla-
tion the form in which it entered the canonical collections:

X, 5, 6, canon 4, *Corpus iuris canonici, ed. cit.*, vol. II, col. 772.

7. See Appendix VII.

8. *Ibid.*

9. Baronius-Raynaldus, *op. cit.*, XX, 385, number 84: Tum litteris ad universos Christi fideles datis, ne quis eos ad sacrum suscipiendum baptisma vi adigeret neve eos festis ipsorum diebus aliave occasione iniuria afficeret.

10. *Ibid.*, XX, 420, number 46: Archiepiscopo Toletano: . . . Judaei existentes in Regno Castellae, adeo graviter ferunt quod de signis ferendis ab ipsis statutum fuit in Concilio Generali, ut nonnulli eorum potius eligant ad mauros confugere quam signa hujusmodi bajulare, alias occasione hujusmodi conspirationes et conventicula facientes . . . mandamus quatenus executionem constitutionis supradictae suspendas, quandiu expedire cognoveris . . . .

11. *Ibid.*, XX, 435, number 48: Sedes Apostolica pia mater ubera charitatis, quibus filios suos nutrit, ad alienos interdum studio pietatis extendit, quos locum sui tabernaculi dilatando in fide nititur parturire, ut si forsan ad aemulationem quomodolibet provocati in adoptionem veniant filiorum, Christusque formetur in illis, et ipsi conformentur eidem, adorentque ipsius pedum vestigia, qui ei aliquando detrahebant.

12. *Ibid.*: . . . Honorius qui suis ad regem litteris illud in Azzachum [Isaac] beneficium se contulisse testatur, memoratoque archiepiscopo mandavit, tum ut illum vexari non permitteret, tum ne Judaeos nova signa gestare compelleret.

13. *Ibid.*, number 49: . . . quocirca Pontifex regem ipsum monere hortarique, fidelium opera in ea re uteretur; non fieri verisimile, ut qui a Christi fide tantopere abhorrerent, se Christi cultoribus fidos exhibeant; eaque de re ad Tarraconensem archiepiscopum Barcinonensem atque Illerdensem episcopum scripsit, ut regem ab imponendo Judaeis eo munere avocarent, cumque Legionis, Castellae, ac Navarrae reges in obeundis hujusmodi legationibus Judaeorum opera uterentur, ab ea re litteris Apostolicis deterruit . . . .

14. *Ibid.*, XX, 446, number 34: Judaei praeferrent signa quibus a Christianis discernerentur, poenis gravioribus imperavit . . . . 450, number 48: Eodem tempore tuendae religionis studio, ne Judaei qui inter Christianos versabantur, suum illis facile virus afflarent, ipsos nota aliqua distingui jussit, quo ab eorum fraudibus caveretur, tum ad expoliendos continendosque mores, disciplinam Ecclesiasticam ne dissolveretur adstrinxit.

15. *Ibid.*, XX, 420, number 47: Et quidem cum nos, quibus Christus, licet immeritus, gregem suum et ovile commisit, exercere inter Christianos, patiamur innumeram legis tuae

hominum multitudinem ritus suos, ut in hoc nostrae ac tuae gentis non sit dispar conditio, sed aequum hinc inde humanitatis solatium, non te decet difficilem, sed potius favorabilem et facilem inveniri.

16. X, 5, 6, canon 18, *Corpus iuris canonici, ed. cit.,* vol. II, col. 778, Potthast, *op. cit.,* number 9673, and X, 5, 6, canon 19; *ibid.,* Potthast *op. cit.,* number 9674.

17. See Appendix VIII.

18. Baronius-Raynaldus, *op. cit.,* XXI, 285, note 1: Anonymus Erfordiensis, Circa festum S. Michaelis, rex Franciae propter nimiam studii sui (Judaeorum . . .) jactantiam XXIII carractas librorum suorum Parisiis incendio jussit cremari.

19. *Les registres de Grégoire IX,* éd. L. Auvray (Paris, Thorin et Fils, 1896–1910), vol. I, cols. 142–143, number 230: . . . Judeos ad remittendum usuras per secularem faciatis potestatem compelli et, donec eas remiserint, communionem sibi fidelium denegari. Porro si qui crucesignatorum Judeis solvere debita nequeunt in presenti, laborare curetis et judices seculares sic eis de utili dilatione provideant, quod post iter peregrinationis arreptum, quousque de ipsorum obitu vel reditu certissime cognoscatur, usurarum incomoda [*sic*] non incurrant, compellendis nichilominus Judeis proventus pignorum, quos interim ipsi perceperint in sortem, expensis deductis necessariis computare.

20. *Ibid.,* II, 165, number 2765; also 33, number 2511; 344–345, number 3074; 529, number 3417.

21. *Ibid.,* I, 218, number 356; 378–379, number 594; 454–455, number 733; 613, number 1052; 797–799, number 1426; and 1427; for related complaints to the King of Hungary, 827, number 1498.

22. *Ibid.,* I, 444, number 707: . . . Ab eis etiam de ortorum fructibus decima nec non de habitaculis fratrum, sicut de Judeorum domibus, contendunt redditus extorquere, asserendi quod, nisi fratres morarentur ibidem, eis ab aliis habitatoribus proventus aliqui solverentur.

23. Baronius-Raynaldus, *op. cit.,* XXI, 89, number 67: . . . Moneri pariter Ferdinandum Castellae ac Legionis regem a Compostellano archiepiscopo praecepit ut Judaeos, qui plura patrabant scelera, coerceret, atque ex Concilii Oecumenici legibus signa, quibus distinguerentur, praeferre juberet; quos tamen in Galiis a populis perfidiae odio in ipsos concitatis religionis specie crudeliter exagitatos clementius haberi jussit, ita enim illorum scelera comprimi voluit, ut nullum in iis insectandis scelus committeretur.

24. *Les registres* . . . , II, cols. 43–45, number 2535; Baronius-Raynaldus, *op. cit.,* XXI, 113, number 20: Hic porro memoria celebrandum non praetermittemus Pontificem, ne ullo modo

a justitiae tramite deflecteret, Judaeis justis de causis ad eum confugientibus, benignum sese impertiisse . . . .

25. *Les registres* . . . , I, cols. 691–692, number 1216: Etsi Judeorum sit reprobanda perfidia, utilis tamen est et necessaria quodammodo Christianis conversatio eorundem, qui Salvatoris nostri habentes ymaginem, et ab universorum Creatore creati, a creaturis suis, videlicet Christi fidelibus, non sunt, prohibente Domino, perimendi; nam, quantumcumque sit eorum perversa medietas, amici Dei sunt ipsorum patres effecti, et etiam reliquie salve fient.

26. *Ibid.*, 692: Est autem Judeis a Christianis exhibenda benignitas, quam Christianis in Paganismo existentibus cupimus exhiberi.

27. *Les registres* . . . , II, cols. 471–473, number 3308: . . . cum aliis crucesignatis adversus Judeos . . . ex inaudite ac insolite crudelitatis excessu, duo millia et quingentos ex ipsis, tam magnos quam parvos, mulieresque pregnantes hostili rabie trucidarunt, nonnullis letaliter vulneratis, et conculcatis aliis equorum pedibus sicut lutum; ac, libris eorum incendio devastatis . . . bona ipsorum auferunt . . . ac pejora facere comminantur, pro eo quod renuunt baptizari . . . ad Apostolice Sedis clementiam duxerunt humiliter recurrendum; this letter was addressed to the King of France and to the archbishops and bishops of fourteen French dioceses, numbers 3309–3312.

28. *Les registres* . . . , II, cols. 779–780, number 3899: Ex parte tua nostris est auribus intimatum quod cum a Judeis regni tui et eorum debitoribus Christianis et ipsorum nomine, non modicum acceperis pecunie quantitatem: quia hujusmodi pecunia ab ipsis Judeis acquisita creditur nomine usurarum, tu, ne peccatum eorum tibi reputetur ad penam, satisfacere de pecunia desideras supradicta . . . multi a quibus Judei predicti extorserunt usuras, cognosci non possint, et pecuniam quam istis restituere teneberis velis in subsidium Constantinopolitani imperii destinare . . . ; see also *ibid.*, cols. 953–954, number 4205, 1183–1184, number 4641, 1169–1170, number 4601.

29. *Ibid.*, II, col. 385, number 3144: Nivelloni et Anselmo, quondam Judeis, nunc vero discipulis Jhesu Christi. Etsi universis que . . . ; see above (Chap. V, n. 42), legislation of Third Lateran Council, and below (Chap. VIII, n. 39), Pope John XXII, still trying in 1320 to enforce the 1179 reform in County Venaissin.

30. *Chartularium universitatis Parisiensis* (Paris: Delalain, 1889–1897), I, 201–202, number 172, Innocentius IV Ludovicum regem Francorum admonet ut quod Odo apostolicae sedis legatus circa Talmud aliosque libros Judaeorum statuerit

observari curet; see Baronius-Raynaldus, *Annales,* XXI, 284–285, number 40, on Saint Louis and his zeal in this affair.

31. *Ibid.,* I, 202–205; also 209, number 178, for condemnation of the Talmud by the Parisian masters of theology and of canon law.

32. Baronius-Raynaldus, *op. cit.,* XXI, 285, number 41, for text of this letter; it is calendared only in Innocent's *Les registres* . . . , I, 115, number 682.

33. Roger Bacon, *Opus minus, Opera quaedam hactenus inedita* ed. J. S. Brewer (London: Longman, Green, Longman and Roberts, 1859), p. 326: . . . magnam Summam illam, quae est plus quam pondus unius equi . . . .

34. Baronius-Raynaldus, *op. cit.,* XXI, 446, number 34: . . . exceptis iis qui artes mechanicas exercerent, in exilium actos. Quod edictum a S. Ludovico in Oriente adhuc agente emanasse ait, cujus causam hanc affert: "Improperatum enim fuit eidem regi a Sarracenis, quod parum diligimus, aut veneramur Dominum nostrum Jesum Christum, qui peremptores ejus inter nos degere toleramus."

35. *Les registres* . . . , III, p. 314, number 6980: Sicut tua nobis fraternitas intimavit ex conversatione Judeorum in tua provincia, quos aliquandiu de mandato Sedis Apostolice in eadem provincia non sine Christianorum dispendio et multorum scandalo tolerasse te asseris, gravia ipsis Christianis animarum noscuntur pericula imminere. Nos, ad animarum salutem totis affectibus aspirantes, expellendi de ipsa provincia predictos Judeos per te vel per alios, presertim cum statuta contra eos a Sede Apostolica edita, sicut accepimus, non observent . . . .

36. *Ibid.,* II, p. 3, number 4123.

37. *Ibid.,* II, pp. 109–110, number 4664.

38. *Ibid.,* II, pp. 250–251 (for John); p. 132 (for Mary).

39. See C. Roth, *The Ritual Murder Libel and the Jew, The Report by Cardinal Lorenzo Ganganelli (Pope Clement XIV)* (London, n.d.).

40. *Les registres* . . . , I, pp. 420–421, number 2815; text also in the collection *Die päpstlichen Bullen über die Blutbeschuldigung,* published first anonymously and then under the name M. Stern, (Berlin, Verlag Cronbach, 1893; Munich, 1900); in the Berlin edition, our text is number I, pp. 2–5.

41. *Les registres* . . . , I, p. 424, number 2838; Stern, *Die päpstlichen Bullen* . . . , text number II, pp. 6–9.

42. *Les registres* . . . , I, p. 463, number 3077 (calendared only); Stern, *Die päpstlichen Bullen* . . . , text number III, pp. 10–13; Baronius-Raynaldus, *op. cit.,* XXI, 362, number 84; see Appendix IX.

43. *Les registres d'Alexandre IV,* édd. de la Roncière, De Loye, Coulon (Paris, Thorin et Fils, 1895–1959), I, 957.

44. Baronius-Raynaldus, *op. cit.*, XXI, p. 502, number 78: . . .
    crudele facinus, quod Judaei in Hugone puero octenni Christiano Lincolniae commisere . . . . Cujus gestae rei historiam plures alii, atque inter eos novatores [that is, the Centuriators] scriptis commendarunt . . . .
45. *One Hundred English Folksongs*, ed. C. J. Sharp (Boston; New York; Chicago, n.d.), XX, number 8; exposition of "Little Sir Hugh," text, pp. 22–23.
46. For an urbane discussion of Chaucer's art and intent, see R. J. Schoeck, "Chaucer's Prioress: Mercy and Tender Heart," *The Bridge*, II (1956/57), 239–255.
47. *Les registres d'Urban IV*, éd. Guirard (Paris, Thorin et Fils, 1901–1958), II, p. 41, number 2900: . . . vos quodam modo excommunicant dum vobis communicare fideles non sinunt; ex quo illud evenit inconveniens ut, quantum ad hoc, judicari videamini judicio Judeorum . . . .
48. *Register caméral*, p. 57.
49. *Ibid.*, p. 87: clericos . . . per censuram ecclesiasticam, laicos vero per penam in Lateranensi concilio contra usurarios editam . . . Judeos vero . . . districtione compelli et donec ipsas reddiderint, communionem eis fidelium denegari.
50. *Ibid.*, p. 304 (calendared only): Patriarchae Jerosolim. mandat ut Sarracenos et Judaeos pauperes ad unitatem ecclesie converti volentes, per dies in quibus catechizari valeant, ab ecclesiis vel monasteriis Acconensis civitatis et diocesis in vitae necessariis faciat provideri.
51. *Les registres de Clement IV*, éd. E. Jordan (Paris, Thorin et Fils, 1893–1945), I, 4–6, number 15; II, 157–159, number 50.
52. Baronius-Raynaldus, *op. cit.*, XXII, 182, number 33; cf. 181, number 29.
53. *Ibid.*, XXII, 230, number 38: Nonnumquam viduas, statim viris earum viam universae carnis ingressis, ipsarum quoque necnon conjugatarum filias, ut cum personis vilibus, nonnullis hominibus tuis et aliis matrimonia contrahunt; majores insuper de civitatibus dicti regni, ut impudicas mulieres, seu alias, quae de Sarracenis aut Judeis traxerunt originem, sibi matrimonialiter copulent; passim non tam inducis voluntarios quam compellis, ut fertur, invitos.
54. *Les registres* . . . , II, 1579, number 19545: Quanto personam tuam . . . .
55. *Ibid.*, p. 1592, number 19723: Datam tibi de . . . .
56. *Ibid.*, III, 334, number 848: Agit nec immerito . . . Judeorum malitiam . . . de disputatione quam in regis presentia cum fratre Paulo de ord. Praedicatorum multis confictis abjectisque mendaciis librum composuit.
57. On this, see C. Roth, "The Disputation of Barcelona (1263),"

Harvard Theological Review, XLIII. No. 2 (1950), 117–144.

58. See above, Chap. IV, n. 7.
59. See Appendix X.
60. *Les registres* . . . , II, 236–240, number 669.
61. Potthast *op. cit.*, II, 1618, number 20081.
62. *Ibid.*, number 20082: . . . totum Talamud et omnes eorum libros . . . qui de textu Bibliae fuerint et alios, de quibus nulla sit dubitatio quod blasphemias vel errores contineant, Iudaeis restituant; ceteros vero sigillis suis consignatos in tutis locis deponant fideliter custodiendos.
63. (M. Stern) *Die päpstlichen Bullen* . . . , pp. 18–23.
64. *Les registres de Nicholas III* . . . , éd. J. Gay (Paris, E. de Boccard, 1898–1938), V, 408–411, numbers 965, 966, 1004: . . . concionibus et aliis modis conversioni Judaeorum . . . .
65. Baronius-Raynaldus, *op. cit.*, XXII, 444–445, number 78: De istis, si tales inveneris, qui sint, in quibus locis, et sub quorum dominio commorantur, nobis rescribere non omittas, ut circa pertinaces hujusmodi de salutari eorum remedio, sicut expedire videbimus, cogitemus. Ut autem de praemissis avidis nostris conceptibus juxta nostra desideria [satisfiat], frequenter nobis intimare studeas qualiter commissum tibi negotium prosperatur.
66. Petra, *op. cit.*, III, 256: . . . diversus prorsus sunt, compellere ad credendum, et compellere ad audiendum Verbum Dei . . . haec potius sit persuasio, quam coactio . . . eoque magis quia passim videmus Hebraeos in eorum perfidia obstinatos quamvis Praedicationi pluries interfuerint.
67. *Les registres*, II, 342, number 743: . . . Item Judoeos [*sic*] Christianis preponit multipliciter, unde multa mala proveniunt.
68. A. A. Neuman, *The Jews in Spain* (Philadelphia, 1944), II, 94, 114.
69. *Les registres de Martin IV*, édd. F. Olivier-Martin *et al.* (Paris, E. de Boccard, 1901–1935), III, 231–238, number 502.
70. Baronius-Raynaldus, *op. cit.*, XXII, 488, number 18: . . . de hujusmodi haeretica pravitate culpabiles vel de illa notabiliter suspectos . . . conversos quoque Judaeos, et postmodum patenter vel verisimilibus indiciis apostantes a fide.
71. See above, n. 60.
72. *Les registres d'Honorius IV*, éd. M. Prou (Paris, E. Thorin, 1888), 563–564; Baronius-Raynaldus, *op. cit.*, XXIII, 10–11, numbers 25, 26, 27.
73. Baronius-Raynaldus, *loc. cit.*: . . . clericos Arabes, atque alios ex Orientalibus terris lingua discrepantes Parisiis sacris litteris imbui, atque erudiri voluit, ut reversi in Orientem suos excolerent, Parisiensisque Ecclesiae cancellario iis pro-

videre jussit: qua in re Innocentii IV, Alexandri IV, Clementis IV, Gregorii X, zelum eximium est imitatus.

74. *Les registres de Nicolas IV*, éd. E. Langlois (Paris, E. Thorin, 1886–1891), I, 58, no. 313 (calendared only): . . . rogat quatenus magistrum Mehir de Ruthenburth, judaeum, ipsius jurisdictioni subjectum, nunc de mandato regio in carcere sine causa rationabili detentum, libertati restituat.

75. Baronius-Raynaldus, *op. cit.*, XXIII, 53–54, numbers 29–31.

76. *Ibid.*, 86–87, no. 49.

77. *Les registres* . . . , I, 612, no. 4184 (Potthast *op. cit.*, II, p. 1888, number 23541) (calendared only): Vicario suo in Urbe mandat ne judaeos Urbis a christianis molestari permittat.

78. *Ibid.*, II, 849, number 6318.

79. *Les registres de Boniface VIII*, édd. G. Digard *et al.* (Paris, E. de Boccard, 1884–1939), I, col. 263, number 778 (Potthast *op. cit.*, number 24091); I, 286, number 848; I, 597, number 1591; I, 620–621, number 1654; II, 566, number 3381; II, 597–598, number 3421; III, 275; III, 655, number 5020; for identical text, see III, 667, number 5039.

80. *Ibid.*, I, 328–329, number 937.

81. *Ibid.*, II, 719–723, number 3617–3621.

82. *Ibid.*, II, 412–413, number 3063: . . . Nos autem, considerantes imbecillitatem vestram et propterea vos, etiamsi divitiis habundetis, impotentium numero ascribentes, volumus ut tanquam impotentibus predicti inquisitores, in casibus in quibus contra vos possent eadem auctoritate inquirere, vobis predictam publicationem faciant nec potentiam ad eam denegandam pretendant, nisi adeo de potentia illius contra quem in dictis casibus inquiretur esset notorium . . . .

Chapter VIII

1. *Cartulaire général de l'ordre des Hospitaliers* . . . , IV, 110, number 4681: Item quia ex ratione naturali colligitur quod congruum foret et rationi consonum quod, ad acquirendum sanctam civitatem Jherusalem, debeat haberi subsidium, si possit fieri, de bonis illorum qui illic Virginis Filium crucis affixerunt patibulo, per quem civitas ipsa sanctificata fuit, erit bonum quod dominus papa ordinet aliquam talliam et contribucionem super omnes Judeos in terris habitantes Christianorum, ad minus usque ad omnium bonorum suorum decimam

ascendentem; licet nos credamus quod non esset nimis si omnium bonorum suorum medietas caperetur.

2. *Ibid.*, 181–182, number 4807: Judeos quoque ad remictendas ipsis usuras per secularem compelli precipimus potestatem, et, donec eas remiserint, ab omnibus Christi fidelibus, quibus hoc per suos diocesanos denuntiatum exstiterit, tam in mercimoniis quam in aliis, sub excommunicationis pena jubemus eis communionem omnimodam denegari . . . .

3. E. Baluze, *Vitae paparum Avenionensium,* nouv. éd. G. Mollat (Paris, Letouzey et Ané, 1914–1927), I, 5: Hoc etiam anno (1306), in augusto et septembri, omnes Judei, nisi forte pauci qui baptizari voluerunt, de regno Francie sunt expulsi; eorumque bona rex habuit et fecit colligi per ministros, nisi quod cuilibet Judeo data est portio aliqua pecunie pro via extra regnum complenda; quorum multi in itinere mortui sunt pre lassitudine vel dolore. *Ibid.*, p. 62: Anno Domini MCCCVJ, in festo sancte Marie Magdalene [22 July 1306], de mandato et ordinatione regis Francie, fuerunt capti omnes Judei ubique in regno Francie quasi imperceptibiliter una die, et confiscata sunt bona ipsorum, quecumque potuerunt inveniri; fueruntque a regno expulsi, ulterius minime reversuri; see also *ibid.*, p. 93.

4. *Regestrum Clementis papae V* (Rome, Typographia Vaticana, 1884–1888), I, number 1139 (calendared only): Cuidam indulget, ut si minus iuste a Iudaeis in terra usa commorantibus aliqua exegerit bona et pecuniae quantitatis, ad restitutionem cuiquam faciendam nullatenus teneatur, dummodo bona eadem in usus eroget pauperum.

5. *Ibid.*, number 491 (calendared only): Mariae remittit, ut pecunias a nonnullis Iudaeis exactas convertat in subsidium Terrae sanctae.

6. *Ibid.*, VIII, number 9134: . . . bonis, que erant apud Iudeos in tua terra morantes, tempore generalis et novissime expulsionis ipsorum et aliorum Iudeorum de regno Francie ad te usque ad summam decem millium librarum Turonen. parvarum pervenisse noscatur, nos tuis supplicationibus inclinatis, ut medietatem huiusmodi bonorum que ad te, ut premittitur devenerunt, retinere tibi et de illis disponere, prout expedire videris . . . reliquam vero medietatem convertere in Terre sancte subsidium tenearis . . . .

7. In Clem. I, 8, canon 1; *Corpus Iuris Canonici, ed. cit.*, II, col. 1147: Clemens V in concilio Viennensi. Quum Iudaei quidam et Sarraceni, sicut accepimus, quod super civilibus aut criminalibus convinci per Christianos non possint, se privilegiis regum et principum tueantur; quia id nedum iuri contrarium, sed et Christianae religioni opprobriosum est quamplurimum et adversum, reges eosdem et principes in

Domino exhortamur, ne concedant huiusmodi de cetero privilegia, vel servent aut servare permittant etiam iam concessa . . . .

8. *Ibid.*, V, 1, canon 1, col. 1179: . . . viris catholicis notitiam
linguarum habentibus, quibus utuntur infideles praecipue
abundare sanctam affectamus ecclesiam . . . scholas in sub-
scriptarum linguarum generibus, ubicunque Romanam curiam
residere contigerit, nec non in Parisiensi et Oxoniensi, Bonon-
iensi et Salamantino studiis providimus erigendas . . .
hebraicae, arabicae et chaldaeae linguarum . . . .

9. See remarks of G. Mollat in his edition of *Bernard Gui,
Manuel de l'inquisiteur* (Paris, Champion, 1927), p. L.

10. *Practica inquisitionis heretice pravitatis,* éd. C. Douais,
(Paris: Picard, 1886), p. 288: Judei perfidi conantur, quando
et ubi possunt, occulte pervertere Christianos et trahere ad
perfidiam judaycam, maxime illos qui prius fuerunt Judei et
conversi sunt . . . ; p. 290: "curse" against Christians in
daily prayers: Benedictus tu, Deus Dominus noster, rex in
seculum, qui non fecisti me christianum vel gentilem. Item:
Destructis seu conversis ad fidem Christi nulla sit spes, et
omnibus hereticis vel non credentibus, accusatoribus vel
bilinguis, id est traditoribus omnibus illud momentum sit,
id est in momento sint perditi . . . ; also, *ibid.*, p. 291:
Notandum autem quod in predictis verbis Judei intendunt
imprecari christianis, quamvis expresse non nominent christianos set sit per circumloqutionem . . . .

11. *Ibid.*, p. 291: . . . quem Judei gallici vocant Maazor, quod
est dictam [*sic*] collectarium orationum, et Judei provinciales
vocant Typhilloth, quod est dictum librum orationum, con-
tinentur supra scripte imprecationes seu maledictiones quas
Judei faciunt contra populum christianum . . . cujus actor
[*sic*] vocatur Salmon, qui intitulatur apud eos *Glosa super
textum legis* . . . quem Judei vocant *Glosas Moysi de Egypto*
et actor [*sic*] illius libri intitulavit *Declarationem et reformationem legis* . . . quem Judei vocant *Glosa David hyspani.*

12. Not without well-founded doubt; see B. Guillemain, *La cour
pontificale d'Avignon* (*1309–1376*), étude d'une société
(Paris, E. de Boccard, 1962), 112–113.

13. See N. V[alois], *Histoire littéraire de la France,* XXXIV, 395,
n. 4; cites *Chartularium universitatis Parisiensis,* II, 427: . . .
Et quia, fili dilectissime, forsan tibi dicitur quod nos non
sumus in theologia magister; audi quid unus sapiens dicat:
"Non quis, inquit, sed quid dicat intendite" (letter of John
XXII to Philip IV). Certainly held doctorate in both laws;
see Guillemain, *op. cit.*, n. 110, and is responsible for the
addition to the *Corpus Iuris Canonici* of the *Liber septimus*

of Clement V, of his own *Extravagantes*, and of the *Extravagantes communes*, which go back as far as Boniface VIII.

14. N. V[alois], *loc. cit.*, p. 542, where the view that it is better to imitate the Virgin than to discuss her origin is recorded.

15. *Chartularium universitatis Parisiensis*, II, 440.

16. Guillemain, *op. cit.*, p. 113 with respect to the working days of the Pope on December 2 and 3, 1334, before his death at dawn on December 4.

17. N. V[alois], *loc. cit.*, pp. 407–408, lists these concerns as poison, magic, alchemy, Judaism, heresy, the exaggerated asceticism of the Franciscan "Spirituals," jealous claims of the secular clergy, independent spirit of temporal princes, the emancipated Empire, and the omnipotent State.

18. *Ibid.*, pp. 408–409: . . . Juif qui avait modelé les statuettes de cire.

19. Guillemain, *op. cit.*, p. 131, n. 178.

20. *Lettres communes de Jean XXII*, Intro. par G. Mollat (Paris, 1921), II, 337, number 8997, *Chartularium universitatis Parisiensis* II, 228.

21. Baronius-Raynaldus, *op. cit.*, XXIV, 127, number 21: Pontifex namque Philippum Francorum regem ob civilia Christianorum regum bella avertebat, ratus funestam aliquam cladem nisi pacatus esset Occidens, exspectandam, nec unius regni vires potentissimis soldanis pares esse aucupandumque videri tempus commodius . . . .

22. A "crusade" of *Pastorelli* is recorded to have arisen in A.D. 1250 under the leadership of a polyglot Hungarian convert to Islam, who was believed to have organized the movement in order to betray a mass of Christians to the Sultan; the crimes ascribed to the 1250 uprising, which are numerous, do not seem to have included the massacre of Jews; see Baronius-Raynaldus, *op. cit.*, XXI, 392, numbers 29 and 30.

23. *Vitae paparum Aven.* I, 128: . . . quidem presbiter qui propter maleficia sua fuerat parrochia sua spoliatus, et quidam alius apostata ab ordine sancti Benedicti . . . .

24. *Ibid.*: . . . Parisius . . . ad Sanctum Germanum de Pratis . . . versus Aquitaniam . . . . Ad partes vero venientes Aquitanie, passim omnes Judeos . . . occidebant . . . versus Carcassonam . . . Tolosam. . . .

25. Baronius-Raynaldus, *op. cit.*, XXIV, 127, numbers 21, 23.

26. *Ibid.*, number 23.

27. *Vitae paparum Aven.* I, 161: Et ut eorum favor amplius cresceret in populo, et zelus aliqualiter appareret, communem fecerunt vocem ut omnes Judei, ubicumque reperirentur, qui nollent baptizari, interficerentur ab eis, nullo alio judicio preeunte; quod et opere impleverunt.

28. *Ibid.* 130: Sed multi de interitu Judeorum gaudentes, dixerunt

quod pro infidelibus contra fideles se opponere non debebant . . . .

29. *Ibid.* 161–162: Perquirentesque Judeos in civitatibus, castris et villis, et nollentes baptizari absque omni judicio trucidabant, bona eorum diripientes et suis usibus applicantes; factaque est strages Judeorum grandis ab eis in regno Francie, et specialiter in provincia Burdegalensi [Bordeaux] et in partibus Vasconie [S. Bazas], et in provincia Tholosana [Toulouse] et in diocesibus Caturcensi [Cahors] et Albiensi [Albi] . . . . Et nisi providentia et potentia majorum de populo obstitisset, procedebant versus romanam curiam apud Avenionem.

30. *Ibid.* 129–130: Judei autem qui evadere poterant, de villa in villam ab eorum facie fugiebant. Tandem ad quoddam castrum . . . in Turri dicta de ejus licentia sunt recepti. Pastorelli vero . . . obsidio non cessavit. Cum autem eis ligna et lapides defecissent, pueros loco lapidum projecerunt . . . dixerunt uni de suis, qui fortior videbatur, quod eos gladio jugularet; qui fere quingentos protinus interfecit, quibusdam tantum pueris reservatis. Qui descendens, quod fecerat, pastorellis nuntiavit, petens cum pueris baptizari. Cui illi: Tu in gentem tuam tantum flagitium perpetrasti, et effugies ita mortem? Statim membratim extitit laniatus; see also Baronius-Raynaldus *op. cit.*, XXIV, 128, number 24.

31. *Vitae paparum Aven.* I, 171.

32. Baronius-Raynaldus *op. cit.*, XXIV, 128, number 24 and 127, number 22; for his letters to ordinaries and officials, see *Lettres secrètes et curiales,* I, cols. 936–938, numbers 1104–1115.

33. *Vitae paparum Aven.* I, 171: Cito autem inconposita et agrestis illa multitudo evanuit; cf. Baronius-Raynaldus *op cit.*, XXIV, 128, number 23.

34. *Vitae paparum Aven.* I, 132: . . . maleficium propter quod in Aquitania omnes leprosi sunt combusti. Ipsi siquidem sunt confessi quod fontes et puteos infecerunt, illo fine ut omnes christiani aut leprosi fierent aut citius morerentur . . . dominus de Parteniaco sub sigillo suo misit regi confessionem cujusdam magni leprosi qui de hoc in terra sua fuerat accusatus, et recognovit quod quidam dives Judeus ad hoc eum induxerat. . . .

35. *Ibid.* 133: quia multi Judei sunt inventi culpabiles in hoc facto in pluribus partibus omnes sine differentia sunt combusti; Parisius autem soli culpabiles.

36. Baronius-Raynaldus *op. cit.*, XXIV, 165, no. 44.

37. *Vitae paparum Aven.* I, 134.

38. N. V[alois], *Histoire littéraire de la France,* XXXIV, 421.

39. *Lettres secrètes et curiales* I, cols. 938–939; see *Extravagantes*

communes V, titulus 2, caput 2; *Corpus Iuris Canonici* II, col. 1290.

40. Baronius-Raynaldus *op. cit.*, XXIV, 165, number 44; *Lettres secrètes et curiales* II, cols. 7–8 and 23–24, numbers 1255, 1256; cf. 1285 for full text, calendared in prior references.

41. N. V[alois], *loc. cit.*

42. See Douais ed., pp. 67–71.

43. *Vitae paparum Aven.* III, 243; Baronius-Raynaldus, *op. cit.*, XXIV, 128–131, numbers 24–30.

44. Douais ed., pp. 170–171.

45. Baronius-Raynaldus, *op. cit.*, XXIV, 128, number 24: Divinae porro justitiae a Pastorellis edita strages adscribi poterit, si atrocia Judaeorum scelera ac blasphemae voces, quas in Christum et Virginem vomebant, perpendantur; utque Thalmudicis fabulis simplicem populum irretire niterentur; there follows the text of Pope John's *Dudum felicis recordationis.*

46. *Ibid.*, 131, number 30: . . . sed Judaeorum improbitate Thalmudica impietas repullularat.

47. See J. Nohl, *The Black Death*, trans. C. H. Clarke (London, Unwin Books, 1926), p. 72, for remarks by Guy de Chauliac, personal physician to Clement VI, on the humiliating helplessness of medical men.

48. Baronius-Raynaldus, *op. cit.*, XXV, 455, number 33.

49. *Ibid.*, 454, number 33: Clemens itaque novo Apostolico edicto docuit nullam immanis adeo suspicionis causam subesse posse, cum lues Judaeos etiam absumeret. . . .

50. *Vitae paparum Aven.* I, 251–252: Et huic malo superadditum est aliud. Nam insurrexit quedam vox quod erant aliqui malefici, et specialiter Judei, qui in aquis et fontibus potiones immittebant, cujus occasione pestis predicta sic incrassabatur. Propter quod multi tam christiani quam Judei innocentes et inculpabiles fuerunt cremati, trucidati et alias in personas male tractati, cum revera hoc non esset nisi ratione constellationis aut divini ultionis. . . .

51. *Ibid.* p. 306: Anno sequenti [1348] Judei per totam Alamaniam fuerunt combusti, quibus imponebatur quod fontes et puteos intoxicassent; et aliqui torti id confessi fuerunt esse verum.

52. Baronius-Raynaldus, *op. cit.*, XXV, 454, number 33: Nullus Christianus Judaeos eosdem invitos vel nolentes ad baptismum per violentiam venire compellat: sed si quis eorum sponte ad Christianos fidei causa confugerit, postquam voluntas ejus fuerit patefacta, efficiatur absque aliqua calumnia Christianus: veram quippe Christianitatis fidem habere non creditur, qui ad Christianorum Baptisma non spontaneus sed invitus cognoscitur pervenire. Nullus etiam Christianus eorumdem Judaeorum personas sine judicio domini regionis, civi-

tatis seu terrae, in qua habitant, vulnerare aut occidere, vel
suas illis pecunias auferre praesumat. . . .

53. *Ibid.*, 455, number 33: Nuper ad nostrum fama publica, seu
infamia verius, perduxit auditum, quod nonnulli Christiani
pestem, qua Deus populum Christianum ipsius peccatis
populi provocatus affligit, Judaeorum falso tossicationibus
seducente diabolo imputantes, nonnullos ex Judaeis ipsis
temeritate propria, non deferentes aetati vel sexui, impie
peremerunt: quodque licet iidem Judaei super hujusmodi
impostura facinoris parati sint subire judicium coram judice
competente; ob hoc tamen Christianorum ipsorum impetus
non tepescit, sed eo furor saevit in majus eorumdem: quo
videtur error eorum, dum eis non resistitur, approbari. Et
quamvis Judaeos eosdem nulli culpabiles aut conscii forsan
essent tanti flagitii, cui vix excogitari posset poena sufficiens,
digna et severa vellemus animadversione percelli; quia tamen
per diversa mundi climata Judaeos ipsos ac alias natione
plurimas, quae cohabitationem Judaeorum eorumdem non
noverant, pestis haec ubique fere communis afflixit occulto
Dei judicio et affligit; proinde verisimilitudo non recipit,
quod Judaei praedicti occasionem tanto flagitio praestiterint
sive causam. . . .

54. *Ibid.*: . . . si quae vero cum iis intercedat controversia, ipsos
in jus vocent, et coram judice litem disceptent.

55. *Ibid.*

56. *Ibid.*, XXVI, 483, number 10: Sacrosancta Romana ac universalis Ecclesia etiam pro perfidis Judaeis ad omnipotentem
sempiternumque Deum, qui et Judaicam perfidiam a sua
misericordia non repellit, saepissime preces fundit . . . novis-
simis diebus adeo efficaces existunt, ut nonnulli ex ipsis
Judaeis de diversis partibus ad partes Italiae accedentes . . .
verae veritatis luce, quae Christus est, summis desideriis
cupiunt illustrari . . . .

57. *Ibid.*: . . . et in signum non fictae, sed sincerae conversionis
eorum pro subsidio Terrae-Sanctae, et ejusdem sanctae matris
Ecclesiae per schismaticos multipliciter lacessitae in remissionem peccatorum eorum de bonis quae habent, libere non
parvam pecuniarum offerunt quantitatem . . . baptizare, et
eis Confirmationis sacramentum conferre procures. . . .

58. *Ibid.*, XXVII, 485, number 2.

59. *Ibid.*: . . . imaginem Dei habent, et reliquiae eorum salvae
fient, ipsorumque conversatio utilis est nimirum in praestandis
obsequiis Christianis. . . .

60. *Ibid.*, 486, number 2: Illos autem ex Judaeis praedictis
duntaxat hujusmodi protectionis praesidio volumus gaudere,
qui nil machinari praesumpserint in subversionem fidei
memoratae.

61. *Ibid.*, 541, number 36: . . . quaecumque per praedicatores contra ipsos Judaeos, ne cum Christianis conversari debeant, . . . districtius inhibemus, ne de caetero talia vel similia contra Judaeos . . . populis praedicare permittant; volentes quod quilibet Christianus Judaeos ipsos humana mansuetudine prosequatur, nec eis in personis, rebus aut bonis suis inferat injuriam, molestiam vel offensam; sed sicut permissum est eis cum Christianis vicissim conversari liceat, etiam mutua commoda alterutrum suscipere.

62. *Ibid.*, XXVIII, 386–388, number 15.

63. *Ibid.*, 553–554, number 5.

64. *Ibid.*, 554–555, number 5.

65. *Ibid.*, 555, number 6.

66. *Bullarium franciscanum,* ed. Conrad Eubel (Rome, 1898–1908), II, 625, number 1206: . . . si quando contingit, ut de iudaeis, mauris, neophitis, Pragensibus aliisve eiusmodi . . . mentionem, etiam illis praesentibus, facerent, consueverunt in spiritus fervore et Dei zelo parum graviter evehi illosque magis maledictis et conviciis irritare quam, impugnetis confutatisque eorum erroribus, iuxta gloriosi Patris et magistri vestri praeceptum in transmissa ad vos regula, ut resipiscant et ad cor reversi veritatem recipiant, examinate prudenterque monere et allicere . . .

67. Baronius-Raynaldus, *op. cit.,* XXX, 51, no. 45.

68. *Ibid.*, XXX, 51–52, numbers 46–48.

69. *Ibid.*, 52, number 50.

70. *Bullarium franciscanum* III, 518, number 1045: Allati sunt nuper ad Nos iudaici quidam libelli "De Talmuth novo" inscripti, in quibus ea de Salvatore nostro Iesu Christo et eius genetrice intemerata Maria perhibentur, quae ut proferre est nefas, ita sine dolore ingenti cogitare non possumus. Nos, ut accipimus, iudaei perfidi quotidie exteriusque impio ore blasphemare non desinunt et in mansuetudinem christianam, quae eos alit et tolerat, ingratissimi, veram religionem improbare non cessant . . . .

71. Baronius-Raynaldus, *op. cit.,* XXX, 91–92, number 21.

72. *Ibid.*, 92, number 21–22.

73. *Ibid.* number 22.

74. *Ibid.*, 139, number 16.

75. *Ibid.*, 180, number 8: Mauricis enim sordibus Hispanias liberasse non contenti Judaica etiam superstitione expiare decreverunt, cum hoc perfidum genus in dies sobolesceret, suaque multitudine Christianam rempublicam aliquando in discrimen adducere posset.

76. *Ibid.*

77. *Ibid.*, 207, number 32: Aliud quod proposuit est, quod ex quo praefatus rex expulerat Marranos de imperio suo, tan-

quam inimicos Christianae fidei, quod mirabatur quod papa,
qui esset caput dictae fidei, illos recepisset in Urbe: et
propterea hortatus est eum, ut de terris Ecclesiae illi sub-
jectis eos expelleret.
78. *Ibid.,* 285–286, number 22: after recounting the trial and
sentence, the chronicler (ultimately Burchard) has this to
say on the Marrano ideology: Objecta porro ei fuere, effutiisse
legem Mosaicam unum habere principium, Christianam tria:
Christum non esse passum, si sit Deus: orando dixisse gloria
Patri, et aliarum duarum personarum divinarum mentionem
omisisse. Comedisse antequam celebraret: diebus prohibitis
carnes esitasse: indulgentias inanes et commentitias esse ad
quaestum confictas: non infernum, non purgatorium, sed
paradisum tantum conditum a Deo. Erant haec Marranicae
haereseos praecipua capita. L. Pastor, *The History of the
Popes* (Eng. trans., London, Kegan Paul Trench Trübner,
1911), VI, 157, was persuaded that the action against the
Marranos reflects Spanish influence.
79. Baronius-Raynaldus, *op. cit.,* XXX, 285, number 22: In tanta
vitiorum libertate, quae Alexandro VI Pontifice vig[n]ere,
Judaei Christianam religionem ementiti, omnibusque flagitiis
contaminatissimi in curiae Romanae officia irrepsisse comperti
sunt: tum quadraginta Marrani, genere Hispani, Marranicae
haereseos infamia insignes comprehensi, qui cum haeresim
publice damnandam parati essent solita clementia in Ecclesiae
sinum recepti fuere.
80. *Ibid.,* 257–258, number 25, 26.
81. H. H. Graetz, *Geschichte der Juden von den ältesten Zeiten
bis auf die Gegenwart* (Leipzig: Oskar Leiner, 1897–1911),
IX, 216; L. Pastor, *op. cit.,* VI, 157.
82. H. H. Graetz, *op. cit.* (German edition), VIII, 364–365.
83. *Rerum Italicarum Scriptores* (Città di Castello: S. Lapi,
1900 ff), XXXII, part 1, vol. 2, p. 224 (J. Burckardi, *Liber
notarum*): . . . ipsique Judei, si christianis pressura obvenerit,
quod Deus pro sua clementia avertat, detrimentum essent
participes et eorum periculo uti nostro res ageretur.
84. *Ibid.:* Judei quoque ab ea impositione immunis esse non
debent, cum inter christianorum dominia constituti liberam
ab eis ducere vitam, in ritibus suis persistere, divitias ad-
quirere multisque aliis privilegiis gaudere permittantur, et
sese denique ex commodis christianorum sustentare ac liberos
et eorum familias alere dignoscantur . . . .
85. *Ibid.,* p. 226.
86. *Ibid.,* p. 505: Martis, XVII februarii et sequentibus diebus,
Judei et ceteri cucurrerunt pro palliis, more solito, et alia
festa bestialia romana habita solemniter.
87. H. H. Graetz, *op. cit.,* (German edition), IX, 38, where

APPENDIX I

POPE GREGORY I

PASCASIO EPISCOPO NEAPOLIM:

Qui sincera intentione extraneos ad christianam religionem, ad fidem cupiunt rectam adducere, blandimentis debent,
non asperitatibus studere, ne quorum mentem reddita plana
ratio poterat provocare, pellat procul adversitas; nam quique
aliter agunt et eos hoc sub velamine a consueta ritus sui
volunt cultura suspendere, suas illi magis quam Dei probantur
causas attendere. Iudaei siquidem Neapolim habitantes questi
nobis sunt asserentes, quod quidam eos a quibusdam feriarum
suarum sollemnibus inrationabiliter nitantur arcere, ne illis
sit licitum festivitatum suarum sollemnia colere, sicut eis
nunc usque et parentibus eorum longis retro temporibus
licuit observare vel colere. Quod si ita se veritas habet,
supervacuae rei videntur operam adhibere. Nam quid utili-
tatis est, quando, et si contra longum usum fuerint vetiti, ad
fidem illis et conversionem nihil proficit? Aut cur Iudaeis,
qualiter cerimonias suas colere debeant, regulas ponimus, si
per hoc eos lucrari non possumus? Agendum ergo est, ut
ratione potius et mansuetudine provocati sequi nos velint,
non fugere, ut eis ex eorum codicibus ostendentes quae
dicimus ad sinum matris ecclesiae Deo possimus adiuvante
convertere. Itaque fraternitas tua eos monitis quidem, prout
potuerit, Deo adiuvante ad convertendum accendat et de
suis illos sollemnibus inquietare denuo non permittat, sed
omnes festivitates feriasque suas, sicut hactenus tam ipsi
quam parentes eorum per longa colentes retro tempora
tenuerunt, liberam habeant observandi celebrandique licentiam.

MGH Epist. vol. II, 383 (XIII, 15).

To Pascasius, Bishop of Naples:

Those who, with sincere intent, desire to lead people outside the Christian religion to the correct faith, ought to make the effort by means of what is pleasant, not with what is harsh, lest opposition drive afar the mind of men whom reasoning, rendered clear, could have attracted. Those who act otherwise and who, under this pretext, want them to give up the customary practice of their own rite, demonstrate that they are concerned with their own enterprises, rather than with those of God!

Now, the Jews dwelling in Naples have registered a complaint with Us, asserting that certain people are attempting, in an unreasonable fashion, to restrain them from some of the solemnities connected with their own feast days, as it has been lawful for them to observe or celebrate these up to now, and for their forefathers from long ages past. If this is the truth, why they seem to be expending their energy on an extraordinarily empty project; for of what use is this, when, even though they have been put under this prohibition, and prolonged usage has been flouted, it avails nothing toward their faith and conversion? Or, why do we set down rules as to how Jews ought to conduct their own ceremonies, if by this means we are unable to win them over? One must act, therefore, in such a way that, owing to our reasoning and meekness, they might desire to follow us rather than to fly from us, in such a way that, showing them what we say out of their own Books, we might be able to convert them, with the help of God, to the bosom of mother Church. And thus Your Fraternity, using admonitions, to be sure, as far as he can, may be afire for conversion with the help of God, but may not permit these men to be disquieted with respect to their solemnities. Rather let them enjoy their lawful liberty to observe and to celebrate all their festivities, as they have enjoyed this up until now, they and their forefathers as well, worshiping through long ages past.

APPENDIX II

POPE GREGORY IV

(Gratian, *Decretum,* pars I, distinctio 45, canon 5. Unde in Tolletano Concilio IV [c. 56] statutum est:)

De Iudaeis autem precepit sancta sinodus, nemini deinceps vim ad credendum inferre. "Cui enim vult Deus miseretur, et quem vult indurat" [Rom. 9 : 18]. Non enim tales inviti salvandi sunt, sed volentes, ut integra sit forma iusticiae. Sicut enim homo propria arbitrii voluntate serpenti obediens periit, sic vocante se gratia Dei propriae mentis conversione quisque credendo salvatur. Ergo non vi, sed libera arbitrii facultate ut convertantur suadendi sunt, non potius impellendi. Qui autem iampridem ad Christianitatem coacti sunt (sicut factum est temporibus religiosissimi principis Sisebuti), quia iam constat eos sacramentis divinis associatos, et baptismi gratiam suscepisse, et crismate unctos esse, et corporis Domini extitisse particeps, oportet ut fidem, quam vi vel necessitate susceperint, tenere cogantur, ne nomen Domini blasphemetur, et fides, quam susceperunt, vilis ac contemptibilis habeatur.

Friedberg ed., Vol. I, cols. 161–162

For translation, see Notes, Chap. IV, n. 12.

APPENDIX III

POPE ALEXANDER II

Omnibus episcopis Hispaniae:

Placuit nobis sermo quem nuper de vobis audivimus, quomodo tutati estis Judaeos qui inter vos habitant, ne interimerentur ab illis qui contra Sarracenos in Hispaniam proficiscebantur. Illi quippe stulta ignorantia, vel forte caeca cupiditate commoti, in eorum necem volebant saevire, quos fortasse divina pietas ad salutem praedestinavit. Sic etiam beatus Gregorius quosdam qui ad eos delendos exardescebant prohibuit, impium esse denuntians eos delere velle, qui Dei misericordia servati sunt, ut, patria libertateque amissa, diuturna poenitentia, patrum praejudicio in effusione sanguinis Salvatoris damnati, per terrarum orbis plagas dispersi vivant. Dispar nimirum est Judaeorum et Sarracenorum causa. In illos enim, qui Christianos persequuntur, et ex urbibus et propriis sedibus pellunt, juste pugnatur; hi vero ubique parati sunt servire. Quemdam etiam episcopum synagogam eorum destruere volentem prohibuit.

PL 146, 1386 D–1387 A (Epistola 101).

For translation, see Notes, Chap. V, n. 9.

APPENDIX IV

POPE INNOCENT III

Regi Francorum:

Etsi non displiceat Domino, sed ei potius sit acceptum ut sub catholicis regibus et principibus Christianis vivat et serviat dispersio Judaeorum, cujus tunc tandem reliquiae salvae fient [Rom. 9 : 3–24], cum in diebus illis salvabitur Juda [Jer. 33 : 6–26], et Israel habitaverit confidenter [Ezechiel 38 : 14], vehementer tamen oculos divinae majestatis offendunt, qui crucifigentium filios, contra quos adhuc sanguis clamat in Patris auribus, crucifixi Christi cohaeredibus praeferunt et tanquam ancillae filius cum filio liberae possit et debeat haeres esse [Rom. 8 : 17; Gen. 21 : 10], Judaicam servitutem illorum libertati praeponunt quos Filius liberavit.

Sane, ad nostram noveris audientiam pervenisse, quod in regno Francorum Judaei adeo insolescunt ut, sub specie usurariae pravitatis, per quam non solum usuras sed usuras usurarum extorquent, ecclesiarum bona et possessiones Christianorum usurpent, sicque illud impletum in Christianorum populo videatur quod in Judaeorum persona propheta deplorat: Haereditas, inquiens, nostra versa est ad alienos, domus nostrae ad extraneos [Lam. 5 : 2].

Praeterea, cum in Lateranensi concilio sit statutum [III Concilio Lateranensi, titulo XXVI] ut Judaei, nec sub alendorum puerorum obtentu, nec pro servitio, nec alia qualibet causa, in domibus suis habere permittantur mancipia Christiana, sed excommunicentur qui cum eis praesumpserint habitare, ipsi et servos Christianos habere non dubitant, et nutrices, cum quibus eas interdum abominationes exercent quas te potius punire convenit quam nos deceat explicare.

Insuper, cum idem concilium testimonium Christianorum adversus Judaeos in communibus causis, cum et illi adversus Christianos testibus Judaeis utantur, censuerit admittendum, et anathemate feriri decreverit quicunque Judaeos Christianis in hac parte praeferret, usque adeo eis defertur in regno Francorum ut non credatur Christianis testibus contra ipsos, sed ipsi contra Christianos ad testimonium admittantur. Quod si aliquando hi, quibus suam credunt pecuniam sub usuris, Christianos testes super facta solutione producant, plus creditur instrumento, quod apud eos per negligentiam aut incuriam debitor reliquerat indiscretus, quam testibus introductis; imo, non recipiuntur etiam testes in hoc articulo contra eos.

Usque adeo etiam, quod cum rubore referimus, insolescunt ut Senoniensi juxta quamdam ecclesiam veterem novam construxerint synagogam, ecclesia non modicum altiorem in qua, non sicut olim priusquam fuissent ejecti de regno demissa voce, sed cum magno clamore secundum ritum Judaicum sua officia celebrantes, divinorum celebrationem in eadem ecclesia non dubitant impedire.

Quinimo, nomen Domini blasphemantes, publice Christianis insultant, quod credant in rusticum quemdam suspensum a populo Judaeorum, quem quidem nec nos pro nobis suspensum ambigimus, cum peccata nostra ipse tulerit in suo corpore super lignum [1 Pet. 2 : 24], sed rusticum moribus aut genere non fatemur; imo nec ipsi diffiteri valerent quin ipse secundum carnem de sacerdotali stirpe descenderit ac regali, et mores ejus praeclari fuerunt et honesti. In die quoque parasceves, Judaei, contra veterem consuetudinem, per vicos et plateas publice discurrentes, concurrentes, juxta morem, undique Christianos ut adorent crucifixum in cruce derident, et eos per improperia sua student ab adorationis officio revocare.

Patent quoque latronibus usque ad noctem dimidiam ostia Judaeorum, nec si quid furto sublatum inventum fuerit apud eos, quisquam de illis potest justitiam obtinere.

Abutuntur ergo Judaei patientia regia, et, cum inter Christianos positi remaneant, hospites suos male cum opportunitate captata Christianos latenter occidunt, sicut nuper dicitur accidisse, cum quidam pauper scholaris in eorum latrina mortuus est repertus.

Ne igitur per eos nomen Domini blasphemetur, nec deterior sit Christianorum libertas quam servitus Judaeorum, monemus serenitatem regiam, et exhortamus in Domino, et in remissionem injungimus peccatorum, quatenus sic Judaeos super his et similibus a sua praesumptione compescas, sic abusiones hujusmodi de regno Francorum studeas abolere, quod habere zelum Dei secundum scientiam [Rom. 10 : 5] videaris et cum leges etiam saeculares gravius animadvertant in eos qui nomen Domini blasphemant, sic animadvertas in blasphemos hujusmodi, quod aliquorum poena metus sit omnium, nec facilitas veniae incentivum tribuat delinquendi.

Ad eliminandos insuper haereticos de regno Francorum potenter insurgas, nec lupos ad perdendas oves sub ovina pelle latentes [Matt. 7 : 15], in terra sua latere permittat regia celsitudo, sed in eorum demonstret persecutione fervorem quo fidem prosequitur Christianam.

Datum Romae, apud Sanctum Petrum, XVII Kalendas Februarii, anno septimo.

PL 215, 501 C–503 A.

___

TO THE KING OF THE FRANKS:

Although not displeasing to the Lord, but rather, acceptable to Him that the Dispersion of the Jews should live and do service under Catholic kings and Christian princes—the remnants of which will then finally be saved [Rom. 9 : 3–24], since in those days Juda will be saved [Jer. 33 : 6–26], and Israel will dwell in mutual trust [Ezechiel 38 : 14], nevertheless, in the eyes of the divine majesty, they give grave offense who give preference to the sons of the crucifiers against whom blood still cries out to the Father over the

joint heirs of the crucified Christ, as if the son of the bondwoman could and ought to be heir along with the son of the
free woman [Rom. 8 : 17; Gen. 21 : 10], and they place
Jewish servitude before the freedom of those whom the Son
has set free.

Now you know it has come to Our hearing that, in the
Kingdom of the Franks, Jews are insolent to the point that,
under color of a wicked usury, through which they extort
not only usury, but usury on usury, they usurp the goods of
churches and the possessions of Christians, and thus what the
prophet deplored, in a Jewish role, seems to have found fulfillment in the Christian people: Our inheritance is turned
over to aliens, our house to those outside! [Lam. 5 : 2].

Besides, although it was enacted in the Lateran Council
[III Council of the Lateran, title XXVI] that Jews, neither
under pretext of nursing children, nor for the sake of service,
nor for any other cause whatever, be permitted to possess
Christian slaves in their homes, but that those who might
presume to live with them were excommunicated, they do
not hesitate to hold Christians as slaves and nurses, with
whom, at times, they carry on abominations it is more appropriate for you to punish than for us to unfold!

Further, although the same Council judged that in court
cases common to both, the testimony of Christians against
Jews must be admissible, since they use Jewish witnesses
against Christians, and decreed that whosoever should give
preference to Jews over Christians in this matter be struck
with anathema, there is deference paid them in the Kingdom
of the Franks to such a point that no credence is given to
Christian witnesses against them, whereas they are admitted
for testimony against Christians. For if, sometimes, those to
whom they have loaned money under usury produce Christian witnesses that payment has been made, more credence
is placed in the document which the indiscreet debtor had
left with them through negligence or carelessness than is
placed in the witnesses introduced; indeed, in this juncture,
witnesses against them are not admissible.

They have become insolent to this point too—We refer
to it with embarrassment—that they have built a new synagogue in Sens beside a certain old church, not a little higher
than the church, and in it they do not hesitate to impede the
celebration of the divine mysteries in that same church by

celebrating according to the Jewish rite their own services
with a great clamor, not in a low voice, as of old, before
they were ejected from the Kingdom.

What is more, blaspheming the Name of the Lord, they
publicly insult Christians on the ground that they have faith
in some rustic, hanged by the Jewish people. We have no
doubt He was hanged for us since He bore our sins in His
body on the tree [1 Pet. 2 : 24], but We do not admit that
He was a rustic, whether by manners or by birth, nor, indeed,
can they fail to confess that He was descended from a priestly
and royal family, and His manners were outstanding and
correct. But on the feast of Good Friday, Jews, contrary to
ancient custom, publicly run through streets and squares,
congregating and everywhere deriding Christians for adoring
in the customary way the Crucified on His cross, and by
their improprieties strive to recall these from their duty to
adore.

Also, the gates of Jews gape open for thieves until midnight, nor, if anything taken by theft is found among them,
can any one obtain justice from them.

The Jews, therefore, are abusing the royal forebearance
and, since they remain located among Christians, are wickedly taking advantage of the situation secretly to kill their
Christian hosts, as is said to have happened lately, for a
certain poor scholar was discovered dead in their latrine.

Lest, therefore, the Name of the Lord be blasphemed by
them, lest Christian liberty be worse than Jewish servitude,
We warn Your Royal Serenity, and exhort you in the Lord,
and unto the remission of sins We enjoin that insofar as you
repress the presumption of the Jews in these and similar
matters, as you thus strive to abolish abuses of this sort from
the Kingdom of the Franks, you will be giving evidence that
you possess zeal for God according to knowledge [Rom.
10 : 5], and, since even secular laws take a grave view of
those who blaspheme the Name of the Lord, so you ought
to view blasphemers of this sort, so that the punishment of
some might be the fear of all, nor let ready pardon provide
an incentive for delinquency.

In addition, you ought to rise up with power to eliminate
heretics from the Kingdom of the Franks, nor ought the
Royal Highness permit wolves, hiding under the pelt of sheep,
to destroy the sheep in his land, but let him show by per-

secuting them the fervor with which he follows the Christian faith.

Given at Rome, at Saint Peter's, the seventeenth day before the Kalends of February, in the seventh year [of Our pontificate].

APPENDIX V

POPE INNOCENT III

Nobili viro comiti Nivernensi:

Ut esset Cain vagus et profugus super terram, nec interficeretur a quoquam, tremorem capitis signum Dominus imposuit super eum, quia Judaei, contra quos clamat vox sanguinis Jesu Christi, etsi occidi non debeant ne divinae legis obliviscatur populus Christianus, dispergi tamen debent super terram ut vagi, quatenus facies ipsorum ignominia repleatur et quaerant nomen Domini Jesu Christi. Blasphematores enim nominis Christiani non debent a Christianis principibus in oppressionem servorum Domini confoveri, sed potius comprimi servitute, qua se dignos merito reddiderunt cum in illum manus injicere sacrilegas qui veram eis conferre venerat libertatem, super eos et filios suos esse ipsius sanguinem conclamantes [Matt. 27, 25].

Verum, sicut nostris est auribus intimatum, quidam principes saeculares, ad Deum cui nuda sunt omnia et aperta [Heb. 4 : 13], oculum non habentes, cum turpe sit* ipsis* usuras exigere, Judaeos recipiunt in villis et oppidis suis, ut eos sibi ministros ad exactionem constituant usurarum, qui ecclesias Dei et Christi pauperes affligere non verentur. Cum autem Christiani, qui a Judaeis mutuum acceperunt, sortem et amplius ipsis solvunt, praepositi et servientes ipsorum potentum saepe, captis pignoribus et interdum eisdem Christianis carceri mancipatis, ipsos compellunt ad solutionem gravissimam usurarum. Quare, viduae et pupilli suis haereditatibus spoliantur, et defraudantur ecclesiae decimis ac aliis obventionibus consuetis, cum Judaei castella et villas detineant occupata, qui ecclesiarum praelatis de parochiali jure contemnunt penitus respondere.

Scandalum quoque per eos in ecclesia Christi non modicum generatur quod cum ipsi carnibus animalium quae mactant fideles, vesci abhorreant ut immundis, istud obtinent principum ex favore quod mactanda carnifices animalia tradunt illis qui, ea ritu Judaico laniantes, ex ipsis accipiunt quantum volunt, relicto residuo Christianis, iis similia Judaeis mulierculis facientibus de lacte quod publice venditur pro parvulis nutriendis. Aliud quoque praesumunt non minus istis detestabile Christianis, quod vindemiarum tempore uvas calcat Judaeus, lineis caligis calceatus, et puriori mero, juxta ritum Judaeorum extracto, pro beneplacito suo retinent ex eodem residuum, quasi foedatum ab ipsis relinquentes fidelibus Christianis, ex quo interdum sanguinis Christi conficitur sacramentum.

Insuper, testes Christianos, quantumlibet bonos et omni exceptione majores, tuti favore potentum, contra se penitus non admittunt. Sane venerabilis frater noster Altissiodorensis episcopus, ut de sua diocesi abominationem hujusmodi removeret, habito prudentum virorum consilio, haec in eadem heri sub anathematis vinculo interdixit, in solemni synodo injungens circumstantibus sacerdotibus quatenus in ecclesiis suis sub excommunicationis poena talia fieri prohiberent. Cui plerique fideles devote parentes elegerunt a praemissis abominationibus abstinere. Verum quidam nobiles ac potentes ac eorum ministri, attendentes ad munera Judaeorum, quae ipsorum corda subvertunt, quosdam fidelium, qui propter bonum obedientiae ac metum sententiae promulgatae, abstinere a talibus decreverunt, terrere minis et contumeliis afficere praesumpserunt, quosdam etiam captos ut se redimerent compellentes ac nollentes dimittere nisi ad beneplacitum Judaeorum, qui ne per excommunicationis sententiam in personas, et interdictum in terras, ab hujusmodi compescantur, se tueri nituntur per appellationis obstaculum ad sedem apostolicam interpositum in clusionem ecclesiasticae disciplinae. Porro Judaei, si propter hoc in Christianos aliquando excommunicationis vel interdicti promulgetur sententia, gloriantur pro eo quod, occasione ipsorum, in salicibus Babylonis ecclesiastica organa suspenduntur [Ps. 136 (137) : 2], et defraudantur nihilominus suis proventibus sacerdotes.

Tu vero, sicut accepimus, qui tanquam vir catholicus et servus Jesu Christi, ob ipsius reverentiam deberes Judaicis superstitionibus obviare, ne inimici crucis exaltarentur in semetipsis contra famulos crucifixi, principaliter faves eis, et ipsi te, in praenominatis excessibus, habent praecipuum defensorem. Nonne contra tibi subjectum accenderetur graviter zelus tuus si tuo praeberet auxilium inimico? Quanto magis, ergo, divinam formidare potes offensam, quod favorem praestare non metuis, qui unigenitum Dei Filium cruci affigere praesumpserunt, et adhuc a blasphemiis non quiescunt?

Volentes igitur subortum ex hoc in populo scandalum de medio removeri, et aboleri tantae praesumptionis excessum, quem in Christum et ejus ecclesiam diceris commisisse, nobilitatem tuam rogamus, monemus, et exhortamur in Domino, per apostolica tibi scripta mandantes quatenus praedicta taliter corrigas per teipsum, a similibus de caetero conquiescens, quod zelum orthodoxae fidei videaris habere ac nos ad correctionem ipsorum non cogamur apponere manus nostras, qui, secundum Apostolum, in promptu habemus omnem inobedientiam vindicare [Rom. 1 : 5] cum ad hoc simus a Domino constituti, ut evellamus quae fuerint evellanda, et quae fuerint plantanda, plantemus [Eccles. 3 : 2].

Datum Romae, apud Sanctum Petrum, XVI Kalendas Februarii, anno decimo.

PL 215, 1291 B–1293 A.
[NOTE: sit° ipsis°—emendation of the printed text: sil ipsius.]

To that noble man, the Count of Nevers:

In order that Cain might be a wanderer and a fugitive over the earth, yet be slain by no one, the Lord set a sign upon him, a tremor of his head, because the Jews, against whom the voice of the blood of Jesus Christ cries out, although they ought not be slain lest the Christian people forget divine Law, ought nevertheless to be dispersed over the earth as wanderers, so that their countenance might be full of ignominy and they might seek for the Name of the Lord Jesus Christ. For blasphemers of the Christian Name ought not to be coddled at the price of oppressing the Lord's servants, but rather be repressed by the servitude of which they have rendered themselves deserving when they laid sacrilegious hands on Him who had come to confer true liberty upon them, calling down His blood upon themselves and on their children too [Matt. 27 : 25].

But, as has been intimated to Our ears, certain secular princes, having no eye for God to Whom all things are bare and open [Heb. 4 : 13], because it would be a base thing for them to demand usury, receive Jews in their manors and towns in order that they might set them up as their own agents for the exacting of usury, and who are not ashamed to afflict the churches of God and the poor of Christ. When Christians, however, who receive a loan from the Jews, pay them the principal and more, the agents and servants of those men of power often, by seizing the pledges and sometimes binding over these same Christians to prison, compel them to the payment of the burdensome usury. Wherefore widows and orphans are despoiled of their inheritances, and churches are defrauded of their tithes and other customary income because Jews, who disdain to respond to the prelates of those churches on parochial right, hold castles and manors.

No small scandal too is generated by them in the Church of Christ in that, since they abhor to eat, as unclean, the flesh of animals which the faithful slaughter, they, by the favor of princes, obtain this, that butchers hand over to them animals for slaughter and they, cutting them up according to the Jewish rite, take what they want from them and the rest is left for Christians, Jewish women of the lower class doing similar things with respect to the milk that is put on public sale for feeding little ones. They also presume to do something else, not less detestable to Christians than are these, in that at the time of the vineyard harvest, a Jew treads out the grapes, shod as he is with linen shoes, and the purer wine taken out according to the Jewish rite, they retain what pleases them, whereas the residue from the same, as it were soiled by them, they leave to the Christian faithful, and from this sometimes the sacrament of the Blood of Christ is confected.

Besides, safe in the favor of men of power, they do not admit Christian witnesses at all, even though they be respectable and beyond all cavil, to testify against them. Indeed, Our venerable brother, the Bishop of Auxerre, having taken counsel with prudent men, in order to remove from his diocese an abomination of this sort, forbade these recently under bond of anathema, ordering in solemn synod the priests in attendance that they should prohibit such things in their churches under penalty of excommunication. Most of the faithful, devoutly obedient to him, chose to abstain from the aforesaid abominations. But certain nobles and men of power and their agents, attending to the gifts of the Jews, which subvert their hearts, have presumed to terrorize with threats and to afflict with contumely certain of the faithful who, for the sake of the boon of obedience and for fear of the penalty promulgated, had decided to abstain from such things. Some too, they arrested and compelled to ransom themselves, refusing to release them except at the whim of the Jews, who are restrained from such doings neither by a sentence of excommunication against their persons, nor an interdict against their lands; they try to defend themselves through the obstacle of an appeal to the Apostolic See, interposed as a block to ecclesiastical discipline. The Jews, in addition to all this, should a sentence of excommunication or interdict be promulgated at times against Christians on this account, glory inasmuch as they have been the occasion that the harps of the Church are hung on the willows of Babylon [Ps. 136 (137) : 2], and the priests are no less defrauded of their income!

You, however, as We receive the report, who as a Catholic man and a servant of Jesus Christ, ought to put a block in the path of Jewish superstitions out of reverence for Him, lest the enemies of the cross be themselves exalted as against the servants of the Crucified, you it is who chiefly favors them and in you they have their most important defender in the aforesaid excesses. Would not your zeal be set afire grievously against a subject of your own who provided aid to your enemy? How much more, therefore, can you fear the divine offense because you do not fear to offer your favor to them who have presumed to nail the only-begotten Son of God to a cross and who still do not rest from their blasphemies?

Desiring, therefore, to remove from the midst of the people the scandal that has risen from all this, and to abolish the excess of so extreme a presumption, which you are said to have committed against Christ and His Church, We beg, We warn, and We exhort Your Nobility in the Lord, We command through these apostolic documents that you yourself so correct the aforesaid, refraining from similar things in the future, that you will be seen to possess zeal for the orthodox faith and We might not be forced to set Our hands to their correction, We who, according to the Apostle have it in Our scope to avenge all disobedience [Rom. 1 : 5] since to this have We been appointed by the Lord, that We might uproot what must be uprooted, and that We might plant what must be planted.

Given at Rome, at Saint Peter's, sixteen days before the Kalends of February, in the tenth year [of Our pontificate].

APPENDIX VI

Pope Alexander III is the author of the oldest extant version of this "Constitution for the Jews," *Sicut Judaeis non*; Pope Innocent III is responsible for the indented introduction and conclusion as well as for the words marked by an asterisk.

Constitutio pro Judaeis:

> Licet perfidia Judaeorum sit multipliciter im-
> probanda, quia tamen per eos fides nostra veraciter
> comprobatur, non sunt a fidelibus graviter oppri-
> mendi, dicente propheta: Ne occideris eos, ne
> quando obliviscantur legis tuae [Ps. 58 (59) : 12],
> ac si diceretur apertius: Ne deleveris omnino
> Judaeos, ne forte Christiani legis tuae valeant
> oblivisci, quam ipsi non intelligentes, in libris suis
> intelligentibus repraesentant.

Sicut ergo* Judaeis non debet esse licentia, ultra quam permissum est lege in synagogis sua praesumere, ita in his* quae sunt concessa illis*, nullum debent praejudicium sustinere. Hos ergo, cum in sua magis velint duritia perdurare quam vaticinia prophetarum et legis arcana cognoscere atque ad Christianae fidei notitiam pervenire, quia tamen nostrae postulant defensionis auxilium, ex Christianae pietatis mansuetudine, praedecessorum nostrorum felicis memoriae Calixti, Eugenii, Alexandri, Clementis, et Coelestini*, Romanorum pontificum vestigiis inhaerentes, ipsorum petitionem admittimus, eisque protectionis nostrae clypeum indulgemus.

Statuimus enim ut nullus Christianus invitos vel nolentes eos ad baptismum per violentiam venire compellat; sed, si eorum quilibet sponte ad Christianos, fidei causa, confugerit, postquam voluntas ejus fuerit patefacta, sine qualibet efficiatur calumnia Christianus. Veram quippe Christianitatis fidem habere non creditur qui ad Christianorum baptisma non spontaneus, sed invitus, cognoscitur pervenire.

Nullus etiam Christianus, sine potestatis terrae judicio, personas eorum nequiter laedere, vel res eorum violenter auferre praesumat, aut bonas quas hactenus in ea, in qua habitant regione, habuerint consuetudines immutare.

Praeterea, in festivitatum suarum celebratione quiquam fustibus vel lapidibus eos ullatenus non perturbet, nec aliquis ab eis indebita servitia exigere, vel extorquere contendat, nisi ea quae ipsi praeteritis facere temporibus consueverunt.

Ad haec, malorum hominum pravitati et avaritiae obviantes decernimus ut nemo coemeterium Judaeorum mutilare audeat vel minuere, sive obtentu pecuniae corpora effodere jam humata.

Si quis autem decreti hujus tenore cognito temere, quod absit! contraire tentaverit, nisi praesumptionem suam condigna satisfactione correxerit, excommunicationis ultione plectatur.

> Eos autem duntaxat huius protectionis praesidio volumus communiri qui nihil machinari praesumpserint in subversionem fidei Christianae.

> Datum Laterani, per manum Raynaldi Acheruntini archiepiscopi, cancellarii vicem agentis, XVII Kalendas Octobris, indictione II, Incarnationis Dominicae anno 1199, pontificatus vero domini Innocentii papae tertii anno secundo.

Basic text of Alexander III: Mansi, *op. cit.*, vol. XXII, cols. 355, 356; additions of Innocent III: *PL* 214, 864 C–865 A.

Constitution for the Jews:

> Although in many ways the disbelief of the Jews must be reproved, since nevertheless through them our own faith is truly proved, they must not be oppressed grievously by the faithful, as the prophet says: "Do not slay them, lest these be forgetful of Thy Law," [Ps. 58 (59) : 12] as if he were saying more openly: "Do not wipe out the Jews com-

pletely, lest perhaps Christians might be able to
forget Thy Law, which the former, although not
understanding it, present in their books to those
who do understand it."

Just as, therefore* there ought not to be license for the
Jews to presume to go beyond what is permitted them by
law in their synagogues, so in those* which have been conceded to them*, they ought to suffer no prejudice. These
men, therefore, since they wish rather to go on in their own
hardness than to know the revelations of the prophets and
the mysteries of the Law, and to come to a knowledge of the
Christian faith, still, since they beseech the help of Our
defense, We, out of the meekness proper to Christian piety,
and keeping in the footprints of Our predecessors of happy
memory, the Roman Pontiffs Calixtus, Eugene, Alexander,
Clement, and Celestine*, admit their petition, and We grant
them the buckler of Our protection.

For We make the law that no Christian compel them,
unwilling or refusing, by violence to come to baptism. But, if
any one of them should spontaneously, and for the sake of
the faith, fly to the Christians, once his choice has become
evident, let him be made a Christian without any calumny.
Indeed, he is not considered to possess the true faith of
Christianity who is recognized to have come to Christian
baptism, not spontaneously, but unwillingly.

Too, no Christian ought presume, apart from the juridical
sentence of the territorial power, wickedly to injure their
persons, or with violence to take away their property, or to
change the good customs which they have had until now in
whatever region they inhabit.

Besides, in the celebration of their own festivities, no one
ought disturb them in any way, with clubs or stones, nor
ought any one try to require from them or to extort from
them services they do not owe, except for those they have
been accustomed from times past to perform.

In addition to these, We decree, blocking the wickedness
and avarice of evil men, that no one ought to dare mutilate
or diminish a Jewish cemetery, nor, in order to get money, to
exhume bodies once they have been buried.

If anyone, however, shall attempt, the tenor of this decree
once known, to go against it—may this be far from happening!—let him be punished by the vengeance of excommunica-

tion, unless he correct his presumption by making equivalent satisfaction.

We desire, however, that only those be fortified by the guard of this protection who shall have presumed no plotting for the subversion of the Christian faith.

Given at [the palace of] the Lateran, by the hand of Raynaldus, Archbishop of Acerenza, acting for the Chancellor, on the seventeenth day before the Kalends of October, in the second indiction, and the 1199th year of the Incarnation of the Lord, and in the second year of the pontificate of the Lord Pope, Innocent III.

APPENDIX VII

FOURTH COUNCIL OF THE LATERAN

Titulus LXVII. De usuris Judaeorum.

Quanto amplius Christiana religio ab exactione compescitur usurarum, tanto gravius super his Judaeorum perfidia inolescit, ita quod brevi tempore Christianorum exhauriunt facultates. Volentes igitur in hac parte prospicere Christianis ne a Judaeis immaniter aggraventur: synodali decreto statuimus, ut si de cetero quocumque praetextu Judaei a Christianis graves et immoderatas usuras extorserint, Christianorum eis participium subtrahatur, donec de immoderato gravamine satisfecerint competenter. Christiani quoque, si opus fuerit, per censuram ecclesiasticam, appellatione postposita, compellantur ab eorum commerciis abstinere.

Principibus autem injungimus, ut propter hoc non sint Christianis infesti, sed potius a tanto gravamine Judaeos studeant cohibere.

Ac eadem poena Judaeos decernimus compellendos ad satisfaciendum ecclesiis pro decimis et oblationibus debitis, quas a Christianis de domibus et possessionibus aliis percipere consueverant, antequam ad Judaeos quocumque titulo devenissent: ut sic ecclesiae conserventur indemnes.

Titulus LXVIII. Ut Judaei discernantur a Christianis in habitu.

In nonnullis provinciis a Christianis Judaeos seu Saracenos habitus distinguit diversitas: sed in quibusdam sic quaedam inolevit confusio ut nulla differentia discernantur. Unde contingit interdum, quod per errorem Christiani Judaeorum seu Saracenorum, et Judaei seu Saraceni Christianorum mulieribus commisceantur. Ne igitur tam damnata commixtionis excessus, per velamentum erroris hujusmodi, excusationis ulterius possint habere diffugium; statuimus ut tales utriusque sexus, in omni Christianorum provincia, et omni tempore, qualitate habitus publice ab aliis populis distinguantur, cum etiam per Mosen hoc ipsum legatur eis injunctum [Lev. 19 : 19].

In diebus autem lamentationis, et Dominicae passionis, in publicum minime prodeant, eo quod nonnulli ex ipsis, talibus diebus (sicut accepimus) ornatius non erubescunt incedere, ac Christianis, qui sacratissimae passionis memoriam exhibentes lamentationis signa praetendunt, illudere non formidant.

Illud autem districtissime inhibemus, ne in contumeliam Redemptoris prosilire aliquatenus praesumant. Et quoniam illius dissimulare non debemus opprobrium, qui probra nostra delevit: praecipimus praesumptores hujusmodi per principes saeculares condignae animadversionis adjectione compesci, ne crucifixum pro nobis praesumant aliquatenus blasphemare.

Titulus LXIX. Ne Judaei publicis officiis praeficiantur.

Cum sit nimis absurdum, ut Christi blasphemus in Christianos vim potestatis exerceat, quod super hoc Toletanum concilium provide statuit, nos propter transgressorum audaciam in hoc capitulo innovamus: prohibentes, ne Judaei officiis publicis praeferantur, quoniam sub tali praetextu Christianis plurimum sunt infesti. Si quis autem officium eis tale commiserit, per provinciale concilium (quod singulis praecipimus annis celebrari) monitione praemissa, districtione qua convenit, compescatur. Officiali vero hujusmodi, tamdiu Christianorum communio in commerciis et aliis denegetur, donec in usus pauperum Christianorum, secundum providentiam diocesani episcopi, convertatur quidquid fuerit adeptus a Christianis occasione officii sic suscepti: et officium cum pudore dimittat, quod irreverenter assumpsit. Hoc idem extendimus ad paganos.

Titulus LXX. Ne conversi ad fidem de Judaeis, veterem ritum Judaeorum retineant.

Quidam, sicut accepimus, qui ad sacri undam baptismatis voluntarii accesserunt, veterem hominem omnino non exuunt, ut novum perfectius induant: cum prioris ritus reliquias retinentes, Christianae religionis decorem tali commixtione confundant. Cum autem scriptum sit: Maledictus homo qui terram duabus viis ingreditur [Ecclus. 3 : 28]: et indui vestis non debeat lino lanaque contexta [Deut. 22 : 11] statuimus ut tales per praelatos ecclesiarum ab observantia veteris ritus omnimodo compescantur, ut quos Christianae religioni liberae voluntatis arbitrium obtulit, salutiferae coactionis necessitas in ejus observatione conservet: cum minus malum existat viam Domini non agnoscere, quam post agnitam retroire.

Mansi, *op. cit.*, vol. XXII, cols. 1054–1058.

FOURTH COUNCIL OF THE LATERAN

Title LXVII. On Jewish usury.

The more the Christian religion is oppressed by the exaction of usury, the more grievously does Jewish disbelief batten on it, in such wise that in a short time they exhaust Christian resources. Desiring, therefore, to make some provision for Christians in this matter, lest they be cruelly burdened by Jews, we legislate by synodal statute that if in the future Jews, under any pretext whatsoever, extort heavy and immoderate usury from Christians, the partnership of Christians with them be withdrawn until they shall have made satisfaction in an effective way for any immoderate burden. Christians too, if there be need, are compelled by ecclesiastical censure to abstain from dealings with them, appeal denied.

We enjoin the princes that they be not hostile to Christians on this account, but rather that they strive to inhibit the Jews from imposing so great a burden.

And under the same penalty we decree that Jews must be compelled to make satisfaction to the churches for tithes and offerings due, which they were accustomed to receive from Christians in connection with their houses and other possessions before these fell to the Jews, whatever the title, so that thus the churches might be preserved from loss.

Title LXVIII. That Jews be distinguished from Christians by their garb.

In some provinces, a diversity of garb distinguishes Jews or Saracens from Christians, but in some, a kind of commingling has so flourished that they are discriminated by no difference. Hence, at times it happens that Christian men have commerce with Jewish or Saracen women, and Jewish or Saracen men with Christian women. Lest, therefore, under the veil of this sort of error, they might have a loophole for the excess of this commerce, so worthy of condemnation, we legislate that such people, of both sexes, in every Christian province and at all times, be distinguished publicly by their garb from other peoples, for it can be read that even Moses enjoined this upon them [Lev. 19 : 19].

On the days of lamentation, however, and of the Passion of the Lord, let them not appear at all in public, for this reason, that some among them (as we hear) on such days are not ashamed to step forth in more than their usual elegance, and do not fear to make game of the Christians who exhibit their memory of the most sacred passion, and show forth signs of lamentation.

This, however, we most strictly forbid, lest they presume in any degree to skip forth in contempt of the Redeemer. And because we ought not to dissemble the opprobrium of Him who has erased our improbities, we command that those who are presumptuous in this way be repressed by the appropriate attentions of the secular princes, lest they presume to blaspheme to any point Him who was crucified for us.

Title LXIX. That Jews be not brought to the fore in public offices.

Since it is too absurd that a blasphemer of Christ should exercise the vigor of power over Christians, on account of the audacity of those who transgress under this head, we renew what the Council of Toledo farsightedly legislated on the matter, forbidding that Jews be brought to the fore in public offices, because under a pretext of this kind, they are usually hostile to Christians. If, however, anyone shall have entrusted such an office to them, let him be repressed by whatever severity is suitable, after a preliminary warning, through the provincial council (which we command be celebrated each year). To any official of this sort, let communion with Christians in commerce and in other matters be denied, until whatever he may have gained from Christians, thanks to his office thus undertaken, be converted to the use of the Christian poor, according to the provision of the bishop of the diocese, and let him relinquish in disgrace the office he assumed without reverence. We extend the same to pagans.

Title LXX. That converts to the faith from among the Jews should not retain the ancient rite of the Jews.

Some, as we hear, who voluntarily approached the tide of holy baptism, have not put off altogether the old man so that they might the more completely put on the new, since, retaining the vestiges of their former rite, they dilute the beauty of the Christian religion with an alloy of this sort. But, since it is written: Cursed is the man who walks the earth in two directions [Ecclus. 3 : 28] and: a garment woven of linen and wool together ought not be worn [Deut. 22 : 11] we enact that such be repressed, by those who are prelates in the churches, from every kind of observance of the ancient rite, so that those who offered the decision of their free will to the Christian religion, the necessity of a salutary compulsion might keep to its observance; for it is a lesser misfortune not to know the path of the Lord, than after once having known it, to retrogress.

APPENDIX VIII

POPE GREGORY IX

Venerabilibus fratribus archiepiscopis et episcopis, ac dilectis filiis aliis ecclesiarum praelatis per Theu-

TONIAM CONSTITUTIS, SALUTEM ET APOSTOLICAM BENEDIC-
TIONEM:

Sufficere debuerat perfidiae Judaeorum quod eos pietas christiana, solius humanitatis intuitu, receptat et sustinet quos hi, qui fidem catholicam persequuntur et nomen domini non noverunt, in suam cohabitationem et consortium non admittunt. Ipsi enim ingrati gratiae ac beneficiorum obliti, nobis pro gratia contumeliam exhibent, et de benignitate impia retributione contemptum, qui ex sola misericordia in nostram familiaritatem admissi, suae deberent agnoscere jugum ex culpa propria perpetuae servitutis.

Accepimus siquidem, quod non sine dolore narramus, et scribimus cum pudore, quod Judaei per Theutoniam constituti, facti sunt adeo insolentes ut illos excessus committere in contumeliam christianae fidei non pavescant, quod non solum dicere sed etiam est nefarium cogitare. Habent enim mancipia christiana quae circumcidi faciunt et judaizare compellunt; nonnulli etiam, non re sed solo nomine, christiani sponte se transferentes ad ipsos, et eorum ritum sectantes, circumcidi permittunt et Judaeos se publice profitentur. Et cum in Toletano concilio sit statutum, et in generali nihilominus innovatum, ne Christi blasphemus publicis praeferatur, cum nimium sit absurdum ut talis in christianos vim exerceat potestatis; nihilominus eis dignitates saeculares et publica officia committuntur, quorum occasione in christianos saeviunt et nonnullos servare faciunt ritum suum. Habent praeterea nutrices et famulas in domibus propriis christianas quae apud eos illa committunt enormia quod abominationi sunt audientibus et horrori. Et licet in eodem generali concilio caveatur, ut Judaei utriusque sexus in omni christianorum provincia et omni tempore qualitate habitus ab aliis distinguantur, sic in quibusdam Theutoniae partibus inolevit confusio quod nulla differentia discernuntur.

Cum igitur nefas sit ut sacri baptismatis unda renatus infidelium ritu vel conversatione foedatur ac religio christiana perfidorum prematur dominio, si blasphemus sanguine Christi redemptum obnoxium detineat servituti, universitati vestrae praecipiendo mandamus, quatenus singuli vestrum in diocesibus, ecclesiis, et parochiis suis praemissos et consimiles Judaeorum excessus omnino reprimi faciatis ne cervicem perpetuae servitutis jugo submissam praesumant erigere in contumeliam redemptoris, districtius inhibentes ne de fide vel ritu suo cum christianis praesumant aliquatenus disputare, ne sub praetextu disputationis hujusmodi in erroris laqueum, quod absit, simplices elabantur, invocato ad hoc, si opus fuerit, auxilio brachii saecularis; contradictores christianos, videlicet, per censuram ecclesiasticam, Judaeos, vero, per sublationem communionis fidelium, appellatione postposita, compescendo.

Datum Anagniae, III Nonas Martii, pontificatus nostri anno VI.

Bullarum . . . Romanorum pontificum amplissima collectio, ed. C. Cocquelines (Rome, H. Mainardi, 1740), III, 280, 281.

———

To Our venerable brothers, the Archbishops and Bishops, and to Our other beloved sons, appointed to posts of eminence in the churches of Germany, health and apostolic benediction:

It ought to have been sufficient for Jewish disbelief that Christian piety, humanity alone taken into account, should receive and sustain them, men whom those who persecute the Catholic faith, and who know not the Name of the Lord, do not admit to live among them, nor to consort with them. For they are ungrateful and unmindful of benefactions; in return for our graciousness, they show us contumely and, by an impious repayment, contempt for kindness; admitted to familiarity with us out of mercy alone, they ought to have acknowledged their yoke of perpetual servitude, the result of their own guilt.

Indeed We hear, and not without sorrow do we recount it, with embarrassment We write it, that the Jews established in Germany have become so insolent that they do not tremble to commit, to the contumely of the Christian faith, excesses which it is wicked, not only to express, but even to ponder. For they possess Christian slaves whom they cause to be circumcised and whom they compel to Judaize; some Christians too, not in reality, but only in name, go over to them spontaneously, and, practicing their rite, permit themselves to be circumcised and publicly profess themselves Jews. And although it was established by law in the Council of Toledo, and this was renewed in a General Council, that a blasphemer of Christ ought not to be brought to the fore in public affairs, since it is exceedingly absurd that such a man exercise the vigor of power over Christians, nevertheless, secular dignities and public offices are committed to them, an occasion they take to play the savage against Christians and to make some follow their own rite. They have, besides, Christian nurses and handmaids in their own houses, who there commit enormities that are an abomination and a horror to those who hear of them. And, although it was provided in General Council that Jews of both sexes, in every Christian province and at all times, be distinguished from others by the style of their garb, confusion has so flourished in the districts of Germany that they are discriminated by no difference.

Since, therefore, it is wicked that one reborn in the tide of sacred baptism be stained by infidel rite or practice, if a blasphemer should detain under servitude one redeemed by the blood of Christ, We order, giving command to your company that you effect the repression of the above and of similar Jewish excesses, each one of you in dioceses, churches, and in your parishes, lest they presume to raise the neck bowed to the yoke of perpetual servitude, to the contumely of the Redeemer, the more strictly preventing them from presuming to dispute with Christians concerning faith or their rite, lest, under pretext of a disputation of this sort, the simple—may this be far from happening!—might slip into the snare of error, invoking to this purpose, should need be, the help of the secular arm and repressing Christians who oppose this by ecclesiastical censure, but Jews by withdrawing communion with the faithful from them, appeal denied.

Given at Anagni, the third day before the Nones of March, the sixth year of Our pontificate.

APPENDIX IX

POPE INNOCENT IV

ARCHIEPISCOPIS ET EPISCOPIS PER ALEMANNIAM CONSTITUTIS:

Lacrymabilem Judaeorum Alemanniae recepimus questionem quod nonnulli, tam ecclesiastici quam saeculares principes, ac alii nobiles et potentes vestrarum civitatum et diocesum, ut eorum bona injuste diripiant et usurpent, adversus ipsos impia consilia cogitantes, et fingentes occasiones varias et diversas, non considerato prudenter quod quasi ex archivo eorum christianae fidei testimonia prodierunt, scriptura divina inter alia mandata legis dicente: Non occides [Exod. 20 : 13; Deut. 5 : 17], ac prohibente illos in solemnitate paschali quidquam morticinium non contingere [Num. 5 : 2; 9 : 6; 19 : 11–16; cf. Agg. 2 : 13], falso imponunt eisdem quod in ipsi solemnitate se corde pueri communicant interfecti, credendo id ipsam legem praecipere cum sit legi contrarium manifeste, ac eis malitiose objiciunt hominis cadaver mortui, si contigerit illud alicubi reperiri. Et per hoc, et alia quamplura, figmentum saevientes in ipsos, eos super his non accusatos, non confessos, nec convictos, contra privilegia illis ab apostolica sede clementer indulta, spoliant contra deum et justitiam omnibus bonis suis, et inedia, carceribus, ac tot molestiis, tantisque gravaminibus premunt ipsos, diversis poenarum affligendo generibus et morte turpissima eorum quamplurimos condemnando, quod iidem Judaei, quasi existentes sub praedictorum principum, nobilium, et potentum dominio deterioris conditionis quam eorum patres sub Pharaone fuerint in Aegypto, coguntur de locis inhabitatis ab eis et suis antecessoribus a tempore cujus non extat memoria miserabiliter exulare. Unde, suum exterminium metuentes, duxerunt ad apostolicae sedis providentiam recurrendum.

Nolentes, igitur, praefatos Judaeos injuste vexari, quorum conversionem dominus miseratus expectat, cum, testante propheta, credantur reliquiae salvae fieri eorumdem [Isa. 4 : 2–3; Jer. 23 : 5–6], mandamus quatenus eis vos exhibentes favorabiles et benignos, quidquid super praemissis contra eosdem Judaeos per praedictos praelatos, nobiles, et potentes inveneritis temere attentatum, in statum debitum legitime revocato, non permittatis ipsos de caetero super iis vel similibus ab aliquibus indebite molestari, molestatores hujusmodi per censuram ecclesiasticam, appellatione postposita, compescendo.

Datum Lugduni, III Nonas Julii, anno V.

(In eundem modum archiepiscopis et episcopis per regnum Franciae constitutis).

(M. Stern) *Die päpstliche Bullen über die Blutbeschuldigung* (Berlin, Verlag Cronbach, 1893), pp. 10–13.

For translation, see Notes, Chap. VII, n. 42.

APPENDIX X

POPE CLEMENT IV

DILECTIS FILIIS FRATIBUS PRAEDICATORUM ET MINORUM ORDINUM INQUISITORIBUS HAERETICAE PRAVITATIS AUCTORITATE SEDIS APOSTOLICAE DEPUTATIS AUT IN POSTERUM DEPUTANDIS, SALUTEM ET APOSTOLICAM BENEDICTIONEM:

Turbato corde audivimus et narramus quod quamplurimi reprobi christiani, veritatem catholicae fidei abnegantes, se ad ritum Judaeorum damnabiliter transtulerunt, quod tanto magis reprobum fore dignoscitur, quanto ex hoc Christi nomen sanctissimum quadem familiari hostilitate securius blasphematur.

Cum autem huic pesti damnabili, quae ut accepimus non sine subversione praedictae fidei nimis excrescit, congruis et festinis deceat remediis obviari, universitati vestrae per apostolica scripta mandamus, quatenus terminos vobis ad inquirendum contra haereticos auctoritate sedis apostolicae designatos, super praemissis, tam per christianos quam etiam per Judaeos, inquisita diligenter et fideliter veritate, contra christianos quos talia inveneritis commisisse tamquam contra haereticos procedatis.

Judaeos autem qui christianos, utriusque sexus, ad eorum ritum execrabilem hactenus induxere, aut inveneritis de caetero inducentes, poena debita puniatis. Contradictores per censuram ecclesiasticam, appellatione postposita, compescendo, invocato ad hoc, si opus fuerit, auxilio brachii saecularis.

Datum Viterbii, VII Kalendas Augusti pontificatus nostri anno tertio.

Bullarum . . . Romanorum pontificum amplissima collectio, ed. C. Cocquelines (Rome, H. Mainardi, 1740), III, 462.

For translation, see Notes, Chap. VII, n. 59.

INDEX

ABELARD, PETER, 11
Abraham Abulafia of Saragossa, 120
Abraham, Patriarch, 8, faith of, 40, 152
Agnellus, Bishop, 45
Albi, diocese, 128
Albigensian heretics, crusade against, 98, 111
Alexander of Hales, *Summa*, 112
Alexander II, Pope, 68–69
Alexander III, Pope, 79–80; *Sicut Judaeis non*, 81, 229
Alexander IV, Pope, 116, 122
Alexander VI, Pope, 15, 144–47
Almohades, Moslem zealots, 52
Alphonsus, Archbishop of Saragossa, 143
Alphonsus I, King of Aragon and Navarre, 12
Alphonsus VI, King of Spain, 65
Alphonsus VIII, King of Castile, 100
Ambrose, Saint, Bishop of Milan, 19, 23
Anacletus, Antipope (Peter Petri Leonis), 78–79
Anales Bertinianos, 52
Anastasius, Roman Emperor, 32
Annas and Caiphas, 90
Antonius, father of Jew from Telesia, 34
Aquitaine, 128, 129
Arcadius, Roman Emperor, 20, 22
Arians, heretics, 35, 41, 51
Aristotle, 39, 40, 95, 155
Assyrians, 156
Astronomical Ring, Maestro Boneto, 146–47
Augustine, Saint, 5, 16, 59, 95, 159
Auxerre, Bishop of, 97
Avignon, 128, 129, 135
BACAUDE, BISHOP, 45
"Badge," 1, 13, 104, 106, 107, 109, 113, 122, 137–38
Baḥya Ibn Paḳuda, 10, 148
Baptism, force forbidden, 54–55, 68–69, 98, 106, 133, 135; Jews' goods confiscated, 111, 121, 130, 133

Barcelona, 52–53; Disputation of (1263), 117–18
Bédarrides, 130
Benedict, Saint, 11
Benjamin of Tudela, 79–80
Berengar, Viscount of Narbonne, 68
Bernard Gui, Inquisitor, 126, 131
Bernard, Saint (Abbot of Clairvaux), 11, 69, 74–78, 81, 152; to touch a Jew like laying hands on Jesus, 75
Bible, versions of, 15, 29, 119; interpretation, "literal," "historical," 150–51; "spiritual," 2, 37, 38, 77, 87–92, 113, 151–52; Jewish, 8–9, 37, 98, 112–13, 150–51
Black Death, 131–34
Blasphemy, accusation, 9–10, 59, 76, 95, 112, 137, 142
Bodo the Deacon, "Eleazar," 63–64
Boethius, 31, 62, 164
Bonastruc da Porta (Moses Ben Naḥman), 117
Bonet de Lattes, "Provenzali," Maestro Boneto, 146–47
Boniface VIII, Pope, 83, 123–24
Books, Jewish, suppressed, 1, 108, 119, 126; returned to owners, 46; translated, 127, 131
Bourges, Archbishop of, 86
Braulio, Saint, Bishop of Saragossa, 57
Bribes, accusation against Jews, 72, 97, 142, 145
Brunichilda, Queen of Franks, 41
Burgos, Bishop of, 101
CAGLIARI, 43–44
Cahors, diocese, 128
Cain, 96, 151
Caligula, Roman Emperor, 6
Canticle of Canticles, 77
Carpentras, 130, 146
Cassiodorus, 31, 62
Castile, Kingdom of, 106, 111, 120, 136, 139
Castle sant'Angelo, 145
Catania, Bishop of, 41

Celestine III, Pope, *Sicut Judaeis non*, 97
Cemeteries, Jewish, 98
Cham, 164
Charles Martel, 51
Chaucer, *Prioress' Tale*, 116
Circumcision, 27–28, 34–35, 64
Claudius, Roman Emperor, 6
Clement, delated as heretic, 61
Clement IV, Pope, 117–19, 122, 151
Clement V, Pope, 125–26
Clement VI, Pope, 131–34
Clement XIV, Pope (Lorenzo Ganganelli), 114
Clergy, privileges, 12–13
Clermont, 67
Clovis, King of Franks, 164
Coelicoli, 23–24
Constantine I, Roman Emperor, 17, 22, 24
Constantinople, Third Council of, 57; Imperial city, 31, 36, 111
Constantius, Roman Emperor, 27
Conversion, of Jews, 2, 47–49, 81, 100, 101, 111, 112, 117, 119–20, 134, 139, 148; suspect, 55, 57–59, 105–06, 132–33, 139; advantages proffered, 47–49, 80, 99, 113–14, 116, 117, 158, 161; of Pope attempted, 120; to Judaism illicit, 23, 25, 105–06, 121–22
Counter Reform, 16, 147
Covenant of 'Umar, 53–54
Cromwell, Oliver, 121
Crucifixion, guilt ascribed to Jews, 1, 71, 93, 153
Cruelty, Christian, 5, 9, 20–21, 110, 128–29, 132
Crusades, 1, 51, 66–82, 98–99, 108–11, 113, 116–17, 125–29, 134, 145–46; 1096 massacres, Altenahr, 74; Cologne, 71, 74; Kanten, 74; Kerpen, 74; Mayence, 71, 74; Metz, 74; Mörs, 73–74; Neuss, 74; Regensburg, 74; Speyer, 71, 74; Trier, 74; Wevelinghofen, 74; Worms, 71; 1104, Blois, 74; Loches, 74; Orleans, 74; Sens, 74; Tours, 74; "Shepherds'," *Pastorelli*, 127–29
Cursing of Christians alleged, 122
DACHAU, 21
Daniel, Rabbi, 80
David, King, 41
De consideratione, Bernard of Clairvaux, 76
Debts, 77, 94–95, 96, 98–99, 108–09, 113
Deuterōsis, "Second Publication," 29
Devil, Satan, 65, 73, 89, 133, 163
Diaspora (Dispersion), 2, 9, 75, 92, 96, 115

Dionysius, pseudo-Areopagite, 95
Disabilities, Jewish, marriage, 25–26, 117; offices, civil, 28–29, 81, 105, 117, 122, 137, 155; domestic, 81, 94, 96, 113, 137; slaveholding, 26–28, 155; witnesses, 81, 97, 113, 137
Divina justitia nequaquam, 114
Donatists, heretics, 30
Duns Scotus, 48
EASTERN EMPIRE, 111
Egyptians, 9, 156
Ekkehard, chronicler, 71
"Elders," Jewish officials, 21, 28
Elieser bar Nathan, chronicler, 71
Elijah, altar to, 41; prophet of zeal, 149
Elizabeth, Queen of Castile, 141
Emicho, Count of Leisingen, 71, 163
England, 111, 121–22, 128
Enlightenment, 18th century, 6, 36
Ephraim bar Jacob, chronicler, 70–71
Eugene III, Pope, 76–78
Eugene IV, Pope, 136–38
Eve, 152
Excommunication, 13–14, 161–62 and *passim*
Expulsion of Jews, papal, 60, 130; from England, 121; from France, 126, 130; from Portugal, 135, 145; from Spain, 51, 135, 143–45, 156
FERDINAND OF ARAGON, 140, 143, 144
Feudalism, 12, 81, 85–86
Flavius Josephus, 129
Florentine merchants and Jewish bankers, 109
Force, "absolute" or "conditioned," 56
France, Jews of the Lord King, 14; Kingdom of, 11, 128, 141
Francis of Assisi, Saint, 139
Frankish Kingdom, 62
Franks, 36; King of, 92
Frederick, Archbishop of Mayence, 60
Frederick Barbarossa, Emperor, 14
Frederick II, Emperor, 84, 104
GANGANELLI, LORENZO CARDINAL, *see* Clement XIV, Pope
Gelasius I, Pope, Saint, 15, 18, 31–35, 99, 157
Germany, persecution of Jews, 69–75, 114–15, 132
Ghetto, 1, 69, 95, 135, 138
Gratian, *Decretum*, 49, 58
Greek Christians, 66, 91–92, 111; pagan, 9
Gregory I, Pope, Saint, "the Great," 15, 18, 31, 35–50, 51, 69, 80, 155, 158; *Sicut Judaeis non*, 35, 97; tolerance, 44, 45, 46, 47
Gregory IV, Pope, 57, 58–59

Gregory VII, Pope, Saint, 65
Gregory IX, Pope, 107–11, 116, 151, 158; "median group" of Jews "perverse," 110, 150; "kindness Christians desire from pagans ought to be shown to Jews," 110
Gregory X, Pope, 119, 122
HADRIAN I, POPE, 58–59
Hadrian, Roman Emperor, 6
Haifa, massacre of Jews, 74
Hakim, Calif, 67
Haman, 25
Hebrew language, for missions, 126, 127, 131; transcription, 15
Henry, Archbishop of Reims, 80
Henry, King of Castile and Leon, 138
Hereditary priests, 93
Heretics, heresy, 14, 61, 96, 118, 139, 141
Herod, King, 89
Hildebrand, *see* Gregory VII
Holy Land, 1, 66, 111, 121
Holy Week restrictions on Jews, 95, 105, 137
Honorius I, Pope, 57–58
Honorius III, Pope, 106–07, 158
Honorius IV, Pope, 121–22, 151
Honorius, Roman Emperor, 20, 22–24, 28
Hoogstraten, 147
Hrabanus Maurus, 63
Hugh of Lincoln, 116
IBN PAKUDA, *see* BAHYA IBN PAKUDA
Ibn Roschd, "Averroes," 52
Innocent II, Pope, 78–79
Innocent III, Pope, 15, 83–102, 103, 153; *principaliter, finaliter*, superior to Emperor, 85; beyond man, less than God, 85; tolerance, 83; "Vicar of Christ" habitual style, 86; Fourth Lateran Council, 103–06
Innocent IV, Pope, 108, 111–15, 122, 151
Innocent VIII, Pope, 142–43
Inquisition, 61, 118–19, 122, 123, 131, 139, 141, 142
Isaac Beneviste of Barcelona, 107
Isaac, Patriarch, 8
Isidore, Archbishop of Seville, Saint, 57
Islam, 1, 5, 7, 13, 14, 55
JACOB, PATRIARCH, 8
James I, King of Aragon, 117, 119
Japheth, 164
Jechiel, Rabbi, 80
Jeremiah, Prophet, 63
Jerusalem, 67; massacre, 74; Patriarch, 117
Jesus of Nazareth, 3, 8, 10, 75, 91, 92, 149, 151, 152, 153, 157; media-

tion between Jews and gentiles, 88; priestly, royal descent, 95
Jews, guardians of Scripture, 14, 19, 98, 149; scandalized by Passion of Jesus, 89
John, Apostle and Evangelist, 37, 91, 152
John, Bishop of Speyer, 72
John, King of Castile and Leon, 138
John, King of Castile, 143
John Lackland, 164
John, Patriarch of Constantinople, 49
John I, Pope, Saint, 62
John XXII, Pope, 126–31
John XXIII, Pope, 3, 4
John Salvati, Jewish convert, 127
Joseph, Jewish client of Gregory I, 44
Joseph, Patriarch, 4
Judaism, *religio, superstitio, perditio*, 37
Judas, 89
"Judgment of the Jews," 14, 102, 109, 116, 119, 126
Justinian, Roman Emperor, "The Great," 17–18, 27, 29, 32
KNIGHTS OF THE HOSPITAL OF SAINT JOHN, 13, 125
Lacrymabilem Judaeorum Alemanniae, Appendix IX, 114–15, 239–40
Landulf, Prince of Benevento, 68
Lateran III, Council, 79–81, 94, 111, 130
Lateran IV, Council, 25, 87, 94, 103–06, 108, 116
Law, Roman, 17–30, 154–56
Leo VII, Pope, 60
Leo X, Pope, 147
Leon, Kingdom, 102, 107, 111, 136, 139
Lepers, 129–30
"Levirate marriage," 61, 100
Liberal arts, open to Jews, 28
Limoges, Jewish-Christian Conference, 67
Louis, King of France, Saint, 111–112, 113
MACCABEES, 19, 154
Margaret, Queen of France, 123
Marie, Queen of France, 126
"Marranos," 11, 25, 55–56, 140–41, 142–45, 155, 156
Marriage between Jews, 61, 99–100; between Jews and Christians, 19, 25–26, 59, 61
Martin IV, Pope, 121
Martin V, Pope, 135–36, 148, 158
Mary, convert from Judaism at Reims, 114
Mary Magdalene, 91, 92, 152

Mary of Nazareth, 8, 43, 112, 125, 126, 130, 137, 142
Masaba, garrison, 129
Mehir de Ruthenburth, 122
Mendicant orders, 84, 109, 111, 119
Midwives, 81, 137
Mohammed, 140
Mordecai, 25
Moses, Lawgiver, 141, 149
Moses Ben Maimon, Rabbi, 52, 87, 153
Moses Ben Naḥman, Rabbi of Gerona, 117
Moslems, 14, 121, 136, 139, 140, 157; threat to Christendom, 51–53, 64, 68, 69, 82, 153, 155
NAPLES, BISHOP OF, 47
Narbonne, 42; Archbishop of, 62, 68, 69
Navarre, 107, 111, 141
Nazis, 4, 159
"Neophytes" (heretics), 139
Nevers, Bishop of, 99; Count of, 92
Nevers, Prior of Saint Nicholas, 114
"New Christians," 55, 138, 143
Nicaea II, Council, 58
Nicholas I, Pope, 59–60
Nicholas III, Pope, 119–20
Nicholas IV, Pope, 122–23
Nicholas V, Pope, 138–39; tolerance, 139
Nimis in partibus Anglicanis, 121
Nivello, Jewish convert, 111
"Nourenberk," Nuremburg, 74
Novarum, 130
Nurses, Christian among Jews, 81, 94
"OLD CHRISTIANS," 138
Oriental languages for missions, 126, 127, 131
Otto of Freising, chronicler, 74
PABLO CRISTIA, 117
Pagans, paganism, 14, 18–19, 23, 30, 42, 65, 110, 132, 138
Paris, 116, 128, 129–30; Abbey of Saint Denis, 79; Bishop of, 94, 99, 111; Jewish books burned, 108; massacre, 74; university, 112, 122, 126, 127
Parousia, 5, 14
Passion of Jesus, *see* Crucifixion
Parthenay, Lord of, 129
Pastorelli, see Crusades, "Shepherds' "
"Patriarch," Jewish dignitaries, 21–22
"Patrimony of Saint Peter," 31, 35, 36
Paul, Saint, Apostle to the gentiles, 8, 33, 38, 39, 40, 84, 138, 149
Perfidia, 8, 37, 41, 92, 122
Peter, Bishop of Terracina, 45
Peter, Saint, Apostle, 11, 33, 37, 84,

86, 89, 91, 152, 153
Peter, zealot Jewish convert, 43
Peter d'Aranda, Bishop of Calahorra, 144
Peter Arbues, Inquisitor, 142
Peter the Venerable, Abbot of Cluny, 11, 76
Pfefferkorn, 147
Pharisees, 93
Philip Augustus, King of France, 85
Philip, King of France, 99, 127, 130
Pius (Antoninus), Roman Emperor, 27
Pius II, Pope, 139
Pius XII, Pope, 159, 164
Poisoning alleged against Jews, Pope John XXII, 127; wells, 129–130, 132–133, 155
Pontius Pilate, 79, 88
Portugal, 101, 109, 111, 117, 119, 121, 122, 141, 144, 145
Practica inquisitionis, Bernard Gui, 131
Praguers, heretics, 139
"Priests," Jewish, 22, 65
Privilege, 12–14, 21–22
Pro perfidis Judaeis, Good Friday prayer, 37, 78, 134
Prophets, 2, 9, 112
Proselytizing, Jewish, 23–24, 61–64, 98, 121–122, 135, 155, 160–161
Provence, 146; Albigensian heretics, 98; Jews, 68, 113
Public office forbidden Jews, *see* Disabilities
"Pure blood," 56, 117
QUINIGESIUS, BISHOP, 33
RAYMOND PENAFORT, SAINT, 107
Reccared, King of Spain, 41, 57
Reconquest of Spain, 51, 69, 139–41
Reform (Protestant), 15, 147
Responsibility, corporate, 9, 152
Reuchlin, 147
Ritual murder charge, 95–96, 114, 115
Robert, fugitive monastery serf, 67
Rodrigo de Borja, *see* Alexander VI, Pope
Roman Curia, 126, 128, 144
Romans, pagan, 6, 9
Rome I, Council, 61, 65
Rome, Jews of, 123–124, 144–146; papal suppression of anti-Semitism in, Gregory I, 50; Boniface VIII, 123–124; Alexander VI, 144–146
Rudolph, Emperor, 122
Rudolph, monk, incited massacres, 74–75
SABBATH OBSERVANCE, 22, 50, 106
Sadducees, 93
Saint Bazas, region, 128
Saladin, 139

Salamanca, 126
Salomo bar Simeon, chronicler, 70, 153, 163
Samaritans, 27, 28, 42
Sancha, supposed sister of John XXII, 131
Sanctuary, right of, 119, 121
Sanguisa, *see* Sancha
Sanhedrin, 8, 9, 90, 153
Saul, Emicho (q.v.), a "second," 71
Scribes and Pharisees, 93, 112, 151
"Secular arm," 21, 99, 118, 139
Sem, 164
Sens, Archbishop of, 94, 99
"Sephardic" Jewry, 144
Sermons, conversionist, 1, 119–20
Servi camerae, status of Jews, 14
Service to Jews by Christians forbidden, 137
Servitude of Jews, "perpetual," 54; "temporary," 92–93
Sicily, 40, 142; Franciscan minister of, 119; Jews of, 68
Sicut Judaeis non, Appendix VI, 229–232; 18, 35, 45–46, 81, 97–98, 109, 119
Si diligenter attenderet, 114
Simon de Montfort, 98
Sisebut, King of Spain, 57, 59
Sixtus IV, Pope, 140–42, 158; tolerance, 140
Slaves, 26–28, 39–43, 100–01
Soissons, Count of, 14
Sorcery alleged against Jews, 127, 135
Spain, 1, 41, 68, 101–02, 109, 111, 136–45, 155, 156
Speyer, Bishop of, 72, 147
Stephen IV, Pope, 62
Sufficere debuerat, Appendix VIII, 236–239; 108
Suger, Abbot of Saint Denis, Paris, 79
Suicide by persecuted Jews, 67, 72, 73, 128–29, 134
Sylvester I, Pope, Saint, 86
Synagogues, confiscation of by John XXII, 130–31; licitly possessed and repaired, 19, 20, 22–23, 30, 45–47, 69, 135, 137; forbidden near churches, 45, 95
"Synagogue chiefs," Jewish officials, 22
"Synagogue fathers," Jewish officials, 22
Syracuse, Bishop of, 42
TALMUD SUPPRESSION, 1, 29, 108, 111–12, 119, 131, 142; study of, 120, 121
Tarragona, Archbishop of, 107, 119
Taxes on Jews, 21, 54, 76–77, 125, 145–46

Telesia, 33–34
Terracina, 44–45
Theodebert, King of Franks, 41
Theodoric, King of Franks, 41
Theodoric, King of Ostrogoths, Arian, 31–32, 62, 164
Theodosius I, Roman Emperor, 20, 25
Theodosius II, Roman Emperor, 23, 24, 28; Code of, 18; *Novellae* of, 19
Thomas Aquinas, Saint, 127
Tithes, 62, 101, 109, 121, 122
Titus, Roman Emperor, 6
Toledo, Councils, 105, 108, 155; IV, 58; VI, 57; XVII, 52
Toleration extolled by Popes, Gregory I, 44–46; Alexander II, 68–69; Innocent III, 83, 99; Honorius III, 107; Gregory IX, 110; Nicholas V, 139; Sixtus IV, 140; Alexander VI, 146
Tomás de Torquemada, *see* Torquemada
Torah, 2, 8, 9, 37, 40, 46, 50, 150, 152, 156; Scroll ceremony, 79; Scrolls destroyed, 1, 73
Torquemada, 144
Torture, juridical, 20–21, 129–30, 141, 155
Toulouse, Archbishop of, 129
Toulouse, province, 128
Tours, Archbishop of, 99; battle at, 51
Trinity, 8, 10, 91–92
Turbato corde, Appendix X, 241; 117, 139
URBAN II, POPE, 67
Urban IV, Pope, 116–17
Urban VI, Pope, 134
Usury, 1, 76–77, 78, 94–95, 96, 98–99, 103, 108–09, 111, 113, 116, 123, 126, 135, 138, 146, 162–63
VALENTINIAN II, ROMAN EMPEROR, 22
Venafro, 34, 46
Vandals, 51
Venaissin, County, 123, 130
Vespasian, Roman Emperor, 6
Vienne, Archbishop of, 113, 114; Council, 126
Vincent Ferrar, Saint, 143
Vinea Soreth velut, 119–20
Visigoths, 36, 51, 155
Volterranus, 143
WEAKNESS OF JEWS DESPITE WEALTH, 123–24
Weil, Simone, 161–62
Witchcraft alleged against Jews, 132, 134
Worms, *see* Crusades; *see also* 147
ZACHARY I, POPE, SAINT, 61
Zorobabel, Prophet, 63